Historical Pursuit of the Purpose of God with Reference to West Africa

William Allen Poe, B.D., Ph.D.

Parson's Porch Books
www.parsonsporchbooks.com

Historical Pursuit of the Purpose of God with Reference to West Africa
ISBN: Softcover 978-1-949888-45-4
Copyright © 2018 by William Allen Poe

All rights reserved. No part of this book may be reproduced or transmitted in any form or by any means, electronic or mechanical, including photocopying, recording, or by any information storage and retrieval system, without permission in writing from the publisher.

All Scripture quotations, unless otherwise marked, are from the Revised Standard Version of the Bible, copyright © 1946, 1952, and 1971 National Council of the Churches of Christ in the United States of America. Used by permission. All rights reserved worldwide.

Scriptures marked (NJB) are taken from The New Jerusalem Bible, published and copyright 1985 by Darton, Longman & Todd Ltd and Les Editions du Cerf, and used by permission of the publishers.

"This is the purpose that is purposed
concerning the whole earth;
and this is the hand that is stretched out
over all the nations.
For the LORD of hosts has purposed,
and who will annul it?
His hand is stretched out,
and who will turn it back?"
—Isaiah 14:26-27 (RSV)

"You change your works, yet
Your purpose is unchanged."
(St. Augustine of Hippo, *Confessions*)

In Dedication

To my beloved wife of sixty-six years, Beth Kelley, and to her brother, Dr. Page Kelley, my college housemate through whom I met Beth. Both are now deceased. In life, both served as missionaries—he in Brazil and she in West Africa with her husband, the author.

Table of Contents

Preface 9
   Creation and Close Of Day

Chapter 1 13
   Divine Creation and Beyond

Chapter 2 39
   God of Creation

Chapter 3 57
   What Then Went Wrong?

Chapter 4 78
   God's Way of Righting Wrong

Chapter 5 104
   To Call His Name Jesus

Chapter 6 129
   Pioneer Of The New Testament Gospels

Chapter 7 162
   Cornerstone Of A Christian West

Preface
Creation and Close of Day

In the unparalleled biblical account of creation, there was always the day followed by night; there was morning and evening followed by a new day. This continued through six days of divine activity followed by God at rest. That which God had created in perfection later was corrupted through the disobedience to God's bountiful handiwork. This says much about the nature of creation, that God had endowed His highest creation to exercise a vast freedom of choice. This property or freedom given to humans became the source of both the good and evil that has ever since characterized human civilization. It belies the vast amount of power for both good and evil that was endowed in humans and that led to the reality of evil. Herein lays the root of the history of the world, which entails both good and evil. For modern minds, few things are more baffling and difficult to explore than is the origin of evil.

God is the final judge of both good and evil in the universe. The earthly ministry of Jesus as recorded in the Gospels was somewhat a parallel. First there came what the older scholars called "The Galilean Springtime," which proved ephemeral and transitory, giving away to something leading to a strong determination to kill Jesus by the Jewish religious authorities. The Gospels depict at one point large crowds following Him, only to be followed by the steady rise of hostility toward Jesus of Nazareth. This continued until that day from the cross He uttered the resounding cry, "It is finished."

The young Christian Church was not a neophyte to this run of life; for three full centuries until early in the fourth century the Church experienced ups and downs as far as its relations with government. Emperor Constantine bestowed legalization to the Church in the Roman Empire early in the fourth century. It would be, in the fourth century, historically inaccurate not to note that occasionally there were regions where the Christian religion was wiped out; far more notable, however, is the revival of the faith in such regions later.

A mortal life is not unlike that pattern followed by Jesus Christ. There are years of creativity and accomplishment, and how meaningful they can become when lived in the will of God! It was just because of this that Jesus taught us to pray daily, "Thy will be done." When this is done, the day that gives summation and completion to other days does follow.

The author has arrived at the point in life where at least the account of creation can be read with insightful meaning. When one has moved into the nineties, one's wife of sixty-six years has gone on to God, children have long since embarked upon their own and are doing well, then perhaps it is time for such noble sentiment as this. When one takes the backward look and is made to see that things one formerly preached and taught to keen young Africans and to American college students at William Jewell College and Northwestern State University in Louisiana were deeply true, then there is a page to absorb, and to look at sunset and the close of another day. When honest, one will recognize that there were those things done on the trail of life that could have been pursued in a more excellent or elevated manner, with a deeper faith, and more persistent trust in the Lord of the harvest. One sees more clearly down the trail of life that God does work all things together for good to those who love Him. This trek is never engaged in by sight alone but is also a walk of faith that God does work all things together for good.

This book offers the author's theological and biblical thoughts, informed by a unique perspective based on his knowledge of what was achieved when a strong missionary society agreed to cooperate with a sympathetic government in advancing Christian schools in West Africa. In the early eighteenth century, the British government was successful in claiming this prosperous part of West Africa, which they identified as the Gold Coast. This period of history, centered in the eighteenth century, came to be known by historians as "the scramble for Africa," and a scramble it was. Germany gained colonies that were then snatched from her at the end of World War I. Italy, Belgium, Portugal, and others likewise gained colonies, but by any measure, Great Britain gained the upper hand, the largest population, and most prosperous territory. Out of it, France emerged with the largest territory.

One of the most prosperous areas for Great Britain was a revival of the ancient territory "the Gold Coast." With the coming of independence, this country changed its name to Ghana, in recognition of an ancient kingdom by that title. By any measure Ghana, with its capital in Accra, has proven one of the most stable on the African continent, far more so than Nigeria, where American missionaries were heavily involved for long periods of service. Nevertheless, Jesus is Lord, and commitment to this led to a progress of a small missionary school to become one of the best high schools in Ghana. This ensued many years ago when an African school needed forty acres of land for necessary expansion of an enlarging boarding school. After long months of failure from the government of Ghana, seven men went to their church and prayed about this issue before proceeding to face the government, who had power to release the land.

(This author has observed that most African chieftains appear to hold an authentic desire for the best for their people.) I am grateful to have served in West Africa at a time when such sentiment was increasingly the case; likewise, concern for women and their role in society was steadily on the rise. God's purpose was at work, even though less pointed or obvious. One thing about all divine purpose is that it moves at the eternal will, and at His pace, whatever historical situations may develop in the yet unborn cycles of time.

In the creative life, it is suggested by Christian practice that for six days one sees things by faith, but in the seventh one no longer sees through a glass darkly. What was done in faith on the trail of life is transformed into verities and reality itself. On the seventh day, one sees time in its true light. All of this is true in that one has come to see through the eyes of Him who is the Alpha and Omega of all things. Jesus Christ remains always the centerpiece of history; it was that same history in which Jesus Christ was made the center, and from which God will once again create a new heaven and a new earth, wherein dwells the righteousness of the Eternal God. It is that same historical stream which in the fullness of time God sent His beloved Son not only to define the Incarnation, but to fulfill history's course until time shall have reached its appointed end.

In the course of history on earth there were all but unbelievable trials and various vicissitudes in order that the kingdom might become established. Sometimes the unfavorable winds were too much for the kingdom seed to survive at the time, but God always has His own time. For example, in reviewing the past one wonders how any Christianity could have endured the bitter ferocious persecution it at times faced; admittedly there are instances in which the Christian religion was uprooted and wiped out. However, disappointing such places are, the Kingdom of God will come just as Jesus taught us to pray. It is Jesus' parable again, some seed falling on bad soil. Nevertheless, Jesus is always Lord of the Harvest. The ultimate promise of God is that the kingdoms of this world will become the kingdoms of our Lord and He shall reign forever.

Chapter 1
Divine Creation and Beyond

The quote, "He has founded it upon the seas," coupled with the awesome and sublime opening verse of Genesis, "In the beginning, God created," set forth one of the most stalwart assertions for divine creation imaginable. Theism asserts that there is but one God whose power, wisdom, and goodness have no limit. The universe owes its existence to the power and self-existence of this one Being. The view of the universe they declare is one of intelligent design: a miraculous creation brought about by the hand and word of a single, all-powerful, and channeling God. For millions of believers throughout the world, God is not only nature's creator but is also its preserver and is actively involved in guiding and directing His creation. For centuries, the three Abrahamic religions—Christianity, Judaism, and Islam—have all firmly adhered to the belief in a divine creation, as well as the basic principle of theism (the belief in one deity) although the deity of Islam, Allah, is a false god and not the same entity as the Judeo-Christian God. The revelation of a creator was not given to each of these faiths at the same time, but rather passed from one group to another over the centuries, first to the Judeans, then to the followers of Christ, and finally, to the Mohammedans. The case for theistic belief regarding the Christian faith was well presented in a series of lectures presented in Edinburgh during the mid-1800s: "Christianity itself rests on theism; it presupposes theism. It could only manifest, establish, and diffuse it in so far as theism was apprehended. I believe that the rational beauty of the cosmos indeed reflects the Mind that holds it together."[1] Also, one should note the array of distinguished scientists, such as John Polkinghorne of Cambridge University, who have been strong defenders of theism and divine creation.[2] Christian theism is the expression of God's divine purpose, but how are we to look for signs of His purpose?

What is the purpose of God? How did the universe get here? Does the world explain itself, or does it lead the human mind beyond

---

[1] Robert Flynt, "Issues Involved in the Question to Be" (Edinburgh: 1877) Kindle Ed.
[2] John Polkinghorne, *Belief in God in an Age of Science* (Yale University: 1998) Kindle Ed.

itself? Without doubt, these questions are among the oldest that mankind has grappled with, and the proposed answers to them have run a wide gamut ranging from the superstitious to the scientific. However, while tellers of folklore and men of science have suggested numerous responses to these questions, only revealed religion has been able to give definite answers, and even then, some variance exists between those answers. In the early days of the Church, a small group of men claimed that angels had created the universe and were also responsible for the Fall of Man. Miles away in India, the ancient Upanishads believed that the universe was derived from a changeless, eternal being known as Brahman. Early church fathers, such as Origen of Alexandria, believed that the universe was not created but was eternal and that other worlds may have existed prior to it. [3] Another famous early Christian, Anselm of Canterbury, thought God was greater than anything that could be conceived and therefore could not be understood by man.[4] Still other ancients believed that, as a web is woven from a spider and sparks arise from a fire, so from one soul proceeds the universe.

One of the most perceptive and acute early American theologians was William G. T. Shedd, a Congregational and later Presbyterian pastor who died in 1894. His Christian doctrinal volumes long held a potent influence on American theology. Shedd published a highly influential two-volume history of Christian doctrine in which the Christian faith never succumbed to the once-popular view that history was cyclical. Some leading early Christians had held to the view that there were earlier worlds before the Genesis creation. Of these early Christians, none had been more influential than Origen of Alexandria. His father was executed for being a Christian when Origen was about sixteen. He sought to be martyred with his father and was prevented from this only because his mother hid his clothes from him. Origen became one of the most loved and noted early Christian theologians. In modern-day parlance he is not generally reckoned a theologian, but among early Christians he was regarded as one of the first or foremost. He died in 254 A.D. and is not technically looked on as a martyr, but few scholars regret his being often reckoned as such because of his cruel sufferings.

---

[3] Henri De Lubac, *Origen on First Principles* (Gloucester, Mass., 1973) pp. 83–86.
[4] Anthony, Kenny *A Brief History of Western Philosophy* (Oxford: 1998) p. 120.

Some early Christians, principally Origen, believed in the existence of souls prior to Adam; originally, they were angelic spirits. Origen was a strong believer in this and sought to defend it with Holy Scripture. Some of his argument for this was that Adam was a generic term and did not necessarily denote a human being. Rather, he was the image of the race. Origen interpreted Paul's "groaning and travailing in pain" as the condition of spirits who once held a higher level.[5]

The New Testament addressed this panorama of history with a resounding finality, "so Christ having been offered once to bear the sins of many."[6] From the beginning, Christian faith has remained *teleological*, or maintaining that God's purpose preceded the birth of time, but this purpose is acted out in the framework of time. That is, time is being continuously moved toward this purpose or goal. If God's purpose is at work, history can mean nothing less than that, within its framework, the hand of God moves creation toward some paramount goal or final post. While He is eternally moving His purpose toward this goal, it would be nonsensical to suppose that the purpose could not be thwarted or delayed through disobedience. The reality of the freedom God allowed to His creation was irrevocable, and humanity was given wide discretion to make choices.

One New Testament scholar saw this as the very essence of the mind of Jesus, and the purpose of God.[7] Such a view precludes any authenticity to the great idea of the freedom of mankind. If this were discarded, the whole philosophy of sin becomes preposterous. The freedom given to man issues from none other than God Himself, when, in that pristine time, He bestowed a divinely-ordained freedom upon man, His highest form of creation. There can be no more stabilizing stance in life than the assurance that one exists in a universe brought purposively into being by an Absolute Power. Throughout the millennia of human history, most men have been unable to believe that the mighty universe, so startling with its adjustment and adaptation, was the product of chance, blind force, or dead matter. The biblical rejoinder to this is, of course, that God *created* the heavens and the earth, rather than merely obliterating the

---

[5] William G. T. Shedd, *A History of Christian Doctrine: Volume 2* (Birmingham, Alabama: 2006) pp. 3–10.
[6] Hebrews 9:28.
[7] J. Armitage Robinson, *Commentary on Ephesians* (Grand Rapids: 1903) pp. 7–8.

empty darkness with which Genesis opened. In other words, the universe came into being through words spoken by God. One of the highlights of New Testament theology is the Apostle John's pronounced use of the Greek *logos,* Jesus as "the Word," as well as his claim that, "Without Him was not anything made that was made."[8] For many centuries, at least since the time of Homer, *logos* was used in Greek civilization to imply finality and the ultimate. What then does this tell us? In applying this profound word to Jesus Christ as the Ultimate, John sets forth the claim that Jesus is the climax of history, beyond which no higher thought can be imagined. In Hebrew, the language in which the account of creation was originally written, God is known as *Elohim,* a name that later, with the rescue of Israel from her Egyptian bondage, would largely give way to *Yahweh.* The latter represents the more personal covenant relationship that God established with Israel. It was a name frequently used by the great prophets of the eighth century.

Genesis reveals basic principles by which God set the universe in motion. These are something placed there by God Himself. For example, there is the strong principle of continuity as opposed to static fixation. There are basic long-standing principles; Immanuel Kant saw the moral principle as being innate or inherent in man. One sees spirit vs. matter, the affirmation of Deity, and in the opening words we confront the deed of creation. The beginning is something that baffles thinkers or philosophers but makes possible the concept of history, progress, and progressiveness.

The rest of the Old Testament, after Genesis, chronicles a partial revelation of this absolute and immaterial Being and His relationship with Israel; while the New Testament forays into the life of Christ and subsequent ministry of His disciples. Origen gave considerable attention to the latter. As previously noted, he raised the possibility of there having been other worlds before Adam. Through the centuries, Origen has been questioned on various doctrines he espoused or set forth at one time or another, such as his thought on the soul. It should be pointed out, however, that he lived at a time when Christian theology was still undeveloped and inchoate. When one considers the long duration in which the Mediterranean churches did not adhere to the same canon of

---

[8] John 1: 1–13. This represents what has long been called the "Prologue" to John's Gospel and abounds in
Greek thought.

Scriptures, Origen and others' mistaken beliefs become more understandable. A practical consideration as to why the Church did not arrive at a consensus earlier is the long struggle against Gnosticism in which it was engaged. Irenaeus was deeply involved in this struggle; this is well evident in his major writing, *Against Heresies*. The same could be said of some of other best people of the Church.

Philosophically, the question may be raised as to whether revelation would have become necessary had God's creation continued in its perfect state rather than meandering from its original purpose. As we know, creation chose the latter, and thus the sin of Adam and Eve became the most far-reaching negative in all of history. The move, so distant from the purpose of God, brought about an unquestionable need for divine revelation, if creation were to ever again know its Creator. This transitional era "in which sin reigned" became epochal and was characterized by the birth of "natural religion." In short, the misstep of the first couple inaugurated the need for mankind to find something to fill the vacuum in their hearts.

The opening words of the Bible established the claim for a theistic approach to the nature of the universe in a powerful way. As mentioned previously, the awesomeness with which the Old Testament opens, "In the beginning God," makes use of the term *Elohim* for Deity. Notice, this was not the beginning of God, for He has neither a beginning nor an ending. However, most Christians recognize that one of the earliest questions a young child might ask is, "Who made God?" Of course, we adults know that God is the absolute and ultimate, beyond which one cannot think. This is known as *divine transcendence*, something that always lies beyond the reach of man or the possibility of human experience and expression. Throughout the step-by-step, or as Genesis puts it the day-by-day creation, one sees the immediate, direct, personal operation of Elohim, which made all but impervious an unabridged theistic approach to the origin of all things, for which the Bible, in its entirety, is noted. The divine act of creation involved no change in the Being of God Himself. Despite the disobedience of Adam and Eve, God's will is always determined from within, not swayed from outside.

As previously acknowledged, from the beginning of religion itself, the idea of one God was transmitted and did not originate separately in the various religions. The elegance of Genesis 1:1 comprehends that which was before time and material. William Wordsworth acknowledged that he was haunted upon first hearing the sounding cataract above Tintern Abbey. How pressed one may be to find lifting words that can convey the emotion of hearing, "In the beginning God created," which with its briskness, vitality, and reality state how the universe came to be. The most brilliant times of science in the West have not dimmed this majesty. The preponderant belief concerning the origin of the universe has staunchly followed this remarkable trail of thought, while its detractors have been unable to derail its awesomeness. The Creator God must be distinct from His creation. To say it another way, God was as much God before the universe came to be as He was when it was completed. Karl Barth referred to that which was before God as the perfect God.

A British historian of the century recently passed wrote, "The meaning of history must be sought in the nature and purpose of God. This purpose is always transcendent. History is the anvil which beats out God's purpose. On this anvil a transcendent God beats out His eternal purpose."[9] He is the God of His being, essence, actuality, or existence. Man exists, but God *is* existence. His being has nothing to do with what He does. Of course, He can do nothing that would represent an antithesis to His being. God's being is all that Deity was, prior to there having been a creation. The eternal God is never beyond being in that He is being itself and is, therefore, not contingent on creation. The false philosophy of *pantheism* makes little distinction between God and creation, suggesting they are one. Creation is dependent upon Him for existence. The economy of God is all that He does, whatever the activity or action may be.[10] The word *economy* is infrequently used today about Christian theology, but was widely employed among the early Church fathers, as in *providence*, or in "economy of God." Both Origen, and later John Chrysostom, were fond of using the term in the sense of God's actions.

In the course of its long history, there has been persistence in the West toward the belief in pantheism. However, the Genesis account of creation speaks nothing of this. Rather, it affirms a God who is supra-temporal, calling into existence all that is material. In an undiluted theistic view, the existence of God and the reality of the

---

[9] E. C. Rust, *The Christian Understanding of History* (London: 1947), p. 17.
[10] Ibid.

Historical Pursuit of the Purpose of God

world are entirely separate. The world could never be an emanation from God but is instead a creation by Him. Those adhering to this view think of the world as a reality other than God.[11] Not before the brilliance of the seventeenth century was this view widely questioned, and even then, the ancient European circle that did develop the belief in pantheism was quite limited in number. However, for most of the classical world, it was infrequent to find thinkers who rejected the account of creation and approached the nature of the world from another view.

There are certain great axioms of faith to which the Bible has unrelentingly held throughout its long narrative, such as the idea of a created universe. The Good Book also refuses to surrender its thesis that the universe was directed from a dark void teleologically by the mind of God. To repeat, the biblical narrative is fixed; it is set and sustained by divine power and does not waver in the affirmation that it is guided forward toward an eternal purpose, or *telos*, set by the Creator Himself. The commencement of Genesis conveys the assertion of God's reality, as well as the assuredness that He is the author of all things. The firmness of this biblical stance is not unlike Descartes' assumption at the beginning of early modern philosophy as he moved from a state of doubt to his famous, "Therefore God is."[12] Other fundamentals follow, such as the idea that man is the chief jewel and glory of God's creation. The Bible is unyielding in its assertion that God established the standard for this relationship and took the initiative in restoring it when it was broken by mankind's disobedience. We were intended for a pilgrimage on earth, which God ordained as an abode for His earthly creation. As deep calleth unto deep, there is an enduring part in mankind (either his soul or spirit) that calls and yearns after God, and He answers. Most importantly, God answered this call in the person of Jesus, who said, "I am the bread of life."

To look for a moment at an early Church Father, Athanasius, who was born in the latter part of 299 and died May 2, 373.[13] He wrote on the incarnation of Jesus of Nazareth in which he set forth an early and strong argument for divine creation. Though

---

[11] Hubert S. Box, *The World and God: The Scholastic Approach to Theism* (London: 1934), p. 179.
[12] Frederick Copleston, S. J., *A History of Philosophy* (New York: 1960), Vol. 4, pp. 90–92.
[13] John Behr, *On the Incarnation: Saint Athanasius* (New York: 2011), p. 19.

he was chiefly concerned with the strongest support for God's incarnation in Jesus of Nazareth, he also held profound views on divine creation out of non-existing material at a time when much of the Greek world was focused on creation out of preexisting matter. Athanasius saw it as of priority that "God is transcendent to all creation beyond all being and human thought. Yet this transcendence is not such that it makes His presence in creation, nor the creature's knowledge of God, impossible."[14] Though best known for his writing on the incarnation, in general Athanasius was a major figure in guiding the Church toward its future Nicene faith including creation, then currently much influenced by Greek thought.

Athanasius held to the fact that God created the universe through His Son, Jesus of Nazareth, but over a period, creation followed the mind of fallen mankind, from whence arose evil, which ultimately triumphed over creation.

The Book of Ephesians is home to some of the most towering thoughts in the Bible or in literature itself. The Apostle Paul could peer into the future to a time when all things will be gathered and reunited with God. Paul capped this vision in another writing by saying "Then cometh the end, when he delivers the kingdom to God the Father after destroying every rule and every authority and power."[15] Viewed from this angle, creation and redemption may be looked upon as "God on mission." As will be seen later, although creation went astray, the eternal purpose of God was not thwarted. One of the weightiest books of the early twentieth century was *The Purpose of God* by English philosopher and chaplain to the king, W. R. Mathews.

The universe as the creation of God has been a captivating thing for humanity to ponder. It is intriguing that, in the modern-day missionary movement, missionaries have so often chosen to begin their work with the story of creation rather than use a more direct evangelic message. An excellent nineteenth-century example of this resort to nature was the superb work of missionary Thomas Birch Freeman, who went to what was then one of the most benighted regions of West Africa. Freeman, the son of an African father and a European mother, showed greater endurance to the African climate than did earlier missionaries in the region. Most of

---

[14] John Behr, *On the Incarnation: Saint Athanasius* (New York: 2011) pp. 26–27.
[15] I Corinthians 15:24.

these pioneer European missionaries, whose monuments stand as a witness of the dangers of foreign mission work, died within weeks or months of their arrival in the Dark Continent. Thomas Freeman worked in the southern part of the British Gold Coast colony (now Ghana), where the West African slave trade had been as intense as any place on the continent. The people with whom Freeman worked were the Fanti, and beyond them in the central part of the area, (now Ghana) were the Ashanti people.[16] The latter were known for their resistance to slavery and boasted that none of them had ever been sold into it. Yet, the Ashanti were some of the most notorious slave trade dealers of the West Coast. Paganism reigned supreme among these West African people, famous for their Golden Stool, which supposedly descended from heaven. The Ashanti capital was Kumasi, known for its violent ways and oftentimes referred to as "the bloody city."[17]

Thomas Freeman and his wife arrived at the Gold Coast in January 1838, at a time when the longest-surviving missionary had just died after only thirteen months in the colony. Thus, Freeman found a vast land of pagans before him where the chances of survival for white missionaries were slim. When Freeman would go to a pagan village, he would begin teaching not with Jesus Christ or God's love, but with the story of creation. Despite their pagan faiths, these West African people seemed receptive to the idea that some great Power had brought the world into being. Although the natives did not utilize a philosophical understanding of God's act of creation, many of them did hold the belief that something or someone brought the universe into being. For example, the Fanti believed the world was brought about via some power greater than their own. This alone speaks volumes to the idea of God giving a general revelation to all the earth. Of course, general revelation has always been limited in what it made known, but mankind has always held a solid belief in a higher power.

From the beginning, Thomas Freeman's work on the Gold Coast was highly successful, with large numbers turning from

---

[16] The author had the privilege of spending the happiest segment of his missionary life among the Ashanti in Kumasi.
[17] The Ashanti fought valiantly against British encroachments in the nineteenth century and were subdued only after a number of wars with the British, who sent some of their most noted military leaders such as Sir Garnet Wolseley.

paganism to English Methodism.[18] In modern times since independence has come to so many African lands, Ghana has stood out as a model independent state, and, unlike so many other African states, has not experienced revolution. In a sizeable pagan town some distance from Kumasi, Freeman displayed a unique tactic for evangelism. He held a large banana leaf in his hand as he began his sermon and asked the audience if anyone among them could create one like it. After indicating that they could not, he explained to them God and His creation.[19] Freeman set up a base of operations in a large village in the Gold Coast some distance from Kumasi. Due to the work of Thomas Freeman and other missionaries, the Gold Coast rapidly became one of the most Christian regions in West Africa, producing such names of distinction as James E. K. Aggrey, an educator and Christian spokesman for Africa.[20] The endurance of Freeman's legacy is well evidenced by the fact that Christianity has become deeply rooted in the region and that present day Ghana remains one of the most politically stable, promising countries on the African continent.[21]

For many ages, religion has been such a far-reaching phenomenon as to have become in part tantamount to human life and our history on earth. Some scholars maintain that there has never been a time when religion was unknown on the earth. Sam Higginbotham, a distinguished English missionary to India, took some of the same approaches as Freeman in teaching the relationship between the earth and religion to his boys at the agricultural school he founded.

Kenneth Scott Latourette, in his magisterial *History of the Expansion of Christianity*, was masterful in his narrative, explaining the close connection between religion and the world. Let it be said that religion was born into the world at creation! This notion has become an essential part of the accepted social and professional assumptions

---

[18] The author's fondest years were in Kumasi where he observed with depth the tremendous transformation Methodist missionaries, along with others, had brought to Ashanti land.
[19] Allen Bertwhistle, *Thomas Birch Freeman: West African Pioneer* (London: 1950), pp. 38.
[20] The school, which the author founded in Kumasi, is today the Divinity Department of one of the country's fine universities.
[21] After decades of British rule and the flamboyant days of Kwame Nkrumah, the country moved quickly toward economic stability and a democratically run government.

in many parts of the globe. Anthropologists and sociologists have studied the number of generations required to move from animism and other pagan customs to Christianity. In widespread religious parlance, it has long been traditional to suggest four generations in evaluating the maturity of Christian congregations. As for West Africa, this judgment appears to have proven plausible.

As mentioned earlier, Thomas Freeman's method of evangelism may seem unexpected and certainly very different from that of other pioneer missionaries, who began with a more direct message about the cross and redemption. Even so, Freeman's approach to mission work remained somewhat standard well into twentieth century, when great scientific discoveries increasingly leapt to the front of the Western mind. The growing awareness of these new matters, which were looked upon as conflicting with religious doctrine, gave birth to bitter disputes between orthodox religion and science. The groundwork was laid for this in the seventeenth century, when for the first time a tremendous gulf seemed to open between the new emerging science and religion. In that century, the significant issue was the age of the earth; with each subsequent century seemingly producing a new area of contention between Christianity and science.

In the seventeenth century the chief divide between religion and science had been over the approximate age of the earth. Ussher, the Archbishop of Armagh, dated creation at 4004 B.C., signifying an early example of a Christian seeking to understand the first eleven chapters of Genesis. It was these chapters that narrated the account of creation, and what had gone wrong with it. Ussher's long-established date would appear on the opening page of the King James Version of the Bible in 1607. Well into the twentieth century, this version was the most widely-used in the West. For centuries, scores of minds looked upon Ussher's 4004 B.C. date as part of their inspiration and accepted this date as necessary to the biblical text itself. As late as the coming of World War II, this version was the most commonly-used version in the United State and Western Europe.

The author recalls an incident from years past, when a brilliant college freshman whom he was advising came to his office. The young man was determined to major in geology but was a devout Christian from a conservative church. When the author explained to the freshman that the 4004 B.C. date printed in the margin of his Bible was not in the text, the student's anxiety was mitigated, and the young man went on to graduate in a geology major at the head of his class. Much more solid work needs to be done in pointing out how inessential and superfluous has been the bitter conflict between science and the Word of God, which have both done so much over the years to enrich modern society. Thankfully more recent decades have shown several foremost scholars accomplishing rewarding work in this area of study.

One of the less noted pieces of modern history was the ministry of Harry Emerson Fosdick at Riverside Church in New York, who publicly rejected the accuracy of Ussher's estimate.[22] Another scholar who challenged Ussher's calculation on the age of the earth was John Ray, a professor and Anglican minister at Cambridge. Ray placed the beginning of time at 75,000 years ago, making the creation seem alien or implausible to his contemporaries. Ray's effort to placate the anxiety between religion and science may have presaged some of the nineteenth century conflict over Darwinism. On the other hand, one of Ray's best writings sought to point out the wisdom of Deity in the act of creation. Nevertheless, Ray's calculation had the effect of making religion and the Deity appear to be extremely detached and impersonal. Palpably, this notion of a distant God was one thing Jesus intended to clarify when He pictured Him as "Our Father," a term of familial closeness.

To return to North America, the conflict between religion and science rose to new crests both in the United States and in Europe in the decades following the War Between the States. Before the devastating conflict, Southern ministers had often experienced intimidation from their liberal Northern counterparts, who scoffed at Dixie's holding fast to its time-honored "Old Time Religion." After the War, during the decade of Federal occupation of the former Confederacy, these same ministers were frequently discomfited by what they perceived as the radicalism of the North regarding the Bible and their interpretation of it. Fervent and ardent disputes were brought about between the two regions, most often over religious issues such as divine creation versus Darwinism.

---

[22] For this, Fosdick endured much scorn from many conservatives in the United States. The author recalls that while in college, those who read Fosdick's sermons were often condemned. Much is said these days about how much the world has changed in the past century. However, many things, such as a change in the attitude between science and religion, have been positive.

Religious insecurity manifested itself strongly in Protestant sermonizing during this era in much of the Anglo-Saxon world. These quarrels, coupled with biblical literalism, were often begun to defend scriptural statements. This led to widespread polarization, making it all but impossible to reach a common ground among the numerous theological circles. In return, this polarization led to a rupture in many theological institutions, with new rival institutions springing up, each claiming to be defenders of the old faith. Several institutions of higher learning were founded in protest to what appeared to many a departure from the old orthodox religious beliefs. Incidentally, this practice has had a long pedigree in America, beginning with the founding of Yale University in 1701 as a protest against Harvard. Cotton Mather once wrote to a wealthy Englishmen, Elihu Yale, stating, "If what is forming at New Haven might wear the name of Yale College, it would be better than a name of sons and daughters." Such a gift from Yale might be a perpetuation of his major religious parlance.

    In the twentieth century, indications of partial healings were taking place in religious circles, with learned professors defending the compatibility of teaching both science and religion. However, some Protestant denominations, which had experienced bitter separations before and during the War Between the States, continued their alienation through this period.[23] It was only late in the century that some reunions began to occur, particularly between the Southern and Northern branches of the Methodist and Presbyterian denominations. One of the renowned men who sought to advance this healing process was Herbert Butterfield of Cambridge University. This is ironically fitting in that it was at Cambridge that the conflict originated in the seventeenth century. Butterfield, a devout Christian, came from a conservative Methodist church in northern England. He came to be acknowledged as one of the foremost historians of the twentieth century, holding consistently to a strong belief in the providence of God throughout history. Butterfield's widely-read and respected work on this subject

---

[23] Perhaps the most consequential of these was the formation of the Southern Baptist Convention, which was formed in 1845. Of the major denominations that split during the nineteenth century, it alone remains separated from Northern congregations.

brought to him extensive acclaim in the West, as well as the respect of liberal audiences despite his highly conservative views.[24]

Another modern Cambridge scholar who sought to resolve the divide between Christianity and scientific discovery was John C. Polkinghorne, who was a distinguished scientist as well as Anglican clergyman. In him was seen something of the continuing demonstration of the reconciliation of science and religion, when he recognized that creation may have taken place several billion years ago with a hypothetical "big bang." Much of his public lecturing was geared toward the harmonious nature between science and religion. He saw them as "The thinking reed of humanity" in which religion and science both sought an understanding of Truth. He said that although one did not find many things in the world stamped with "Made by God," the evidence of His handiwork was indeed everywhere in the findings of science. He made an interesting comparison of how the Church struggled in its first five centuries through several theological controversies before coming to accepted doctrines. There were parallels, Polkinghorne suggested, between the Church and science on how each had struggled to define itself over time.[25] For these poignant evaluations, he was looked upon as a highly reputable English scholar, deeply respected for his faith even by those who were not themselves religious.

One's fixation about God and the universe may become so deeply entrenched that it becomes disturbing to learn of anything that departs from a long-held view. The author recalls a fascinating college class more than seventy years ago at a small, highly recognized institution in which freshmen were discussing such issues. Regarding a question about the origins of the earth, the wise professor commented, "Give me the first four words of Genesis, and I will walk with you a long way in the search for truth."[26] These four words, "In the beginning God," offer a sense of security for anyone who has lived in the past two centuries and witnessed the unbelievable, far-reaching change brought by them. The most fundamental groundwork for such times is to accept that God is in control of all of history. The divine mind is not limited to religious

---

[24] *The Origins of Modern Science: 1300–1800* (New York: 1951) p. 187.
[25] John C. Polkinghorne, *Belief in God in an Age of Science* (based on Lectures at Yale 1996) Kindle Ed.
[26] Professor Sarkiss at Howard College (now Samford University) in Birmingham, Alabama.

things alone, but to every aspect of historical occurrences. The often-heard phrase "history is His story," goes too far by suggesting that God is responsible for the dark times of history in addition to its triumphs. To claim that all of history is "His story" is to deny the reality of freedom of the will and the accountability of humanity to God. Perhaps it would be more suitable to say that "His story is written within history." While that which is called religious history may speak more of God's special revelation, it must not be forgotten that the Deity likewise reveals Himself through the channels of general revelation, which may relate more distinctly to the mundane things of life. It is wisdom to accept the fact that God chose to create, rather than obliterate, the chaos with which Genesis opened its narrative. Supposedly, this too, was an option open to Him. "The heavens declare the glory of God, and the firmament showeth His handiwork."[27]

Historically, the subject of creation has long retained a significant niche in theological thinking about God. Origen, dying in 254 A.D. and having written First Principles, has long been regarded in many circles as the first systematic theologian.[28] He wrote much about creation, even suggesting there may have been earlier worlds before the existing one. Origen was deeply influenced by classical Greek philosophy, which regarded the universe as eternal, a position he took. In fact, Origen was in that small circle which witnessed the young Church move from Hebraic biblical expression to a new era in which the Church relayed its message in direct Greek terminology. This came about because by the close of the first century Christianity had become predominantly Gentile rather than Jewish

Still centuries later than these Fathers, following Luther's break with the Catholic Church (in the West in 1517), it again became necessary to define theology for the new Protestantism. Philip Melanchthon was the most gifted of Luther's associates in the realm of theological definition, and it was he who made the first attempt to do this for Protestantism, as Origen had earlier done for the Church at large. Guardedly defining its dogma and doctrine in *Loci Praecipus Theologici*, Melanchthon devoted a chapter of his work to creation. It was well that he should have done so in that the following century introduced the Scientific Revolution of the

---

[27] Psalm 19:1.
[28] Other historians of the early Church would afford this title to Irenaeus.

seventeenth century, which brought new anxiety for all branches of Christendom.

Melanchthon's opening words on the divine creation were, "God wished to become known and recognized. Therefore, He created all creatures and, in the process, used great artistry to convince us that things do not just happen by accident, but there is an eternal mind, and architect, a good and righteous One."[29] He saw history as the chief vehicle in the divine economy. About creation, his famous phrase, "Out of nothing," became standard logo for centuries as classic Protestant theology. "For he spoke, and it came to be; he commanded, and it stood forth." This word from the psalmist stood as a prooftext among Protestants for centuries.[30] Melanchthon maintained that not only did God create but sustains all things; he regarded this as "a general action of God," and not bound to secondary causes.[31]

It was in the century following Melanchthon that the age of the earth became the burning issue of the day. As previously noted, it was Archbishop Ussher who had already calculated this and placed creation at 4004 B.C. The author recalls seeing this date in his Bible at the opening of the Book of Genesis, when as a child he attended Sunday school in a small rural church in Tuscaloosa County, Alabama. Seldom, if ever, did one hear this questioned in a portion of the South where life continued much as in ante-bellum days. Here cotton was king and rural ways of life were built around that reality with a long practiced religious dynamic still much in vogue. Only the King James Version of the Bible was used, and it alone considered orthodox. Six miles from the campus of the University of Alabama in Tuscaloosa, such was the standard worldview, at least in the largely rural areas, until the coming of World War II. Not until entering college did one hear anything to question this. How fallacious the common practice of periodization of history can be!

One of the most significant developments of history of the West, however, was the launching of the Scientific Revolution in the seventeenth century. As logical, in the course of events, this was confined to a small circle of the learned, knowledgeable, inquisitive minds, and to university circles such as Oxford, Cambridge, Paris,

---

[29] Philip Melanchthon, *Creation and the Fall into Sin*, Loci Praecipus Theologici (Kindle ed.).
[30] Psalm 33:9.
[31] Melanchthon, *Theologici*.

and Padua. For the first time since the Aegean civilizations, men began to ask searching questions about the universe that had been little, or not, thought of in previous centuries.

The scientific revolution in the West was unique; throughout much of the twentieth century increasingly it continued to be recognized for this, steadily receiving additional focuses, and study. It was not a movement from no science to a lot of it; there had long been a lot of it. Nor was it a sudden shift from error to truth. Alternatively, it was not a break from *a priori* thinking and reasoning to empirical reasoning. Neither was it a shift in experimentation as these were made in the ancient and medieval world. They, too, produced observers who discerned what was about them. The scientific revolution of the seventeenth century was revolutionary in that science ceased to be esoteric and tight-lipped. Indian and Chinese science had been the property of a few, but not so with the scientific revolution in the West. It rapidly became widely disseminated. These scientific discoveries quickly led to a new world picture, or view of the world. Galileo used the term "world system."

Attempts were now made to describe various aspects of the world in a manner that was both harmonious and consistent. Increasingly there were attempts to relate everything to everything else. This symphony and coherence must have some degree of harmony or accordance with the phenomena one sees, and which human beings accept. It must harmonize with the basic ideas of philosophy and religion, or it does not endure long. An example is the moral effect on the world, and the effect of the world on morals.[32]

How did the universe get here? Without doubt, this is the oldest question humankind has pursued, and historically the answers have run a wide gauntlet, ranging from the superstitious to the sublime. From the least advanced paganism to the most erudite scientists, the question was kept alive. Christian faith never succumbed to the once popular view that history was cyclical, and that it periodically repeated itself. The ancient story of the phoenix bird, which supposedly lived in a distant place in Arabia, reflects this view of history. The New Testament addressed this panorama of history with a resounding finality, "So Christ having been offered

---

[32] The author is deeply grateful to the late Dr. John Ramsey, graduate professor in European history at the University of Alabama, who directed his dissertation and thinking along these lines.

once to bear the sins of many."³³ Christian faith has from the beginning remained teleological, maintaining God's purpose preceded the birth of time, but was enacted out in the framework of time, being continuously moved toward a purpose or goal. If God's purpose is at work, history can mean nothing less than that within its framework the hand of God moves creation toward some paramount goal or final post. While He is eternally moving His purpose toward some goal, it would be nonsensical to suppose that the purpose could not be thwarted or delayed through disobedience. Such a view precludes any authenticity to the great idea of the freedom of humankind. If this were discarded, the whole philosophy of sin becomes farcical. The freedom given to man issues from none other than God Himself; when in that pristine time He bestowed a divinely ordained freedom upon His highest form of creation, mankind.

One of the greatest of the pre-Nicene Church Fathers, Origen, held to the view that the world was eternal. Following the Council of Nicaea in 325, however, the Fathers, for the most part, began to break with Origen's view, and with that of the classical judgment that the world had been created out of pre-existing material. Some two centuries following Origen's death, his name once more became highly esteemed in the Christian Church.

The fourth century, was one of the greatest ever for the Christian faith and its worldview changed, becoming almost unanimously that of creation *ex nihilo*, (out of nothing). His belief that there had been a plurality of worlds is a classic one. In the fourth century, many of the teachings of Origen became suspect and the dominant view became that the world was created out of nothing. With that, Origen's noteworthiness faded, and for a time he himself was regarded by many as heretical. It must not be forgotten, however, that he had taught well before Nicaea. To take the long view, Origen's fame faded for a few centuries, but prior to the sixteenth century reformation his niche in church history was fully restored, and Origen gained in reputation in the Church. His reputation reached a high point and gained even greater momentum after the Protestant break with Rome in the sixteenth century.

One of the conspicuous things throughout the entire process of creation was God's ecology remained good, and at its

---

³³ Hebrews 9:28.

finality was pronounced "very good." This is diametrically opposed to the contemporary view of the great ecological imbalance in the cosmos and of the current threat, it imposes to human society. Whatever flaw developed in creation stemmed not from a negligence of the Creator but from man's response to His creation.[34] Thus, it becomes representative of a continuing disobedience on the part of the created to the Creator. One of the long-enduring properties of Christian faith has been God's constant care over His universe. Here one notes a major difference in biblical thought from Greek philosophy, which did not lay stress on a continuing divine care of the universe, even Stoicism its most moral philosophy did not. From mythology and folktale of the past, only the Old Testament rose to the acme of conceiving of a higher power calling the world into existence and likewise manifesting a divine care over it. There is real merit in the comparison by the Christian student of the creation stories in Genesis with the much later discovered Near Eastern myths addressing this. Their rediscovery in modern times, however, through the work of Samuel Noah Kramer and others gave a real misapprehension to some later Christians who felt threatened by such discoveries. The discovery of *The Epic of Gilgamesh* by Austin Henry Layard and the start of its decipherment by Henry Rawlinson received widespread attention in Victorian England.[35]

A major teaching of Christian faith is the fact that it regards God as a creator, not an artificer creating from something already in existence; rather He is the author of all matter and Christian dogma asserts that He continues to create. One of the interesting enigmas of modern-day science is its insistence that something like ninety-five percent of matter is now considered missing.[36] Genesis, in an eye-catching moment, portrayed God as resting after His work was done; Jesus, in a later and more elevated revelation once said, "My Father works."[37] Thus, creation may be thought of as an ongoing divine process. The anthropomorphic depiction of God scrutinizing His work and seeing it, as Genesis said, "Very good," must not be

---

[34] This will receive greater detail, subsequently under the theme of a great disobedience in the universe.
[35] N. K. Sandars, *The Epic of Gilgamesh* (New York: 1960), pp. 9–11. This work attracted the assistance by George Smith who made large contributions to the understanding of the Old Testament.
[36] Calvin Blake, *Beyond a Material Reality: Dirac's Universe* (1996), Kindle Ed.
[37] John 5:17.

viewed as the implication of an eternal cessation from God's labor. To do so would transform the Deity of the Old Testament into a lone Greek figure musing in His solitude.

Very early Christian practice, at least before the second century, appears not to have reckoned much with suppositions about how the universe came into being. The readers for whom they wrote, in an age to a degree little remote in sentiment from Victorianism, did not expect this. In total contrast, scientific advances and the discoveries of a post-World War II world called for nothing less than a major scrutiny. E. Y. Mullins, perhaps the most distinguished American theologian of his day, writing at the end of World War I did not see anything wary about the understanding between Christian faith and science.[38] For this, Mullins was often considered too liberal; he lived at a time when the conflict between religion and science was yet very much alive in the United States. Moderate as his theology was, it stimulated the growth of fundamentalism in parts of the United States.

Christian faith about the universe has never been a singular belief held by everyone. Western civilization has been characterized, as no other in history, by its varying beliefs and hypotheses about almost everything. Perhaps Stoicism was first to warrant notice of the difference between its views and Christian interpretations. It set forth many ideas and produced great individuals whose character of thought would have been a credit to Christianity. A distinguished student of the history of thought and morals wrote, "The great practical difference between the schools lies [sic], not in the differences they inculcate, but in the different degrees of prominence they assign to each, in the different casts of minds they represent and promote."[39] Perhaps the prince among Stoics was Seneca, who lived into the Christian era, but never mentioned Christianity.[40] Stoicism may be said to have represented the hunger in the world for those things which shortly thereafter Jesus of Nazareth encapsulated when He said, "I am the bread of life; he who comes to me shall not hunger."[41] It seems reasonable to suggest that Stoicism awakened

---

[38] Edgar Young Mullins, *The Christian Religion in its Doctrinal Expression* (Philadelphia: 1918), pp. 25– 26.
[39] William Edward Hartpole Lecky, *History of European Morals: From Augustus to Charlemagne* (New York: 1955), p. 128.
[40] Ibid., p. 336.
[41] John 6:35.

the hunger for things about the world that Seneca's not-so-distant contemporary, Jesus of Nazareth, satisfied to the utmost. Could that have been one of the objectives Jesus had in mind in His great and beloved saying, "I am the bread of life?"

God's creation with man at its summit was one without limits; and it possessed an attractiveness and allurement that made the tempter's temptation to Adam and Eve so realistically tantalizing. In these Genesis accounts of creation, with its two narratives, does it really matter whether the author is thinking in the framework of Sumerian cosmology or not? "In the beginning God," continues to be just as majestic in the twenty-first century, which has witnessed the exploration of outer space, as was true at the saga of creation. No more sublime and imposing explanation of how the universe came to be has ever been offered by thinkers than that with which the Pentateuch opens. It constitutes the strongest possible avowal or testimony for the existence of God. The universe affirms God. This impregnable thesis has proven unassailable despite the might and main of long and straightforward attacks against it. Thus, concerted efforts to dethrone it have been unable to annihilate the concept of the reality of God.

It should be noticed that this assumption is not an argument for the existence of God, but rather the acceptance and affirmation of this belief. Nowhere did the Old Testament propose to prove the existence of God. That would have been quite contrary to the ancient Hebraic way of thinking and more in line with modernity, which asks, "Where is the evidence?" In the Semitic mind it was, "The fool hath said in his heart, there is no God." To embrace this and not to accept the lofty concept of God's being is to surrender something innate and intrinsic within humanity. One of the things that impressed the nineteenth century missionary explorer, David Livingstone, in his long treks across much of central and southern Africa, was the fact that he never found a people who did not hold to some form of belief in God. Other pioneering missionaries of the modern-day mission enterprise, representing different parts of the globe, commented on this same characteristic, whatever the difference between their variant stages of civilization.

Rene Descartes was not thinking of this innateness of God when in his famous seventeenth century syllogism, he declared, "Therefore God is." This was around 1596, long before missionary connections with the western and central African populations began to demonstrate just how widespread was the belief in God. Difficult indeed it would be to state anything that has been more historically characteristic of human beings than that. This theistic approach to an understanding of the universal belief appears to be about as widespread as anything on earth ever has, and only in passing times has it been otherwise questioned. Atheism was deeply entrenched among some of the most radical eighteenth-century philosophies; and in an increasingly secular world of the present century, one finds an ascending number who state that they do not believe in God. Nothing is farther, however, from the truth when one considers history wholistically. The lateness of these groups and their vein of thought are not to suggest that no atheism appeared in societies in early times. Never, however, in the growing secularism of modernity has it been the dominant creed of any Western society.

How did the universe get here? Christian faith has been steadfast in its insistence that it was spoken into existence or decreed by a paramount Power. The craving and panting for the God of creation, among those who have not known His revelation in Christ, are but a part of this innately-driven quest which the divine planted within the highest form of His handiwork. Across the globe, one finds much the same affirmation and searching for God, both in the most elegant and most crude language. Without doubt, the psalmist said it best, "As the hart panteth for the water brooks, so panteth my soul for Thee, O God."[42] During the author's tenure in West Africa, he noted many names for God among the different language groups; their understanding of Him varied according to their social development. One thing that stood out, from the least developed to the most advanced people, was that West Africa was a place where the belief in God/gods and a created universe was universally prevalent. Yet how divergent were the concepts and degree of rationality in their beliefs! While many of these ideas were quite simplistic, others showed higher elevation and development. Had there ever been any doubt whatsoever, living in West Africa made the author realize that belief in deity was as ingrained and intuitive as anything ever was. Less clear to the author were the African avenues to the propitiation of the gods and their diverse, and conflicting, methods of attaining this. Some appeared to regard it as

---

[42] Psalm 42:1.

stemming from the nature of deity itself, while others seemed to suppose that human beings had been responsible for some affront to deity that must be atoned. Interestingly, one sees in these pagan conceptualizations much that is primary to Christianity, namely, the reality of God, the fact that He has been offended, and the necessity for reconciliation with Him. This, coupled with the fact that one could enjoy the Deity's favor or bitterly experience His disapproval, is to some degree, the elemental core of evangelical Christianity. Paganism showed considerable variation in the thought of the extent that the gods could become placated and appeased. An interesting example comes to the mind of the author.

In the boarding high school over which the author presided at Kumasi, Gold Coast (now Ghana), some of the students went each Thursday afternoon to the neighboring villages to mingle among the people, seeking to witness for Jesus Christ. One village, Akokoamong, was some seven miles from the school and had no church of any kind. Near the center of the village was a large pagan altar to which village folk frequently went seeking assuagement from some wrong they might have done. The students were concerned about this but were advised not to refer to the shrine's presence in the village whatsoever. The village chief gave permission to our students for preaching in the village, at a place not far from the shrine. The number of village folk who attended the student services steadily increased. While this was going on, a pastor from a church in Memphis visited the Gold Coast and was taken to Akokoamong. With enthusiasm he said that his church would provide money to build a small church building; however, the author advised him not to say this. Rather he should tell the village folk that if they would build the mud walls straight and thick enough that the rains did not deteriorate them, his Memphis church would provide money to enable them to have a metal roof for the small building, instead of the typical thatch roof. The little building was completed, and with interest, we noted that fewer and fewer people visited the pagan shrine. Steadily, the number seeking training for the Christian life increased until the congregation was organized into a church. Within a couple of years, the pagan shrine simply disappeared with larger numbers coming to the church.

When something is permitted to isolate the creation from the will and purpose of its Maker, reconciliation becomes imperative, but this cannot occur until there is some degree of revelation. While the beauty and wonder of nature may speak of God, it does not reveal His being and character. Creation was depicted as having taken place by fiat or divine warrant, without any outside assistance; rather it emanated from an eternal purpose and plan that stemmed not from the speculative thought of philosophers and theologians. The term "theism" came to be applied to this approach. The Apostle Paul in the New Testament Book of Ephesians first reached the apex of such a sublime mystery. The opening lines spoke of a time "Before the foundation of the earth."[43] One may speak of the creation of a universe; or more commonly the creation of a legacy, or a masterpiece of art or music. At the popular level, one is heard to say, "She has created a reputation for herself."

Throughout the entire Bible, one may follow this great revelation and affirmation of creation that over a period the Bible describes as days. By no means were affirmations of creation limited to the Book of Genesis. God spoke the universe into existence, and in the Prologue of the Gospel of John, it affirmed that the Word was the *Logos*, which introduced a Greek concept into the biblical doctrine of creation. In the narrative of the days of creation, one finds certain great principles of the universe. For example, "There was evening and there was morning," the bringing about of a second day in which the principle of advancement and moving forward is seen, as opposed to fixation. The ancients believed in the cyclical view of time, but Christianity has always taught the continuity of history. It does not repeat itself but moves forward. Genesis reveals physical and scientific, as well as moral and spiritual principles of creation. Immanuel Kant saw the moral principle as being inherent in humanity, as something built in by God, just as these other principles were. The "waters gathered together" brings to remembrance the old adage, "Birds of a feather flock together," and their coming together produced the oceans. One of the most pragmatic dictums is that of the greater and lesser, as in that of the greater and lesser light. Genesis 1:26, where God makes man in His image, made him the centerpiece of creation. To have dominion is the basis for humanity's centrality in the cosmos. It also provided the basis for one of the most intellectual debates of the nineteenth century, that of evolution. Faith in the validity of man became the

---

[43] The author, as perhaps the majority of scholars, and certainly unanimous among conservative thinkers, accepts Paul as the author. In the twentieth century, this attracted debate, but remains a theological stronghold.

Historical Pursuit of the Purpose of God

basis for man's claim to its high place in the cosmos. The night and day thesis, making the claim for darkness and light, provides the principle of separation or distinctiveness in the cosmos.

Echoed throughout the Genesis creation narrative are the inspired words, "And God said, 'Let there be...'" which confirmed that He was systematically bringing the world into existence out of nothing. It may, however, come as a surprise to some to realize that the most moving, powerful, and best-remembered words concerning creation come not in Genesis but centuries later from Deutero-Isaiah and the Psalms.[44] *Ex nihilo*, to use early Christian terminology, was a prominent early Christian belief held by most of the Church Fathers. Those who did not, such as Origen, were the exception and came early while much under the influence of classical Greek philosophy. The biblical affirmation, which preceded Greek teaching on creation, is constant in its insistence that it materialized not from some previously existing material. Greek paganism was willing to acknowledge that God created the world but insisted that He required matter to accomplish this. This Classical Greek thought, was heard throughout the fifth and fourth centuries B.C. It was likewise the belief of Stoicism, which did more than any other ancient philosophy to establish a high ethical code in the ancient world. An ancient Hebrew writing declared: "God created, and He provides; He made, and He sustains."[45] The great rival to the Stoic philosophical fraternity were the Epicureans, who believed that the world came into being accidentally and had no goal. It has been a hurdle in any age to find a predominant segment of society adhering to such a view as the Epicureans espoused. Generally, they have been thought to look to an opposite pole from most Greek ethical thought in several areas.

The "how" of creation is not of supreme importance in Christian dogma, and certainly leaves no ground for what the later centuries called "conflict of religion and science," which reached its pinnacle in the Victorian Age. Even though the theory experienced some precocious signs of rejection early on, it had powerful influence on religious thought and perhaps more significantly succeeded in dividing Christians into two divisions of thought.

---

[44] The author accepts that not all of the Book of Isaiah came from the same pen. Deutero-Isaiah commences with the 40th chapter of the book.
[45] George Foot Moore, *Judaism in the First Centuries of the Christian Era: The Age of the Tannaim* (Cambridge: 1950), Vol. I, p. 384.

Often vehement hostility has identified the camps and earmarked them as liberals and conservatives.[46] Such cleavages are usually long in healing, but happily, progress has been made in the last half century of western civilization. Nor, is the amount of space in the Old Testament devoted to creation of great impact. Later Old Testament writings portray a more mature concept of God's creation than do the Genesis narratives.

Perhaps this points to a wide general acceptance of the belief that no need was seen for a rejection of earlier biblical truth. The number of times a statement is made has nil to do with its authenticity. Certainly, in later Scriptures of the Old Testament, greater emphasis is placed on creation, notably in Deutero-Isaiah. In neither the creedal statements of Israel nor those of the early church was the doctrine of creation brought to the forefront of doctrine; after 150 A.D., the Church considered this doctrine as part of its creed, and in 325 at the Council of Nicaea, it was formalized into creedal usage.[47] This is not to say that the Fathers did not attempt to assuage philosophical thought and biblical truth. This they did, even to a degree in creation. Gregory of Nyssa attempted to explain in some detail the six days of creation; his brother, Basil, had dealt with this earlier, but with perhaps less clarity. One thing became noticeable among the church fathers regarding creation. While the Old Testament had attributed this to God, they placed the work of creation on the Logos, so weighty a Greek contribution to the development of primitive Christian doctrine. It was through the Logos that God manifested His economy, which is His activity in the universe.

---

[46] Hindsight has proven that this was religious futility and should never have raised its ugly head.
[47] Christoph Barth, *God with Us* (Grand Rapids: 1991), pp. 9–11. Likely, such teaching accounted for the fact that the Church felt the need to solidly its dogma of creation.

Chapter 2
God of Creation

Of significance is the fact that no biblical need arose for the necessity to defend God as Creator of the universe. Only sparingly, if at all, does holy writing allude to those who did not accept this tenet, as for example, "The fool has said in his heart there is no God."[48] Genesis 1 and 2 are at a popular level generally considered the best account of creation in the Bible, but Deutero-Isaiah (Chapters 40-66 of the Book of Isaiah) elevate creation to its highest theological tone of the Old Testament. Here in impeccable fashion God was depicted as Creator, and with unsurpassable majesty. Likely, no other property of God in the Old Testament identified Him more distinctly than does Creator.[49] It was not Yahweh's regality, nor His providence, or His *chesed* love that defined Israel's God more than did the creation of the cosmos. For an even more rewarding understanding of the Old Testament concept of creation, one might compare it to the Babylonian epics and one of their gods, Marduk.

Until the seventeenth century the biblical doctrine of creation was the universal belief of almost all people of the West; it was only in that century that this hitherto universally accepted thesis came under scrutiny. With that arose the question of the age of the earth. Only in late years of the twentieth century was serious thought given to just how unbelievably long ago the beginning of the universe might have been. Polkinghorne, a former professor at Cambridge University, wrote: "Behind this fruitful universe, whose fifteen-billion year history has turned a ball of energy into the saints and scientists, and that this purpose is at work in the world."[50] It was his belief that ten billion of these years were spent in evolving to the place that life could be born. Both Ussher and Polkinghorne were for a time Anglican parish priests. The Eastern Church has gone further than did the Western Church in its emphasis that in the teleological vision of God, creation will share in the life of God. The Apostle Paul may have been thinking upon such lines in the

---

[48] Psalm 14:1.
[49] It was once fashionable for older theologians to speak of the attributes of God. More recently the properties of God became practice.
[50] John Polkinghorne, *Belief in God in an Age of Science,* Kindle edition.

magnificent passage in Romans where he wrote: "We know that the whole creation has been groaning in travail together until now."[51] Only here in the New Testament is the picture of God's creation groaning and travailing in childbirth awaiting something new to be formed.

In the New Testament, Jesus spoke little of creation, though He assumed it, but made no reference to its beginning, but realized its beauty. He was deeply aware of its forms of life. Like William Wordsworth, Jesus was an insightful lover of nature and made comely references to it in his own teaching. Incidentally, Jesus' employment of nature in his teaching suggests vividly that he was a rural man familiar with its flora and fauna. In one of His most famous references to the natural world, Jesus insisted that from its observation one should learn what the birds already knew; that was, not to be anxious about their daily needs for tomorrow.

Polkinghorne advanced a very interesting and thought-provoking thesis about the fullness of creation. "To acknowledge that by bringing the world into existence, God has self-limited divine power by allowing the other [the universe] truly to be itself. The gift of love must be the gift of freedom, the gift of letting-be."[52] He went on to suggest that later aberrations and catastrophic events might have been the result of freedom bestowed on the universe that through its changes and alterations developed the properties that later led to cosmic disaster. It is, to be sure, an intriguing thesis; however, does it not raise the complex question of God having created something with potential growth and development that could lead to a large natural disaster? One must ask if God could not have created such a universe lacking the potentiality of such devastation. It is, however, during such far-ranging thought that one must recall that man is man, and God is God. Indeed, God did create humanity with a wide-ranging freedom that culminated in the disobedience of Adam and Eve in the Garden of Eden.[53] Suffice it to say, there are few more gnarled or problematical concepts in theological thinking than the balancing of God's will and man's freedom.

According to scientists since the 1920s, there has been a distinct emphasis on the evolvements in the universe stemming from

---

[51] Romans 8:22.
[52] Polkinghorne, Ibid.
[53] Ibid.

the changes in nature. Obviously, the universe can produce systems of unspeakable complexity that balanced with man's ability to live in it. Had this balance not have remained precise, it would have obliterated the possibility of human life on earth. According to the Anthropic Principle, such things as the color of the sun, earth's place in the solar system, its magnetic field, and the fact that after each stage of creation earth would be unsatisfactory for human habitation.[54]

Across the globe, both in the crudest and most elegant language, one finds the same deeply rooted assertions about eternal issues. The deepest concerns of life are often expressed in the most common fashion, for example, in parts of America it has long been customary to hear God spoken of as "the Man upstairs." Likewise, these same concerns have been set forth in the most sophisticated philosophical terminology. In the course of century's long revelation, as portrayed in the Old Testament, many different terms for God were introduced into the Hebrew language. The awesomeness with which the Old Testament opens, "In the beginning God," makes use of the term *Elohim* for Deity. It was not a beginning of God, for He knew neither beginning nor has an ending. Yet one of the earliest questions a young child might ask is, "Who made God?" God is the Absolute and only Ultimate; He is the Beyond. He is that beyond which one cannot think. Always divine transcendence lies beyond the reach of man or the possibility of human expression.

What a variety of approaches have been used among philosophers to elucidate God's transcendence, but this lies beyond possibility, otherwise He would not be transcendent. Just as the universe is beyond the mind, so God is above the universe.[55] Transcendence is often contrasted with Immanence, and with Pantheism. God can never really be transcendent, but always immanent, so close is the identification of God and the universe. Clearly, we cannot think of transcendence without thinking of something that is transcended. The obvious answer to the question "What does He transcend?" is that He transcends the universe.[56] Lacking divine revelation God remains incomprehensible, though

---

[54] In the Genesis narrative, at each stage of creation it was stated that God saw that it was good. Inevitably, this, too, was a part of the goodness God saw.
[55] Hubert S. Box, *The World and God: The Scholastic Approach to Theism* (London: 1934), p. 28.
[56] W. R. Matthews, *God in Christian Thought and Experience* (London: 1930), p. 130.

existing before all beginnings. No one has expressed this aspect of divine transcendence better than did Alfred North Whitehead almost a century ago.

> Religion is the vision of something, which stands beyond, behind, and within, the passing flux of immediate things; Something, which is real and yet waiting to be realized Something, which is a remote possibility, and yet the greatest.[57]

This meant that history would be a major channel of divine revelation. In the eleven chapters before Abraham, there is little that would be considered history as the term is accepted today.[58] The sacred name, "Yahweh" was not known in Israel before Moses; this came only after one of the great theophanies of the Bible in which God disclosed Himself to Moses who experienced Him at the burning bush, in one of the most beautiful of Old Testament litanies. Theologians have from ancient of days distinguished between general and special revelation with most acknowledging that general revelation is not saving revelation. In one of the most general indictments of mankind in the entire Bible, the Apostle Paul made the argument that humanity did not heed what nature had obviously made known of God to them. "So, they are without excuse."[59] So sacrosanct did the name "Yahweh" become that its guarded use brought hesitancy as to how it was originally pronounced. Yahweh was invisible, while the older term for God, *Elohim* was not.[60] With the giving of the Decalogue to Moses, great care was made that the name Yahweh, given to Moses in one of the most beautiful theophanies of the Bible, would not be taken in vain. It was for the purpose of Moses becoming God's spokesman to Pharaoh that he was given this deeper revelation of God. God's purpose may be identified in a single act of history, as well as in long historic spans of time. Thus, it is: those who embark on service to God seemingly

---

[57] Alfred North Whitehead, *Science and the Modern World*.
[58] This is not denial of the truth of this part of the Book of Genesis but recognition that their genre is not historical in nature.
[59] Romans 1:20. After the birth of Calvinism in the sixteenth century, most Calvinists in behalf of total depravity of man found formidable support in Romans 1:18–32.
[60] H. Wheeler Robinson, *The Religious Ideas of the Old Testament* (London: 1913), pp. 60–61.

come to know Him most intimately. The name was given to Moses, not for pride of learning, rather as a property of a divinely-given call to deliver Israel from bondage in Egypt. What a challenging task this was in that through Egypt's long, checkered history, the power of Egypt was at one of its peaks.

Through a long-dedicated line of Egyptologists, such as the pioneer historian J. H. Breasted, scholars have become much closer to the event of the Exodus of the Jews from Egypt than once they were. For example, the generally accepted date of the Hebrew exodus is not as remotely put as once it was. The pharaoh who welcomed Jacob to Egypt in the time of famine represented an Egyptian dynasty, the Hyksos, who were kindred to the Hebrews. At the time of the Exodus, this political posture had changed, and once again, native Egyptians were in power.

No other term received greater reverence in the Old Testament than Yahweh. The rest of the Old Testament became a continuing divine revelation given by God to humankind, His highest form of creation. Never, however, in all the revelation did familiarity reduce the sacrosanct regard for Deity. Perhaps, in modern America few more discrepant contrasts could be made with antiquity than the holiness of the Hebrew mind for the name of God, and the frequent flippancy with which it is used in America. While much of the Old Testament would be reckoned as general revelation, most of the sacred writings of the Jewish people are considered special revelation. Generally, theologians do not consider general revelation saving revelation; in contrast, special revelation is so regarded. This is not to say that authentic information about God cannot be conveyed through general revelation. The regularity of nature would be but one example of a general revelation to all.

The great mountain peaks of special revelation would be its theophanies, such as God's appearance to Moses at the burning bush, and again to Isaiah in the Temple in Jerusalem. Revelation was progressive until the coming of Jesus of Nazareth. From that point, a higher revelation cannot arise. Some religions do make the boast of being later revelations of God than that found in the New Testament, but this claim has never been accepted by mainline Christianity. This is not to suggest, however, that all Christian people, since Jesus' day, immediately reach the peaks of what Jesus Christ revealed about God. There is a growing up to Him, and unfortunately, some believers, as well as some Christian groups, never ascend the height very far. Those who do climb higher never ascend the towering peak of divine revelation in the temporal world. A favorite old evangelical hymn declares, "There are heights of joy that I may not reach, till I rest in peace with Thee." Christian apologetics acknowledges that relatively few saints on earth ever reach their potential in the knowledge and likeness of God while bound to that which is earthly. Perhaps it would not be amiss to add that undoubtedly the intent of much of the Pauline Epistles of the New Testament is to motivate their readers to press on. Still another old evangelical hymn, once so widely sung in American congregations, is "I'm pressing on the upward way, Lord, plant my feet on higher ground." Much of the spirituality of the European mystics throughout the Middle Ages was a call to the soul to press on to a higher spirituality, and more intense sense of the presence of God.

General revelation is that which God has given to all people universally; it is open to all, and even those who have never heard of the name of Jesus Christ have come to believe through nature and providence that there is a God. For example, when one concludes from an examination of nature, or otherwise, that there must have been a God who brought something to pass, that would be a general revelation. "The heavens declare the glory of God," is a splendid example. As has been seen, general revelation is not what theologians have called saving revelation. Most theologians have reckoned special revelation as an experience equivalent to religious conversion in the New Testament. Jesus Christ becoming incarnate on earth and living for a span of years among human beings is unanimously believed among Christians to have been the supreme pinnacle of God's revelation; from that high peak none ever can rise higher.[61]

The Book of Hebrews, by an unknown author, reaches a theological peak in declaring that while in the past God's revelation was partial; however, in Jesus of Nazareth the summit was reached and ceased to be partial; representing the very fullness of God's nature and being. No self-revelation can ever transgress or supersede that apex. That alone made Jesus of Nazareth unique—there can be no denial that God has spoken through other religious figures, but

---

[61] This of course applies only to Christians. Some other religions were established on the belief that they, too, were revelations from God.

none have ever gone beyond Jesus, though living centuries later than He did. Though humanity has all too often tarnished that divine revelation through their interpreting of it, nothing can blemish the revelation of Jesus and its standing in history. Nor is it feasible to imagine that in some future millennium one might indeed emerge who towered above Jesus in some of His teaching. That is true because in Jesus Christ, the eternal broke into the temporal. From that which is temporal, nothing can ever emerge or evolve to replace the Logos, which was in the beginning was with God. That powerful statement is buttressed with the apogee affirmation, "And the Logos was God."

Historically, there have appeared those who boasted that they provided a more complete revelation than that given in Jesus of Nazareth; this is a denial of the most fundamental claim of the Christian religion. The claim is the absolute certainty that in Jesus of Nazareth God was fully realized and that nothing new can ever emerge from that which was found in Him to widen or bolster such a bold assertion. This is not a denial of the truth that always there is ample room for continued growth and understanding as to what one does find in Jesus of Nazareth. Paul's admonition to what has been considered his most admired church, the one at Philippi, exemplifies this possibility. "Let this mind which was in Christ Jesus dwell also in you."[62]

Undoubtedly, the greatest threat Christianity has ever faced along these lines was second-century Gnosticism, which was a conglomeration of much past thought from Greece and the Near East. Christianity, not without a historic struggle however, refuted Gnosticism. It should be once more noted that this was the century in which Greek philosophy became master of Christian thought with Judaism having virtually closed its doors to the faith. There are few Judaic Christian writings or homilies stemming from Judaism as virtually all the interpreters of the faith were Gentiles in this century.[63] None were more to the forefront against this than Irenaeus in the second century. His greatest writing, *Against Heresies*, little read among Christians today, was heavily directed to the Gnostics.

---

[62] Philippians 2:5. The New Jerusalem Bible translates it, "Make your own the mind of Christ Jesus."
[63] This is not to say that the century did not know Christian writings, but not other Christian revelation.

As just noted, general revelation, though not to be equated with saving revelation, is worldwide; wherever on the planet there has been the search for God undoubtedly represents a seeking after Him from the fact that mankind was made in the image of God and is humanity's response to that echo yet remaining in creation. "We always knew there was a god," is a saying common in the missionary lore and experience from across the world on being introduced to the God and Father of Jesus Christ. General revelation is open to all who come to sense through nature and providence that there is a god, even those who have never heard of the name of Jesus Christ. The author witnessed much of the reality of this when working among the rural people of West Africa. One of the somewhat enigmatic teachings of Paul the Apostle, who knew Gentile life at close hand, is that they did not measure up to that which they had learned of God through general revelation. The fullest biblical exposition on this general revelation to pagans was by the Apostle Paul about the middle of the first Christian century.

> "For what can be known about God is plain to them, because God has shown it to them. Ever since the creation of the world his invisible nature, namely, His eternal power and deity, has been clearly perceived in the things that have been made."[64]

General revelation was highly pragmatic in that humanity cannot by searching find God. The hunger is there, but not the satisfaction. It was Deity who took the initiative in making Himself known to humanity. Such revelatory acts are a continuation and parallel of God's deed of going forth to search for Adam and Eve when they had fled from Him. It was guilt that made them hide from God in the Garden of Eden, but it was grace by which God sought them out. Though humanity is incapable of finding the Deity, there is within him the insatiable desire to do so. From the oldest book of the Bible, Job laments, "O that I knew where I might find Him."[65] One of the oldest and perhaps most bitter of the post-reformation theological disputes was how much of the likeness of God, in which

---

[64] Romans 1:19–20.
[65] Job 23:3.

Historical Pursuit of the Purpose of God

man was created, was destroyed in the Fall of Man. Part of Calvinism insisted that it was "total depravity," as it came to be known. Another following was of the view that it was only partial, much of the image of God remained in him after the disobedience of Adam and Eve.[66] Of all the early Church Fathers, none surpassed Irenaeus in analyzing this primitive portion of the biblical story. He pointed out that part of the tempter's suggestion to Adam and Eve was that they would be "like God," if they ate the forbidden fruit of the tree. Thus, this was the allurement to satisfy one of the innate things about humanity, namely, its desire to find God. Irenaeus argued that part of the temptation of Adam and Eve lay in the fact that they would become like God by their own means. The theology of the Apostle Paul was rich in using such words as "glory" to relate how God's plan for the redeemed was to make them, degree by degree, like God. Thus, the disobedience of the primeval couple was their unwillingness to follow God's command in rejecting His wisdom of what was best for them in the divine plan for the race's perfection.[67]

God's plan was foreign to those in the Book of Genesis who would build a tower that would reach heaven, and thus bring about their own way to God. God's way was a life of obedience that in the fullness (*pleroma*) of time would make humankind like Him. The ancient biblical temptation to be like God, but in the wrong way, is something deeply sealed within the human heart, and must be a residue of that which the fall of man did not displace. The Old Testament Book of Job, already mentioned as likeliest the oldest piece of literature in the entire Bible, reveals that deep craving or hungering for the divine. Job lamentably cried out for help in finding God. "Will no one help me to know how to travel to his dwelling?"[68] That constitutes life's strangest paradox, the deepest longing for that which lies beyond the bounds of human possibility. Robert Browning once expressed gratitude for having craved for that which he could not achieve.

To argue for such a divinely implanted thesis is at once to rekindle the oldest and most long-lasting debate earth has known; that of the origin of mankind. Commensurate with that is how the universe itself came to be. As far as the author's knowledge, there has never been a poll or census on how the universe came to be. Is

---

[66] Horace Bushnell in America epitomized this view.
[67] Dennis Minns, *Irenaeus: An Introduction*. Kindle Ed.
[68] Job 23: 3, New Jerusalem Bible.

there a conflict between the hearts and minds of men on this? For people of faith, how tersely set forth are the Bible's opening words, "In the beginning God." One of the most majestic of all the Psalms declares that God was: "Before the mountains were brought forth, or ever thou hadst formed the earth and the world, from everlasting to everlasting thou are God." John Calvin commented that no matter how hoary the mountains might be, God was from the ancient of days. This affirmation of God, nevertheless, sets forth the basic biblical view in the opening chapter of the Bible, and one held by most Christians in the world. For such a huge and disparate audience, how tersely set forth are the Bible's opening words, "In the beginning God created heaven and earth."[69] The rest of the Bible may be succinctly stated as the self-revelation of this God to mankind, the crown of His creation.

The Bible also has much to reveal about mankind's response to this self-disclosure of God. Throughout all the Bible, and indeed earth's history, one finds the scaffolding for man's long quest to find God. In early modern times when men began to explore the earth to a degree never known, they found religions that had been produced by mankind. This led to the introduction of courses in comparative religions in American colleges whose study proved beneficial in the development of a deeper understanding of culture and mankind's propensity for religion. Human hands lifted by man toward God can never do more than arrive at nature religions. The evidence for this through the ages and across the globe is ubiquitous. Such, however, were religions that led not to God, but only deepened the intense thirst for Him. The biographies of pioneer missionaries in Africa south of the Sahara and in the Orient are especially rich in depicting the hands that had been lifted toward heaven. The stories related to their new founds joys upon hearing of the Hand let down from Heaven were deeply poignant.

In returning to the theme of creation it should be noted that the "how" of creation, so vital in scientific studies, was of almost no concern to the biblical writers. They were more inclined to praise earth's glory than to search for its origin. "The heavens declare the glory of God."[70] After the close of the Old Testament came the brilliant birth of Greek philosophy which did turn its thought to

---

[69] Genesis 1:1, New Jerusalem Bible.
[70] Psalm 19:1.

these esoteric mysteries of the universe. In the Golden age of Greek philosophy, the giants arrived pretty much at the consensus that God created the earth out of pre-existing material. This was the view of Plato, the Stoics and most of the other well-known thinkers. That is the thesis set forth in Plato's Timaeus. Nevertheless, the primary purpose of Plato was to give a religious and theological view of creation. It was the view of W. R. Matthews, eminent philosopher in England about a century ago, that "The Timaeus contains some of the greatest sayings on the subject of creation which have ever been uttered." The following is an example. "Let me tell you, then, why the Creator made this world of generation. He was good, and the good cannot have jealousy of anything. And being free from jealousy, he desired that all things should be as like Him as they could be."[71] Neo-Platonism, which had an enormous influence on early Christian thought, made it easy to identify the God of Genesis with Platonic thought.[72] Neo-Platonism was the later development by Plotinus of Plato's philosophy; and one of its interests is that Plotinus was much nearer the time of Christ than was Plato. It does not seem inapt for Christians to identify aspects of Plato's Timaeus with God's general revelation of Himself. The Apostle Paul, in his letter to the Church at Rome, appears to have held this same view.

Questions not of concern to the ancients later received explanation and interpretation through myth, ancient Near Eastern creation accounts, and notably in Greek philosophy. After the Scientific Revolution of the seventeenth century questions never raised by biblical writers became one of the most fertile grounds for academic wrangling in modern civilization, a highly fertile and pregnant seventeenth century broke with the past as no century before had ever done. Within about half a century two remarkable figures, Galileo and Newton, wrote works that reversed the accustomed thought of centuries. In 1632 Galileo's "Dialogue" appeared and in 1687 Newton's Principia. Nothing had ever stirred the interaction of science and religion as did these works. Assumptions of prior ages were challenged that soon led to the recognition that a new world had been born. Philosophical assumptions that had once been universally accepted and become a part of Christian theology were now debated. Thomas Aquinas

---

[71] W. R. Matthews, *Studies in Christian Philosophy: Boyle Lectures 1920* (London: 1928), p. 207.
[72] Desmond Lee, Plato: *Timaeus and Critias* (London: 1965), p 7.

(1225-1274) had represented the epitome of medieval thought where a synthesis between world knowledge and theology had been reached. The scientific revolution of the seventeenth century laid all this aside, and in doing so created vast anxiety. In addition, its removal of old scaffolding made room for the thought of the modern world[73].

This influential century proved to be the fountainhead for the centuries-long conflict between science and religion that has not fully abated yet but has been waning. Given its context, there was never rationalization for this conflict of religion and science, which ensued. The primary agitating issue varied from century to century, such as the age of the earth in the seventeenth and evolution in the twentieth. Christian theology suffered much in its stature from this, but in quite recent decades has shown signs of a resilient recovery. By no means, however, has this billion years ago been ubiquitous or universally welcomed in all Christian communions. There are conservative Christian communities in much of the world that yet renounce science as a foe of religious faith. Happily, the last century has produced several brilliant scientists, as well as being devout Christians, who have helped heal this open sore of modernity. Herbert Butterfield and John Polkinghorne, both of whom taught at Cambridge were of this persuasion. With the latter's suggestion that the earth was created fourteen billion years ago as a result of the big bang, conservative religion pulled away rapidly from modern religious thought. The fact that Polkinghorne was also an Anglican clergyman did much to soften this thesis with more moderate Christians.

Prior to creation, the biblical avowal was that all was chaos. God could have simply chosen to obliterate the chaos; instead, He chose to create. This speaks notably of the kind of Deity the Christian God is. Had he chosen obliteration over creation, He would have continued to be the supreme invisible, indefinable God. In keeping with His nature; however, He chose to create just as he chose to go in search of a disobedient Adam and Eve. The deeply moving thought of James Weldon Johnson that God was lonely and resolved to create becomes more plausible after thinking along these lines.[74] Every believer should develop a prayer something like this.

---

[73] Ian G. Barbour, *Religion and Science: The Gifford Lectures*, Kindle Ed.
[74] James Weldon Johnson, "The Creation." The emotional beauty and thought of this poem by one of the

"Lord, give me grace to become creative in every situation and setting, which my life may confront me with."

In the Old Testament, in fact, we have two accounts of the creation of man. Both are much more committed to the truth of the revelation that mankind was created for fellowship with God, rather than with any concern *modus operandi*. Of all God's creation, mankind is the only part of it with any capability for fellowship with God, as he was made in the likeness of Him. The New Testament appears to re-affirm that the likeness unto God will be restored at the end when:

> Everything has been subjected unto Him,
> then the Son Himself will be subjected
> to the One who has subjected everything
> to Him, so that God may be all in all.[75]

In these accounts of creation, the question must be raised, does it really matter whether the author is thinking in the framework of Sumerian cosmology or not? Genesis 1: 1 is just as majestic in the world of twenty-first century exploration of outer space as ever it was in the days of a more modest cosmology. No more sublime an explanation of how the universe came to be has ever been offered by thinkers than Genesis offered. The Bible opens with the strongest possible avowal for the existence of God. It assumes His existence. It should be noticed that this assumption is not an argument for the existence of God, but rather a call for the acceptance of this belief. To state this in another way, it is an embracing of an innate idea of man that God is. Rene Descartes after spending the famous winter in his stove during the Thirty Years War pondering the theological ideas he had been taught arrived at his famous philosophical conclusion, "Therefore God is." Most people do not arrive at their conclusion of the existence of God in Descartes philosophical manner. They hold, indeed, to an ingrained belief in the reality of God, and of which life has given them no reason not to do so but has buttressed belief in Him.

---

primary contributors to the NAACP, born in Florida 1871, did not receive the universal acclaim in Christian circles that it might have. In the opinion of this writer, it is at least a minor Christian literary work of art worthy of becoming better known by younger Americans.

[75] I Corinthians 15: 28.

The revelation of God that is displayed in the Old Testament was intermittent and always partial, but it was progressive and ongoing. It was also a revelation given most copiously through and in history. One may with reason argue that had God chosen some other vehicle of revelation, history would never have played the role it has played in Western Civilization. Finally, it was a revelation, which through many centuries failed to reach its culmination in the Old Testament; only with the New Testament and the coming of Jesus of Nazareth that such a fulfillment may be said to have been reached. Additional revelation came not by plowing still more deeply into history, but only with the backward look to ascertain the mind of Jesus.

Such questions as were raised above were faced by the young Christian Church, and this became more pronounced when after the first Christian century the Church increasingly resorted to Greek philosophy to define its own dogmas. Origen would have considered these moot questions, as there never was a "time" when the universe did not exist; as he believed it to be eternal. Origen was not alone among the Church fathers who were of this opinion. Opinion on this has historically differed in Christian thought, with the more, by far, orthodox view being that the universe came into being in the realm of time, as an act from the Diving Being. Some Christians, along with some of their predecessors of Greek philosophy, have looked upon the universe as having no beginning; rather it was eternal. This was the most common view of classical Greece, when history's most renowned philosophers occupied the stage of Mediterranean thought. However, from the least developed paganism, to the most erudite schools of theology and philosophy, such questions continue to be raised.

Origen of Alexandria believed that the universe was eternal.[76] In holding to this concept of an eternal universe, he was in company with well-known Greek philosophers. If this were the case, creation was eternal just as God was, and beyond the realm of the

---

[76] In spite of Origen having been recognized as the first theologian, so much of his thought is confusing.
For example, he wonders if there have not been worlds before this one, and if ever there will be a time when there is no world at all. Another source of confusion is the revision later done by Rufinus, and to some extent statements made by Jerome. Still another point to be considered is that there are Greek and Latin texts on De Principia, which do not agree.

rational. Likewise, it would seem to justify the claim of Pantheism. One of the best of many sources on Origen is *De Principia*.[77] The question of creation was, therefore, beyond the realm of the rational for Origen. Just as God was eternal, likewise was the cosmos. Origen's view was contrary to the Christian rationale of *ex nihilo*, creation from non-existent material. Thus, the Christian God is a direct Creator, not a divine Artificer. From a modern-day perspective, the Father of Christian Theology was heretical; from his own panorama not so, as many significant dogmas of the faith had not yet become dogmatics, and would not until the next century, following the Council of Nicaea in 325. Most novices in the study of Church History have been fascinated by the story of Origen's desire to accompany his father to martyrdom, which was prevented by his mother hiding his clothes. Origin was about seventeen at the time, but in the middle of the third century, he did become a martyr c. 252 during the Decian persecution.[78]

Another question, which arose concerning creation, was the issue of whether matter was evil or not. Since Christianity taught that God created the world out of non-existent material, the issue became a weighty one for those who accept that matter was evil. Such was the view of the most prominent Greek philosophers. It was out of this assumption that other issues arose. From this dualism developed the concept of God in opposition to evil matter. Such was the platform on which Mani developed the religion of Manichaeism; and it may be noted that for almost a decade of his life Augustine of Hippo was a follower of Mani. It was only his disappointment with the sect's esteemed teacher, Dr. Faustus, whom Augustine met, that he turned away from the religion.

In contrast, almost universally, the major Greek philosophers held to the view of creation out of pre-existing material. This was the view of Plato in The Timaeus. Nevertheless, the primary purpose of Plato was to give a religious and theological view of creation. It was the view of W. R. Matthews, eminent philosopher in England about a century ago, that "The Timaeus contains some of the greatest sayings on the subject of creation which have ever been uttered." The following is an example: "Let

---

[77] Henri De Lubac, *Origen on First Principles* (London: 1975), p. 27.
[78] Due to the fact that Origen died as a result of his tortures, and not directly from instant martyrdom some have questioned his claim to this. The consensus of historians is that he was a true martyr.

me tell you, then, why the Creator made this world of generation. He was good, and the good cannot have jealousy of anything. And being free from jealousy, he desired that all things should be as like him as they could be."[79] Neo-Platonism, which had an enormous influence on early Christian thought, made it easy to identify the God of Genesis with Platonic thought.[80] Neo-Platonism was the later development by Plotinus of Plato's philosophy; one of its interests is that Plotinus was much nearer the time of Christ than was Plato. It does not seem inapt for Christians to identify aspects of Plato's Timaeus with God's general revelation of Himself. The Apostle Paul, in his letter to the Church at Rome, appears to have held this same view. In North America, much of such religious thinking regarding a single battle was widely popularized through the introduction of the Schofield Bible.[81]

The cornerstone of Christian faith remains steadfast, that there can be no more stabilizing influence in life, than the assurance that one does live in a universe brought purposively into existence by an absolute eternal being. Is it not but axiomatic that if God did indeed bring the universe into being, there must have been some purpose in His doing so? Since He is divine, likewise the purpose must be divine, as it is beyond comprehension that God could act out of His character. From this, the Apostle Paul concluded that the Gentiles, "Have no excuse for their ignorance of God."[82] Theologians would consider this general revelation; not necessarily, would it be regarded as Salvation History.

Since the time of Copernicus, the earth has not been regarded as the center of world, and nature itself has been looked upon as a vast complex system. With its ceaseless line of causes and effects, which have no beginning or ending, the question has been posed, "Does it still make sense to speak of the creation of the world and of man?"[83] Human thought has had a long line of believing that

---

[79] W. R. Matthews, Studies in Christian Philosophy: Boyle Lectures 1920 (London: 1928), p. 207.
[80] Desmond Lee, Plato: Timaeus and Critias (London: 1965), p. 7.
[81] The Schofield Bible continues to be widely circulated with various plans and institutes of study.
[82] Romans 1:20 Paul gave three examples of God's manifestation of himself since the time of creation.
His invisible attributes, God's eternal power, and his divine nature.
[83] Erich Frank, Philosophical Understanding and Religious Truth (Oxford: 1945), p. 55.

Historical Pursuit of the Purpose of God

nothing comes of nothing. Christian faith, however, has always held to the belief that God created the universe; and that which has long been the historical faith was transcendently stated in the opening words of the Genesis narrative.[84] It should be noted that the sublimity and loftiness of these opening words of the creation narrative display a theistic approach to the nature of the universe. Likewise, it implies a religious view of the cosmos that calls for communion with Him. If this were true, then the personal nature of God is retained, allowing Him to have fellowship with His finite creatures that were bestowed with real freedom of choice.[85] Likewise, the narrative knows nothing of an eternal world.

Could there be a wider cleavage in human thought than those who follow the theistic (the opposite is atheistic) route to the origin of the universe, and those who adopt a modus operandi explanation that eliminates the divine hand?[86] One of the conspicuous things about the Genesis narrative of creation is the fact of the day-by-day creation, there is the immediate or direct, personal operation of God in all that came to be. Of course, to say, "God saw" is to make use of anthropomorphic language. Both theologians and philosophers fully recognize the pitfalls in making use of anthropomorphic language. Nevertheless, however sophisticated or erudite, they acknowledge they are driven to this and cannot escape anthropomorphism. The idea is incurable and necessary.[87] Throughout the creation narrative, however, there is the unabated, almost personalized, theistic approach to the origin of the universe. From the long study of natural religion, studies gathered from unique, and widely variant, parts of the earth, the unrivalled view of almost all people has been that of creation, though often expressed in pagan terminology.

How did this universe get here? It was brought into being through creation by a Supreme Being (the Ultimate), whom we call God. The rest of this book, which we call the Bible or the Writings, will be the record of His self-revelation to us. It will also show something of man's response to this revelation. The "how" of

---

[84] Ibid. pp. 56–57.
[85] Ibid. p. 204.
[86] Novice students might note that in the ancient Greek to place the letter "a" at the beginning gives the opposite meaning to a word. Gnostic and agnostic is another example.
[87] W. T. Stace, *Religion and the Modern Mind* (Philadelphia: 1960), p. 17.

creation is not of supreme importance and certainly leaves no ground for the centuries later so called "conflict of religion and science." God could have chosen simply to obliterate the "chaos" which existed prior to creation. Had he done so, he would have continued to be God—self-existent—but instead he chose to create. What a revelation about God, and the kind of Supreme Being He is! Lord, help me in every situation of life in which I may find itself to choose to be creative.

Chapter 3
What Then Went Wrong?

Trevor Kletz wrote a book asking this same question. His was a study of major industrial errors that produced explosions or other disasters in recent centuries that for many people resulted in their death. The book revolutionized the way the industrial world viewed safety and how such disasters could be avoided.[88] God's perfect creation, likewise, witnessed something gone wrong. In this case, it was through the disobedience of man and not a mechanical or industrial error. In His creation God allowed mankind to exercise a full freedom of choice, something no other portion of creation could claim. The question as to why God allowed such a high privilege to mankind is to ramble among the mysteries of the universe. Musing over this, man came to know that was the most proffered decision ever bestowed upon it. It is that which distinguishes the difference between the human world and the animal realm. It has been said that responsibility is being able and required to give an account to someone for something.

It follows that meeting such disparate, oftentimes discordant, views as have been noted, made one recognize the complete necessity for a divine revelation because natural thoughts of God are as divergent as imaginable. Concepts of God varied enormously among the diverse groups of people the author came to know in West Africa. Perhaps the foremost and ubiquitous attitude was the absolute necessity of placating the gods by making use of the proper charms. In Lagos, Nigeria in 1952 on the campus of the Baptist Girl's School, there was a huge tree that needed to be taken down; had it fallen, it would have crushed one of the buildings. On the morning that the wood choppers were to begin their work a pagan priest was brought in by the workers to assure that such an accident did not happen. Periodically, the priest blew fresh "juju" on the tree to prevent such misfortune. Hours later, when the tree began to fall it fell precisely where the cutters wanted it. Among the many watching the cutting were pagans and Christians. The latter were

---

[88] Trevor Kletz, *What Went Wrong?* (London: 1956).

convinced that it was God who prevented a calamity, while the pagans were confident that the juju had worked.

One might call it a tie that day between paganism's god and the Christian Deity as there was no empirical proof as to why the tree fell into the right place. However, over the long range of history there is little doubt as to which has shown greater care over its devotees. Though there has been a continuous and widespread existence of paganism, there can be little, if any, rational evidence that its values have surpassed the benefits Jesus Christ brought to the earth. In typical paganism, one finds an almost total absence of what Christians have so long loved to call grace or God's unmerited favor. While no dogma of Christianity has a stronger foundation than this one; in Christ God did something through *agape* love for humans totally unmerited. Undoubtedly, this must be the strongest contrast between paganism and Christianity as each religion has lived out its time on earth. Because this is true, little wonder that John Newton's hymn, "Amazing Grace," became the most beloved hymn in Christendom.[89] The contrast between the two systems of religious thinking could not be sharper or more illuminated than what Christians call grace. Christians, too, acknowledge West Africa alienation between humanity and Deity, but likewise readily accept that it was immitigably overcome in the incarnation of Jesus of Nazareth. This age-long alienation between humanity and God recognizes that, historically, it was arched over at a definite point in history through the Incarnation of Jesus of Nazareth who took upon Himself the offence of us all. When one entered a predominantly Christian village in West Africa the contrast to a pagan one was distinctly realized. Such a unique diverseness, among an otherwise common people, was deeply sensed.

Divine revelation was an absolute prerequisite for humanity to move beyond its crude and frightful concept of Deity. Granted this psychology, it is of little wonder that Adam and Eve sought to hide from God. Apart from eternity's resounding words of Jesus, "Come unto me," humanity would have continued desperately groping for a satisfactory knowledge of the God whom paganism knew to exist. Rooted among such forlorn people was the futile sense that the gods needed to be placated if there to be was peace in

---

[89] John Newton was noted as a notorious slave trader in West Africa in the eighteenth century.

the village. In a Christian West, a child's beloved, "God is love," would have been a total anomaly or something freakish to paganism. This was one of the most inherent things early nineteenth century anthropologists saw in their early investigations across the globe as when men began their journeys across the oceans. In the middle of the twentieth century one still found in West Africa numerous villages where no church of any kind existed.

Less clear to the author was the West African reason for the propitiation of the gods. Some appeared to regard it as stemming from the nature of deity itself, while others seemed to suppose that human beings had been responsible for some affront to Deity that must be atoned for. Interestingly, one sees in these pagan conceptualizations much that is primary to Christianity, namely, the reality of God, the fact that He has been offended, and the necessity for reconciliation with Him. This, coupled with the fact that one could enjoy the Deity's favor or bitterly experience His disapproval, is to some degree, the elemental core of evangelical Christianity. Paganism showed considerable variation in the thought of the extent that the gods could become placated and appeased. An interesting example comes to the mind of the author.

In the high school, boarding school over which the author presided at Kumasi, Gold Coast (now Ghana) some of the students went each Thursday afternoon to the neighboring villages to mingle among the people, seeking to witness for Jesus Christ. One village, Akokoamong, was some seven miles from the school and had no church of any kind. Near the center of the village was a pagan shrine, which had been there perhaps for generations. The students were told not to make mention of it all, or to get into a dispute as to how much power its gods had.

In the systematic process of creation, there was never any suggestion of an emerging flaw or blemish in the creative process that might suggest some future difficulty. No disfigurement of any degree had made an intrusion at any point into the handiwork of the Creator. Whatever flaw later arose in creation stemmed not from any heedlessness of the Creator, but from man's response to that work of the divine. Here one notes a major difference in biblical thought from that of Greek philosophy. Stoicism, nearer in thought to Christianity than other Greek philosophies, did not think of the origin of things as necessarily ever having been flawless. Nevertheless, in Christian thought, God's ecology remained good

Historical Pursuit of the Purpose of God

throughout, and in the end, its finished work was pronounced "very good."

The Stoics agreed with other great classical philosophers that creation was out of pre-existing matter. This philosophy did bequeath to Western Civilization something of its ethical system, but of course, western historians are in large agreement that it was minimal in comparison with the contribution of the Christian religion to ethics and morals. Stoicism was the faith that most Romans turned to when desiring some belief higher than the old traditional paganism that bound the Romans together for such a long era. It had a tremendous impact on the development of Roman law and life. Stoicism long remained a significant part of the European educational concepts that the upper classes followed, and there can be little doubt that it had some influence on Christian thinking in the early centuries of the Faith. For example, the first head of the influential theological school in Alexandria, Pantaneus, had once been a Stoic.[90]

Of the ancient approaches to creation, it was only the Judaic sacred writings, which approached it from the idea of having been created out of non-existing material. In Christian theology, this has been, as the oldest theological thinkers put it, creation "ex nihilo." Incidentally, that is about the highest paradoxical statement anyone could make of anything.[91] There is evidence to suggest that Justin Martyr, prominent second century Christian martyr, perhaps held to this position, as did his successor, Athenagoras. Justin appeared to believe that there had been a scattering of divine truth among the Greek philosophers, and he remained a Platonist even after he embraced the Christian faith. His understanding of God was so Platonic that he thought of the Deity as unknowable and transcendent.[92] It was the reading of the Old Testament that led Justin to Jesus Christ.

The biblical assertion is that God spoke the world into being over an unknown period. This concept very early on became one of the great landmarks of Christian dogma, where it has ever

---

[90] A strong tradition among the early Christians was that Pantaneus had once travelled in India. If that were the case, perhaps he encountered Indian mysticism and religious thought.
[91] D. M. Baillie, *God was in Christ* (London: 1947), pp. 110–111.
[92] Leslie William Barnard, *St. Justin Martyr: The First and Second Apologies* (New York: 1997), pp. 14–16.

Historical Pursuit of the Purpose of God

since retained its cornerstone. Biblical theology looks upon this work of creation from God, as not that of an artificer, but as a divinely spoken creative word from the eternal realm. No biblical writer ever departed from the dogma that it was divine; for Deity gave the universe its existence. In Judaism, any other thought would have been very alien as seen in the forceful, "The fool hath said in his heart there is no God." Through all the centuries, that has remained a solid footing for all Christian thought. There are suggestions that some things in the first eleven chapters of Genesis may have been influenced by Babylonian creation myths, but the prominence of God as Creator is not one of them.

The anthropomorphic depiction of God scrutinizing His completed work and finding it "very good" must not be an eternal cessation from His labor. Such would transform God into the ancient Greek mold in which He is seen as a solitary figure brooding in thought. Jesus of Nazareth repudiated such an idea in a pithy and succinct statement, "My Father still goes on working, and I am at work too."[93] Eighteenth century Deism has its place in history for its depiction of God as remote and characteristically distant from the operation of the world, but the God of the Bible is revealed as attentive and always assertive with the affairs of earth. Elijah, in ancient Israel, teased or bantered with the prophets of Baal about their god not being responsive to their summons for help on Mt. Carmel. One of the feeling things about the Christian religion for those who may sense little concern for doctrine, or church history is the assurance that God is attentive to their daily cries for help. In Psalm 107 the Psalmist, where deed after deed is enumerated of what Yahweh has done for Israel, is a beautiful testimony of this divine economy. Some cried to Yahweh out of their distress, while others were in darkness, gloom, affliction and irons. The thesis of the Psalm is the readiness of God, whatever, the need of the moment. Much of the Psaltery abounds in such a portrayal of the Deity yielding to the cries of distress from the humble of the earth, and their praise of thanksgiving for His having done so. A total contrast in the ancient world were the Epicureans, who differed sharply with the Stoics in their understanding of the world as ethical and looked upon the impossibility of any higher power manifesting its concern for the

---

[93] John 5: 17, New Jerusalem Bible.

distraught ones of earth. To them, the world existed only by accident itself, offering little room for the altruistic whatsoever.

The one indisputable doggedness of the creation narrative is that it lies beyond the power of human intellect to fathom its mysteries or ruminate on how long such a state of perfection may have continued before it came to its end. The most stringent Christian belief is the assertion that its Maker had previously and innately endowed humans with a total, unbridled freedom of will. This issue of freedom of the will has been one of the most persistent and nagging issues that human minds have ever faced. One has only to remember the Pelagian controversy of Augustine with Pelagius, the British monk over this issue in the fifth century. When one follows rationally all the arguments stemming from this, it is not an issue easy for the mind to grapple with. This freedom given to humanity was never something concocted or contrived, but a genuine gift from God that carried responsibility. Perhaps one of the most ringing voices of modernity in advocating the reality of this freedom given to humankind is that of John Polkinghorne erstwhile Anglican priest and professor at Cambridge. He suggested that God might have limited Himself in bestowing such freedom. It meant, he said, that nature must be allowed to be itself even when reeking disaster in creation. Polkinghorne saw this freedom as reaching to the lower realm of creation, even allowing the universe to develop tendencies that might ultimately threaten God's own will.[94]

The present writer's favorite definition of responsibility is one learned in his first year of theological study: "To be responsible is to be required and able, to give an account to someone for something."[95] Never was the freedom God bestowed to Adam and Eve intended to be a puppet show, but a credible and realistic choice for His highest creation to exercise. The couple was given full option, at creation, for humanity to exercise this responsibility, which some have seen as a limitation upon God Himself. It was humanity's violation of this wide-ranging freedom that brought its fall through a resultant power to exercise unsound and erroneous choices. This is a superb commentary on the profoundness of freedom of choice, innately and divinely bestowed on humans. A full and complete acceptance of this fact is one of the most striking

---

[94] John C. Polkinghorne, Ibid.
[95] Professor Olin Binkley at Southern Seminary, Louisville, Kentucky, 1950.

realities of the depth of the creation narrative. In approaching the biblical account of the Fall of Man, it appears to the writer that the over-towering peak in the entire range of God's revelation of Himself must surely be that from His vantage point, something very monstrous and extreme had gone incongruous with His creation. The twin peak in this range was that God would not leave it thus but purposed its redemption and restoration. Thus, of all the purposes of God in the long run of history, this plan to redeem His own creation must be foremost and fundamental to all subsequent divine goals.

Among the narratives of humans there have been various tales that spoke of a long-ago, but now faded golden age on earth. Perhaps this represents the human nostalgic and re-emerging remembrance of "things most precious," which human beings have shown their capacity for retaining, and with which the race was endowed. Shakespeare made one of his characters say, "I cannot but remember that such things were things most precious to me."[96] Nothing in all the archives of grievous blow has captivated the imagination of humanity more than the Fall of man. Quite apart from biblical references to it; other literature retains the remembrance of things that once were, but now removed from their pristine perfection. Since the seventeenth century, the influence of John Milton has helped keep this drama awake in Western Civilization. Even with a fading fondness for Milton in contemporary times, the Fall of Man remains one of the unfathomable enigmas from earth's long undated past. The complete fullness and wholeness of Deity itself, with all its divine attributes, were fully reflected in Milton's fall of a perfect creation. Equally so, the seamy and squalid side of human possibility is displayed in the biblical account of the fall. With the words of Adam that it was the fault of the woman, the age-long blame game was born with its unending line of heirs.

When one considers the wide array of discrepancies and contrast between the ancient Jewish rabbinical interpretation of the fall and the narrative of Genesis, it appears wise to avoid seeing the account as a literal depiction of what occurred. The Rabbis saw the fall of Adam and Eve as the result of fallen angels having sexual relations with men, and for which they, too, were cast down. Thus,

---

[96] In the play when McDuff observes that his castle has been burned.

it was their seduction of men that brought on the fall. In addition, the angels, according to rabbinic tradition, had sought to prevent the creation, but once this was done, the seduction took place. According to the rabbinical tradition, the result of the fall was God's withdrawal of the Shekinah glory from earth to the first heaven.[97] From this glance at the thought of the ancient Rabbis, it becomes transparent that one should waver before applying a literal interpretation to the episodes of the first eleven chapters of Genesis. As noted elsewhere, with chapter twelve one does arrive at far more firm historical ground in the Book of Genesis. None of such an interpretation may be said to have done violence to the profound truth of Genesis. The universe is here by the authority and power of God. Mankind was given the highest place in the universe, even that of being the cause for it to go astray. God chose to create humanity with the highest endowment of any other part of creation, and to bestow on humanity a vast freedom of will in the exercise of choice. These are perpetual and undaunted peaks of divine revelation as to the kind of universe one lives in; they need not become entangled with pseudo attempts, even when well intentioned, to reconcile the biblical narrative with the rationality of human understanding.

What happened in the "Fall of Man," remains but one of multitudinous mysteries in the inscrutable ways of God to humankind, which after all was His highest form of creation. A vital ingredient of good religion is to reverence that sense of awe and mystery which comprises its very essence. Lacking that, it ceases to be religion. In contrast, some of the mystery religions of early civilizations set forth their proud boast to have unraveled some of the enigmas, which form the core of good religion. The Christian religion set forth an entirely different concept. Perhaps the account of Moses removing his shoes before the biblical theophany of God is a prompt to a modernity that is trained to probe every detail in the emergence of such mysteries. The finest of the Church Fathers reveled in their effort to balance the transcendence of God with their own limited understanding of His being. Those whose propensity is to interpret literally this brief narrative given of Genesis concerning the misdemeanor of Adam and Eve surely have not fathomed its mystery. The significant thing is that something did occur in the Garden of Eden, which brought a deep declension to the splendor

---

[97] Alfred Edersheim, *The Life and Times of Jesus the Messiah*. Kindle Ed.

of God's creative action. In spite, however, of its profound reality at the time, God did not accept this as an enduring fixity or lasting reality but purposed to redeem it. Over the ages, much has been written about the purpose of God. Surely, following the malfeasance that the Fall His central design became that of redemption. Herein is seen the crux of the matter on which theologians and philosophers have written about the purpose of God.[98]

It is important to recall that the pioneer attempts of writers to unravel the profundities of the divine truth of God pointed to another direction, toward a more critical understanding of history. In some cases, the dating of historical events was revised by hundreds of years as history adopted new critical methods of study. It is of basic significance to grasp that the foundations of biblical criticism proved to be the guiding lights to a critical understanding of history. Biblical higher criticism preceded such advances in the writing of history. One reason may well be that quite often pioneer historians were also Christian ministers as well. Regarding the early critical approach, both biblical and historical, Germany made a real contribution as the leader in this field. All of this becomes germane when one recalls that it was history as the primary arena in which God has acted as part of His revelatory character, as to who He is and what He was doing in the world. Until the consummation of time, history will likely remain the most significant field in which God completes the work of an eternal economy. The Church Fathers were emphatic that God's revelation was not made directly to the mind of men but inferred from His work and activity. They employed the term: "economy" (*oikonomia*), meaning to oversee or regulate an office. Sometimes the term was used in connection with the providence of God.[99]

Modern students of historiography and the critical method unhesitatingly are quick to recognize their indebtedness of early biblical scholars who pioneered in applying critical methodology to the study of the Old Testament.[100] Quite apart from any theological

---

[98] None have surpassed the quality of W. R. Matthews work in England almost a century ago while a professor at Cambridge. His *Purpose of God*, published 1935, remains a magnus opus.
[99] G. L. Prestige, *God in Patristic Thought* (London: 1964) pp. 59–61. The term economy was used by the church fathers as late as the time of Chrysostom.
[100] While pursuing the Ph.D. the author was amazed at how much historical criticism had derived from biblical criticism, which he had studied earlier in theological seminary.

evaluation of truth, this has been an invincible tool in the evaluation of religion to human society, namely its verifiable roots in history. God entered history with entrenching purpose, to redeem that miscalculation for which Adam and Eve were responsible. The author recalls reading in high school days what for him was an entrancing book, *And God Goes Marching On*. Like the determined Greek soldiers of ancient history in their long march questing for the sea, a relentless God through history searches for His fallen creation. What He does is always purposeful and measured; it is this that makes the Christian God teleological in all His economy.

Precedence or priority need not fall on the misdeed of Adam and Eve, rather on the vehicle of continuous history that God made use of. It was not at the spot or origin of the misdeed that the teleological hand of Deity was best revealed, but in the long continuous arm of history that followed it. This has proven to be nothing less than a continuous invasion of God into history, of the eternal into the temporal that has not yet terminated its course. Thus, it was, in the teleological plan to redeem, God did not resort to some "quick fix." The chosen means through history would be long, progressive, and achievable, terminating only in God becoming incarnate in Jesus of Nazareth. In a mythical way God came to the Garden of Eden seeking; whereas, in a historical manner He came redeeming. Theologians have named this long chain of God's activity as *Heilsgeschichte*, Salvation History or God's plan to culminate the age long purpose of redeeming creation from its fallen estate.[101] With a human inclination to think of the millennium's long process, the ancient biblical axiom of a thousand years being one day becomes preempt.

In the advance through history, one panorama of theologians depicts an attempt to display God's nature, personality, and being. Here the emphasis necessarily falls on the transcendence of God, His beyondness, otherness, and infinity. Perhaps the exaltedness of Old Testament theology reaches its summit here, with no writer surpassing Deutero-Isaiah. "For my thoughts are not your thoughts, neither are your ways my ways, says the Lord. For the heavens are higher than the earth, so are my ways higher than your ways, and my thoughts than your thoughts."[102] Still another group

---

[101] This terminology first became popular in Germany and most especially after World War II became popular in Western Europe and America.
[102] Isaiah 55: 8–9.

of theologians place the emphasis on God's activity, or what has been His economy. Perhaps in general terms one might say that high-church theology has tended to place emphasis with the first grouping; on the other hand, evangelical Christianity, particularly since the Reformation, has put emphasis on the other front, or with God's economy in the world. One conceived of God in the eternal realm; the latter from the temporal or cosmological angle. Early theologians who tended to think within this range tended to block history tidily into periodization; each new period beginning with the letter "C." (The historical divisions they used were: Creation to God's Covenant with Abraham, Covenant to Christ, to the Creation of time.)[103] This was the cosmic drama of world history understood to follow the divine plan of God in the working out of secular history.

Thus, there has been a distinct historical line of God running through the general course of history that falls within the realm of time. This unique and distinct line separates the teleological activity of God from the general course of history, but this must not suggest that God does not work in the latter secular history as well. "All pathways by His feet are worn."[104] Rather, it advises that God has a continuous and unremitting flow of historical happenings, which run to the plenitude of His purposes. In every successive generation, God works through individual men and women to achieve His purposes on earth. By no means, however, should one conclude that this alone points to the center of God's focus. There are always many rivulets that run to the rivers that flow to the ocean. So, in the course of human history God, too, has His rivulets and rivers that cascade into His larger activities, which in turn lead to the fulfillment of His overarching teleological purpose.

Those times when some man or woman has been able to detect the hand of the Divine in this flow of history are known in Christian terminology as revelation. Christian theologians have long spoken of general and special revelation. General revelation need not be regarded necessarily as saving revelation, but special revelation is reckoned by Christian thinkers to be that. Justin Martyr, in the second century, became the first Christian father to offer his insight on these two distinct lines of revelation. It becomes a divine

---

[103] Ian G. Barbour, Ibid.
[104] Joseph Mary Plunkett, in the poem, "I See His Blood upon the Rose."

revelation in that it was God who made perceptible His hand in some act of history. Western historians, who accept this philosophy of history, generally agree that in the call of Abraham to leave Mesopotamia, some two millennia before Christ, began the long line of special revelation, which reached its triumphant spectrum in Jesus of Nazareth. This long-reaching activity of God, of course, falls within the general drama of human beings on earth, giving substance to the oft-repeated statement that God makes history the arena of His activities. Undoubtedly, there were those events taking place in the ancient Near East that made it fortuitous for Abraham to depart at the time he did in pursuing God's purpose.

The movement of an important ancient chieftain some two millennia before the rise of the Roman Empire would normally have aroused little more than local interest. Such, however, was not the case when Abraham made the significant move of his entire clan. It was his deep belief that this was done at divine direction. Had he advanced in religious perception to some degree beyond his local neighbors? Whatever the answer, God is responsive to our longing to know Him. "As the hart panteth for the waterbrooks so panteth my soul for Thee, O God." Mankind's error in the ancient garden relationship to God did not destroy it, or the fact that humanity had been fashioned in the image of God. Even before God began the search for the hidden couple, they were conscious of wrongdoing. To look centuries ahead, what a turnaround it was for the New Testament to set forth the invitation, "Let us draw near with a true heart in full assurance of faith, with our hearts sprinkled clean from an evil conscience."[105] The unruliness of Adam and Eve left a deep consciousness that things were no longer as once they were with God in that the couple sought to hide from Him. Their error was the human pursuit of fulfillment, followed by the fallacious attempt to repair the damage, which led to the rise of natural religion. In natural religion the search for God is inaugurated by mankind. As has been observed, the human approach alone would suggest that the Barthian concept that through the Fall of Man a total eclipse of any likeness to God had been terminated, was an erroneous or fallacious one. Real religion has always been based on the axiom that God initiated and continues the search for His fallen creation. Older theologians interpreted Genesis 3 as the first word in the Bible about

---

[105] Hebrews 10:22.

God doing something to nullify this, and therefore a first reference to the coming of Christ.

Natural religion is humankind's upward reach toward God; revelation is God's downward reach to those who seek Him. It seems to follow that the infinity of God would necessarily call for a progressive revelation, just as a child pursues its learning progressively. As seen, the disobedience to God portrayed in Genesis resulted in the birth of natural religion, which only widened the chasm between God and creation.[106] As has been noted, perhaps it was not as foreboding as Karl Barth made it in a theology, which saw total obliteration of any God likeness remaining in man, but anyone who has seen the Grand Canyon is moved by the extent of its chasm, across which no human voice is carried. The voice between God and man is likewise silenced or turned down in natural religion. The Tower of Babylon was humanity's effort to bypass the chasm and ended in human unproductiveness. With good reason did John A. Mackay describe this break between God and His creation as, "The Great Rift," in a superb evangelical analysis of the Book of Ephesians.

The Fall of Man did not obliterate humanity's longing for God; thus, a global natural religion advanced across the earth. Some of this religion is perhaps sufficiently mature as to merit the ascribing of it as a philosophy. For example, some of the Upanishads of early India have been thought to reach this description. One of the approaches used by a young couple in their twenties living in West Africa was to look for the deeper longings of the idolatry one saw on every hand. It was the intensity of this longing to cross the chasm that led so many of the Ashanti people of the then-Gold Coast to faith in Jesus Christ.

Few theological themes captured the attention of the early Church fathers more than did that of Adam and Eve, followed by the Fall of Man. Irenaeus, Athanasius, Augustine, and some of the minor Fathers all dealt with this. It should be noted that of these, only Augustine lived after the Council of Nicaea in 325. Even so, whatever the transgression of Adam and Eve in the Garden of Eden., the Genesis story portrayed is one of eating forbidden fruit. Christian theology has almost universally depicted this as

---

[106] Much of the early portion of the Book of Romans constitutes an insightful content of what the Apostle Paul felt to be the result of the Fall.

disobedience to God. Whatever the deed, it was irreversible, universal in application, and irreparable on man's part. It was the most pervasive or cosmopolitan act of humanity ever enacted on earth. In Christian theology, this has been for long centuries known as the "Fall of Man." It is doubtful if anything in the entire Bible is more widely recognized than the story of Adam and Eve. It is the basis for the doctrine of Original Sin, once much more widespread in the parlance of Christians than in modern times. The modern longing to cross the chasm may be seen in the pleasure moderns pursue, wealth to which they bow, the obeisance to power they make, narcissism which fills so many lives, and the vanity, pride, arrogance, and boastfulness characterized by many. The proposed tower in Genesis would supposedly have reached to heaven, but one is never pulled up by our own bootstrap. William Barclay, popular New Testament scholar of Scotland, did so much to popularize religion among a post-World War II secularized society famously said, "What you need is a hand let down from heaven."

The biblical narrative stated that after having disobeyed God's command by eating the forbidden fruit, Adam and Eve hid themselves from the Lord, something revelatory of a sense of guilt having been born into humanity. Genesis was depicting the great truth that it was man who walked out on God, hiding from the presence of the Lord after having been disobedient to Him. Humanity turned away first; but it was God who initiated the search in calling out, "Where are you?" This question is the first recorded in the Bible. The fleeing from God and God's pursuit of Adam and Eve is anticipatory of a once well-known line from Francis Thompson's nineteenth century poem, "The Hound of Heaven." "Lo, all things fly thee, for thou fliest me"

> I fled Him, down the nights and down the days;
> I fled Him, down the arches of the years;
> I fled Him, down the labyrinthine way
> of my own mind; and in the mist of tears
> I hid from Him.[107]

---

[107] This poem, written by Francis Thompson, in 1893 is said to have inspired the famous line, "with all deliberate speed," used in one of the famous desegregation cases of the United States Supreme Court.

Whatever the mystery of the disobedience, Christian theology has tenaciously held to the belief that the hiding of Adam and Eve was characteristic of the pattern those disobedient to the will of God would continuously follow. Certainly, Jonah chose this path over willingness to preach to the people of Nineveh, an Old Testament example of one who would flee from Deity. Equally elevated in the Genesis narrative is the observation that it was God who went in search of Adam and Eve. From their foiled attempt to hide from God came the first question in the entire Bible, "Where are you?" It is considering this prehistorical episode that the New Testament came to place such emphasis on the truth that believers should not fear God. Perhaps the apex of this truth may be found in the words of Jesus, "Come unto me all you that labor and are heavy laden and I will give you rest."[108] Nothing can make us more heavily laden than wrongdoing not confessed to God. Nor has anything brought greater emptiness to societies of the West than the pursuit of secularism. Secularism has been growing since the end of the Victorian Age, but it had its standstills prior to World War II. Following a decade of brilliant growth of religious institutions in the 1960s, secularism has shown a march that has little sign of retardation at this time in history. Atheism is at its highest peak in history in the United States, and church attendance has declined considerably. One may well wonder if secularism is the attempt of the West to flee from God, as did Adam and Eve.

Since the time of Adam and Eve and the entrance of evil into the world, an evil conscience has plagued posterity in every generation the earth has known. As these lines are written, the common news of the day is that of two men fleeing from their escape of a high security prison in Pennsylvania. The public is being constantly reminded that the two are highly dangerous and guilty of murder. From whence came such evil? A quick response might be from their background in the home, but once more where did this have its origin and what has elongated the presence of evil through the millennia? Surely, the attempted escape from the punishment of such crimes must share some relevancy to what the Genesis narrative was attempting to depict in the account of Adam and Eve.

What a turnaround the New Testament made in its far-reaching and global invitation, "Let us draw near with a true heart in

---

[108] Matthew 11:28.

full assurance of faith, with our hearts sprinkled clean from an evil conscience."[109] Something of the same is heard in the beautiful and much-loved words of Jesus, "Come to me, all you who labor and are heavy laden . . . and you will find rest for your souls."[110] The same evil conscience has plagued humanity in every generation since the attempt of Adam and Eve, in that fatal non-historical attempt to hide from God. Thus, in this sense original sin is an historical actuality. It was this ineradicable and far-reaching depth of alienation that created the impassable abyss between God and man. This launched the necessity of God's search for humankind, if creation were not to be a futile thing. Thus, the purpose of God was to restore creation to its pristine beauty.

Some of the most striking and catchy parables of Jesus were built around the theme of someone searching for something, a woman seeking her lost coin, the shepherd in search of a sheep that had wandered away, and a father longing for a prodigal son. Just as the child asked, "What is beyond the rainbow?" the human soul searches perennially for those things that lie beyond life's bounds and are to be found only in that realm beyond the temporal. One of the most enduring axioms of Christian theology is that mankind does not find God but is found by Him. In the parables of Jesus, it was always that someone found that which was missing. To recall, it was God who went in search of Adam and Eve.

Irenaeus thought that through the Fall of Man the disobedient gradually fell into nothingness. One should note here the vast difference between Hebraic thought of the Old Testament and that of early Christian thought, which had become influenced by Greek philosophy, beginning in the second Christian century. In Greek thought to fall into nothingness was equivalent to the Hebrew concept of hell (*Sheol*). Thus, this became his equivalent to hell; Irenaeus, writing about this Old Testament narrative, began with a philosophical approach, as his career fell within that period when Greek philosophy had begun to characterize Christian thought very deeply. This far-reaching trend began to develop rapidly following the fall of Jerusalem in 70 A.D. and took on a stronger tempo in the second Christian century. Irenaeus lived perhaps to the last decade of that century as the Bishop of Lyons and may (or may not) have

---

[109] Hebrews 10: 22.
[110] Matthew 11: 28–29.

died a martyr. Traditionally, he has been characterized as such in Lyons where the crusade against Christians became vicious.[111] Modern evidence seems to point this way.

Turning now to a historical view of how creation and the fall have been viewed in the Church, one notes that in the Patristic writings of the early Church the glory of creation was never left out in the biblical understanding of the glory of the incarnation, and in the earthly work of the Messiah. Even in their staunch proclamation that God was in Christ, early Christian representatives never abandoned the majesty of creation, not even considering the more recent glory of God, which had surrounded the Messiah's birth. Some of the earliest Christian fathers retained creation as one of their central themes. These included Tatian, Aristides, the early apologists, Justin Martyr (a shining light in the second century), and Irenaeus, et. al. Until the destruction of Jerusalem in 70 A.D., the Church largely retained its Jewish stamp, which was the religion of Peter, Paul, and one might argue, to some extent John Mark since he wrote the first Gospel, which bears his name and was written about a decade before Jerusalem was destroyed. It was a Gospel very much in line with Judaism.

The Fourth Gospel was written well after the Fall of Jerusalem in 70 A.D., and it was this Gospel that introduced the concept of the Logos into Christian theology, providing a perfect link with philosophy. The pedigree of the word *logos*, which played a major role in early Christian thought, can be traced as far back as Homer. Some of the later books of the New Testament give evidence of this shift from Judaic thought to Greek. A careful analysis of Christian doctrine bears out the fact that before the end of the first century a shift in Christian theology was under way; setting toward the attunement of its dogma with Greek philosophy. This was noticeable in both Clement of Alexandria and Origen, each of whom served as head of the theological school in Alexandria. Clement had spent many years in Athens after its expansive

---

[111] One of the things that makes Irenaeus is that he was a friend of Polycarp, who had been a friend of the Apostle John and had heard him preach. Irenaeus was familiar with much of Mediterranean Christianity, having been born in the East, spent time in Rome, and died as Bishop of Lyons. Christianity had come later to this Western Roman province, but it had endured bitter persecution, including the death of the aged Plotinus, Bishop of Lyons, and Blandina, the slave girl who had converted to Christianity and faced a brutal martyrdom.

reconstruction by the Roman Emperor Hadrian. At a later stage in the history of the Church, Origen's outstanding legacy was devalued to some degree because of his deep reliance on Hellenistic thought.

Christianity's first, and most threatening, antagonism was Gnosticism, traces of which may be detected in some of the later writings of the New Testament. First- and second-century Gnosticism, in retrospect, may be the first full-blown threat to the truth of Christianity, in which a widely divergent and many-colored view of creation was proposed. For the first time any view of history that might be divinely teleological and purposive was cast aside by an antagonistic view that in effect obliterated the divine majesty of creation. The Gnostic thesis entailed a multiplicity of eons and these were the result of an innumerable number of inferior gods. One of the most regal themes of Old Testament revelation sprang from, "The heavens are telling the glory of God, and the firmament proclaims His handiwork."[112] This is the elegant and imperial manner in which the Bible made its claim for the Creator God. While Gnosticism did represent the first grave threat to the Christian idea of creation, Western civilization has periodically put forth other theories of how the universe came into existence. None ever gained a footing comparable to the Christian view. Challenges to this thesis would not be set forth in Western Civilization prior to the seventeenth century.

The Church owes a vast amount to Irenaeus for his lifework, *Against Heresies*. It is a devastating refutation of the Gnostic ideas of creation and its wearying series of emanations. The Bible is, of course, the longest running account of any deed enacted on earth; yet it never loses its freshness when referring to creation. The oldest book of the Bible, perhaps Job, fixed magnificently upon it.

Throughout the Bible, the biblical portrayal of the sublimity of God's creation is never camouflaged or laid aside. Day by day, the finished work of God in creation was declared good, until the seventh day when it was said to have been "very good."

For those who find emotional comfort in biblical prooftexts, it may be pointed out that the Genesis account of creation parallels neatly the scientific view of a progressive creation. It should be pointed out that God's creation, from incipiency to its

---

[112] Psalm 19:1.

completion remained God's joyful and praiseworthy creation. The Book of Psalms portrays much of its beauty and splendor.

Minor emphasis on creation from any scientific point of view was to a large degree lacking before 1600. It maintained the Jewish stamp upon it, which was the religion of Peter, Paul, and one might argue, to some extent John Mark, since he wrote the first Gospel. Its theology was very much a descendant of Judaism. It is very interesting to observe that the Fourth Gospel was written well after the Fall of Jerusalem in 70 A.D. It was this Gospel that introduced the concept of the Logos into Christian theology. A careful analysis of Christian doctrine bears out the fact that before the end of the first century there was a shift in Christian theology. It was moving from its Hebraic setting toward the attunement of its dogma with Greek philosophy. This to some degree was a factor delaying the scientific revolution until the seventeenth century.

Historically, when writers have written about creation, it has traditionally been designated as "doctrine of creation." This is somehow curious in that God was never concerned to offer a doctrine, but to establish a fellowship. This is to take the backward look; God's concern was not that a doctrine might be understood, but that the Creator of all that is might be known. It is simply beyond human compass to grasp as to why God might have desired fellowship with His creation. However, it appears that the biblical outlook was that Deity did long for fellowship with its handiwork, and more particularly for that part of it which was made in His likeness. Any probing as to why God desired this lies beyond human comprehension. Certainly, it was not that there was some component lacking in God's essence without the universe. Such a thought is the very core of Pantheism's assertion that God and the universe function as one—a great thing about God, who is personal and requires nothing to make Him complete, or what He is in His being. Reality may loom far beyond what is man's most reasonable calculation or thought about anything. For example, there was little reality about Columbus, or his predecessors, in their understanding of how wide the Atlantic Ocean was. This was for them to learn by discovery. Even the most learned might fall far short of humanity's best understanding of the universe and its purpose for being. That is why; if answers were to ever be, divine revelation was a necessity. The doctrine of divine revelation bespeaks of one of the first, or pristine, characteristics of God in His intent to reveal Himself to a part of creation that was made in His image. Older theologies emphasized that one of the purposes in creation was that God might make Himself known and have fellowship with Him. At least, the sentiment expressed in the poem by James Weldon Johnson, that God was lonely and decided to make Him a world, is good theology.[113] Note, nevertheless, the anthropomorphic language Johnson made use of to describe creation; without such resort, it would hardly be revelation to humankind at all.

In creation, God made some things innate, and with man's progress capable of becoming known through human discovery. The deepest mysteries of God, however, do not fall within such a domain, and certainly, the most conspicuous of these is the nature of God Himself. It is due to this human frailty that nature religion was ever born; because, as Augustine said, God made us for Himself, and our heart is restless until it rests in Him. Theology has remained coherent through the centuries only on the premise that God elected to bridge the gap between Him and His erring creation. Even with the distinct and pronounced difference between man and the lower creation, the summit of His creation fell short of its ability to discover the Being of God on our own. Herein lays the vast difference between natural religion and divine revelation. In the former, humanity forlornly launched its own pursuit for reality, but never discovered it. In this regard, such religions may be described as "false" religions, in that they never arrived at a satisfying answer to their quest. For Christians to express this fact in such fashion would not, however, be a propos in addressing the non-Christian population of the world. The world would have been a better community had no religion ever learned to make use of harshness in its characterization of religions at variance with its own. Christianity must acknowledge the fact that during the medieval age, Christianity did this to a degree not paralleled, until the birth of modern-day Islamic fundamentalism.

One's fixation about God and the universe may become so deeply entrenched that it becomes disturbing, and disposing, to hear of anything that departs from a view. The fact that throughout the long discipline of historiography there have been historians who looked upon this as naïve or ingenuous does not undermines its

---

[113] James Weldon Johnson was born 1871, during Reconstruction, and before his death in 1928 grew up to become very active in the NAACP.

truth. Neither does the fact that many first-rate historians, such as the late Herbert Butterfield at Cambridge, affirmed this truth, give it authenticity. Rather it is something of the teleological purpose of God that His hand would be shown, not only in creation, but also throughout its continuance. It is a never-ending process in that at the end of the biblical revelation, the seer John visualized a new heaven and new earth brought about by the God of creation. Never in the tide of history, until that day dawns, will God confront a situation from which His Spirit cannot redeem and retrieve some good.

Deity could have simply annihilated the chaos that existed prior to creation; but God would have still been as much God as He has eternally been. Instead, He chose to create. He depends upon nothing to establish His being and essence. God supersedes all the descriptive power of mankind. Thus, He is beyond description, definition, or portrayal. Think, for example, of a wealthy woman who might require her wealth in order to define who she is, and her standing in the community. Before the nineteenth century, these were the perceptible things most likely to define someone's place in parts of Europe. A college professor stripped of her superb specialized learning would not be a college professor. God isolated from His universe would nevertheless be God. The universe came into being through a spoken word from Him. It does not lie within the realm of human knowledge to determine precisely how long ago this word was spoken, or the length the word at the time may have been. All that one understands with the use of the word "God" is eternal and has never been part of a temporal realm that is evanescent.

Chapter 4
God's Way of Righting Wrong

After each day of creation, God reviewed His "daily" work, evaluated was that it was good, and at its finality, after the seventh day, it was pronounced "very good." How long this state of perfection may have continued before something went awry is locked among the mysteries of God; throughout, however, in the continuing narrative God is confronted with the missteps of Adam and Eve. This actualization became the central focus of God's purpose through all of history, until the temporal realm shall be no more. The purpose of God within history may be said to have begun with the call of Abraham to leave his native land to follow *Elohim*. Through Him the nation of Israel comes to be. "There is a divine process of selection and election at work in history, until gradually a nation is developed now recognizing its God, through great theophanies such as Yahweh. The process of selection worked in history until ultimately it led to Jesus of Nazareth.[114] The purpose of God may historically be interwoven with many other local events that contribute to the larger divine plan. God may well become interwoven with numerous other more moderate or local divine purpose. God's ultimate purpose may, and undeterminably does, extend far outside the bounds of history. One of the most asymmetrical things about history is the vast amount of it that cannot be accounted for; in this way it appears to be much like matter itself, original sin, and predestination. Augustine (354-430) in the fourth century showed strong theological inclination toward much of this, but it was Calvin who formed the system into a dominating one in religious circles; and unlike Augustine his thought spilled over beyond religious borders. In the sixteenth century, Calvin's influence received something like "canonization" in much of the Western world. His doctrines gained powerful footage in the New England colonies and played a protrusive role in the development of its culture including the economic. Calvinism became deeply entrenched in some of the most influential colleges in the American colonies, and in the mind of Jonathan Edwards, as well as other

---

[114] E. C. Rust, *The Christian Understanding of History* (London: 1947), p.137.

Historical Pursuit of the Purpose of God

distinguished colonial thinkers. Calvinism as a system of thought penetrated many additional areas of Western life.

Christian belief, however, is that God did something in Jesus Christ to bring history to its decisive divide, which is still recognized throughout much of the globe. The early Church fathers taught nothing less than that in Jesus of Nazareth came God's invasion of time, and that in Him a Kingdom was established that runs parallel with earthly rule, but which in time will supersede it. Even so, the reality of current evil should not be questioned. Both the experience and thought of Jesus left no room for refuting its reality. No one has ever seen this more clearly than did St. Augustine of Hippo, one of the most influential figures of Western civilization, who was highly gifted. His early years were anything but a paradigm of Christian character. Until he was thirty-three years of age nothing could have been more antipodal than his conduct was to Christian faith. Nevertheless, who can measure the far outreach of his mother, Monica's, prayers?[115] These were redoubtable efforts to bypass the rift, but unlike a detour one might make on the road there was none in the economy of God. This proposition regarding an alienated humanity is likewise a voluminous and capacious theological truth. We can see just how much he had steeped himself in the thought of St. John the Apostle. It was he who made the boast that to see Jesus is to have seen God.[116]

Some of the most mature writing of the entire New Testament makes it startlingly clear that God's search even antedated time itself. Ephesians, in what became in the sixteenth century a divisive theological issue, one that has not been fully abated, declared, "Even as he chose us in him before the foundation of the earth."[117] That provides as wide a panorama as imaginable for God to search for His fallen creation. It reached its summit in the words of Jesus, "I am come to seek and save that which was lost."[118] To follow the literalists, one could only interpret this to mean God's purpose of redemption for a lost or fallen creation will be "gathered up" unto its oneness in Jesus Christ.[119] The unfaltering effort to bring this to actuality was most expressly seen in Jesus' unforgettable

---

[115] His mother was named Monica and year after year, she prayed for his salvation.
[116] "He that has seen me, has seen God."
[117] Ephesians 1:4.
[118] Luke 19:10.
[119] Ephesians 1:10.

parable of a farmer searching for a lost sheep, a woman for a lost coin, and a father for a lost son.[120]

Following the great rift between God and His creation, the remainder of the Bible becomes God's plan to reverse it. It was John A. Mackay, erstwhile president of Princeton Theological Seminary, who so fittingly compared the sin of Adam and Eve to a rift between God and man. Mackay wrote in euphonious praise of the Book of Ephesians which so touched him as a lad of fourteen in Scotland:

> For to this book I owe my life. I was a lad of only fourteen years of age when, in the pages of the Ephesian letter, I saw a new world. I found a world there which had features to a world that had been formed within me.[121]

The devout and young Mackay would in the future offer numerous salient things of a spiritual maturity to many parts of the globe. There is no book in the Bible that more clearly envisioned a new world, which young Mackay envisioned, than the book of Ephesians. All of creation had become bereft of its pristine and unalloyed wholeness. Subsequent centuries that witnessed the emergence of civilization followed this distant state of imperfection, but God's perfection was never effaced from the human thought. It has echoed through such writers as Plato, Dante, and Milton, and in the fables of long-forgotten golden ages of the distant past. This is of significance in that the fall was not absolute, resulting in total depravity as Karl Barth so staunchly argued for in the twentieth century. Emil Brunner argued that the fall was partial and not entirely obliterate, as is the current view of most Western theology. Had the Fall of Man been total or absolute, it is difficult to see how religion could have developed across the globe, as it did. The apogee of all religion has been mankind's sense of needing to be placed on right terms with whatever gods might be known. Natural religion means just that, it came by an indigenous instinct, which had not been extinguished in Adam and Eve's fall from God's grace. This is a foundational plank of evangelical Christianity and to some extent the Christian movement.

---

[120] Luke 15:4–32.
[121] John A. Mackay, *The Ephesian Letter and This Present Time* (London: 1953), p. 21.

The evil that did enter the world is not unlike the wind of which Jesus spoke when He said that no one knows from whence it comes, one hears the sound of the wind, but knows not from whence it came. The source of evil in the world has been warmly contested by discordant schools of thought, but it did not arise from the Godhead, or from any flaw in creation. The narrative given to us in the Bible of the rise of evil in storied form is therefore of equivocal interpretation. Most likely, the oldest book of the Bible is that of Job who struggled with this anguishing problem. Certainly, evil represents a revolt against the will and purpose of God. The Genesis narratives are just as profound as those of the New Testament but must be looked at in another form.[122]

One of the chief propensities of evil is its potency to multiply and advance in the world. Consider, for example, nuclear weapons, first used by the United States in World War II against a belligerent Japan. Three quarters of a century later the world is ominously threatened by its use not from a single power alone. Too, this threat likely comes not from the West where it had its origin but notably from North Korea, Iran, even Israel under certain situations, and potentially elsewhere. Jesus fully accepted the reality of evil and recognized the inevitability of this in His parable of the wheat and tares. Natural growth is not limited to the good alone, but characteristic of evil as well. The sun shines not alone on the good, but the bad as well. It is this law of nature that guarantees the unremitting, steady, and guaranteed increase of evil in the world. One of the difficult pieces of theology for modern man is the explanation of Satan in the universe. Assiduous care must be taken lest it philosophically and ultimately emanate with Deity; more likely, it is an abuse of the freedom of will God gave to creation.

John Polkinghorne advanced an intriguing thesis in his insistence that the freedom of choice given by God must be allowed to occupy its terrain to the full.[123] There is little hesitancy in the recognition of evil in the world; the twentieth century enlarged this to never before known dimensions. The gargantuan portion of this, along with its omnipresence, has made it easy, even logical, for modern folk to accept the reality of evil, due to a widespread cleavage with the Bible, notably in the West where biblical

---

[122] It must be remembered that history as it is defined today had a beginning as did other things.
[123] John Polkinghorne, Ibid.

understanding of evil has been to some extent abandoned in favor of many other interpretive comebacks. One paramount observation is obvious; Jesus never questioned the reality of evil, nor did He fail to personify it. In His own personal struggles, there is no indication that He regarded such metaphorically or emblematically. The Apostle Paul was quite emphatic, "For we are not contending against flesh and blood, but against the principalities, against the powers, against the world rulers of this present darkness, against the spiritual hosts of wickedness in the heavenly places."[124]

Thus far the chapter has sought to clinch the fact that God would not abandon His creation after its tragic disobedience to Him. His was a love that would not let go; in it an eternal love was manifested. We note now once more that the chief arena for God to work was through history. Any number of well-meaning people have often used the line, "History is His-story."[125] Actually that goes too far, though God does work in history, as is acknowledged by illimitable historians. No one can assign a date as to when Adam and Eve may have committed their tragic act. Even so; whatever action it set forth was in the temporal, not the eternal, realm. In all likelihood it was in an era when darkness had begun to give way to dawn that polytheism had its rise. It is not surprising in that we were made for God and "our hearts are restless until they rest in Thee." It appears to have been global, though not simultaneous. Paganism was the hand reaching upward toward God; revelation was God's assuagement of that longing. The author recalls an old Yoruba woman in Nigeria saying to him, "Paganism was the search for God until the path ran out." Revelation is God longing to become known. It reached its summit only in Jesus of Nazareth. In Genesis one is not dealing with a literal history, as if one were reading recent history which told of some devastation that had destroyed a city or area. Here we are in the realm of mythology and not the turf of solid historical ground. Even so, because the human creation did experience "the fall," its effects appear to have deepened with the passing of the ages.

A variety of approaches have been used among philosophers to elucidate God's transcendence, but this lies beyond

---

[124] Ephesians 6:12.
[125] It has been previously noted that the author rejected this as being both too general and lays aside human responsibility. God bestowed humanity with much responsibility on earth.

possibility; otherwise God would not be transcendent. Just as the universe is beyond the mind of man, so God is beyond the universe.[126] Transcendence is often contrasted with God's immanence, and sometime with pantheism in which God can never really be transcendent, but always immanent, so close is the identification of God and the universe. "Clearly we cannot think of transcendence without thinking of something which is transcended. The obvious answer to the question what does He transcend, is that He transcends the universe."[127] Lacking divine revelation God remains incomprehensible, though existing before all beginnings. This necessitated an action from God for the closure of the separateness and wide gulf, which appears to have developed in the Garden of Eden resulting from willful disobedience. Had there not have been this disobedience, presumably there would have been no need for God's revelation. Humanity lacked the means to close the gap; only through a divine and progressive self-disclosure of God was this ultimately healed. Someone has suggested that when Jesus of Nazareth hung on the cross, the hands were pointed in opposite directions, as if to beckon both sides of the rift to find their unity and wholeness in Him. Here one has moved into the impenetrable, a factor always present when God is involved. That is how divine revelation is defined; God answering that deeply implanted longing for that which was not entirely effaced by the sinful step of man's disobedience in the Garden of Eden. Revelation is God healing the self-inflicted wound by which mankind became alienated. In God's search of mankind, something is at work drawing him to accept that revelation of truth. What man receives is only the truth God wishes to give him at the moment. The revelation of God is always partial and limited in scope. Only in Christ was the full and final revelation given. It had been tersely stated that what was needed following the fall was a hand let down from heaven.

Revelation is more. It is the restoration of that innate, internal knowledge of God that was before the breach with Him. Transcendence only widened the gulf between mankind and God with the coming of the fall. As was noted earlier, no one has expressed this aspect of divine transcendence better than did Alfred North Whitehead almost a century ago.

---

[126] Hubert S. Box, *The World and God: The Scholastic Approach to Theism* (London: 1934), p. 28.
[127] W. R. Matthews, *God in Christian Thought and Experience* (London: 1930) p. 130.

> Religion is the vision of something, which stands beyond,
>
> Behind, and within, the passing flux of immediate things;
>
> Something, which is real and yet waiting to be realized
>
> Something, which is a remote possibility, and yet the greatest.[128]

One of the late books of the New Testament was stately in its approach to this problem. The unknown author of the book of Hebrews wrote late in the first century or early in the second, "In many and various ways God spoke of old to our fathers by the prophets; but in these last days He has spoken by a Son, whom he appointed the heir of all things, through whom he created the world."[129] The Apostle Paul once set forth an interesting and telling statement when he wrote, "There are so many kinds of voices in the world, and none of them is without significance."[130] Pragmatically, it becomes a matter of which voice to heed. Wordsworth, a great romantic poet, once wrote of hearing a thousand blended voices of nature. Perhaps the voices one hears may be contradictory or antipodal. There is always, however, the voice of God which the prophet Elijah spoke of as "a still small voice." God's voice may come in the form of a chiding or censure; it may likewise come in the form of a courtship and invitation for the breach between Deity and humanity to be renewed. It is the latter that constitutes the great historical voice toward which all history moves.

The author of the book of Hebrews had a rich panoramic view of the past, and what a portrayal he gave of it! Not only did he see the multitudinous ways in which God had dealt with His people of old, but he understood also the incompleteness of those inaugural

---

[128] Alfred North Whitehead, *Science and the Modern World*.
[129] Hebrews 1:1–2. It is of interest to note that both John and the author of Hebrews were late in writing their works. Both brought creation into their introduction, and at a time when the early Church was beginning to consider such questions under the impact of the Gentile entrance into the Church.
[130] I Corinthians 14:10.

Historical Pursuit of the Purpose of God

revelations, and the latter part of his writing constitutes some of the most beautiful in the entire Bible. He wrote to Christians, probably early in the second century, who were bearing up amid some of the most ferocious persecution the Roman government was to set forth. His word to them was, "Let us run with perseverance the race that is set before us, looking to Jesus, the pioneer and perfecter of our faith, who for the joy that was set before him endured the cross...and is seated at the right hand of God."[131] The variety of God's revelation to mankind spanned Elijah's still small voice, to Isaiah's splendid theophanies in the Jerusalem temple in the eighth century B.C. Ultimately, the Apostle Paul would remind the Corinthians that none of the voices of God ever lacked an appointed significance, which God gave to them at the time of divine revelation.

Over the long course of something like two millennia before the coming of Jesus of Nazareth, the revelations varied greatly. This was true in both the character and content of revelation. Theologians are close to unanimity in recognizing that the revelation of God was progressive, recognizing that only in the One who said, "He that hath seen me hath seen the Father" was the summit of God's Being reached. Nothing in all of history following the man of Nazareth could make the justifiable claim to have gone beyond what he did with regard to making an eternal God known.

After the eleventh chapter of Genesis, the Old Testament narrative of divine Revelation is narrowed to become the narrative of a revelation to one man, Abraham, whose progeny would become a nation. These first eleven chapters of Genesis cannot be dated and must be regarded as "prehistorical," and a vessel of God of His and single-minded revelation to His earthly creation. On arriving at the call of Abraham, one stands on firmer historical ground. Much is known of Abraham's time through the discoveries of Samuel Noah Kramer and his successors.

The call to Abraham to leave Ur and follow God's guidance is one of the most challenging commands ever given to a Hebrew prophet; it is the sustaining root to what follows in the Old Testament. Here God was most purposeful, and it is with Abraham that He begins the long fulfillment of that purpose. The first ten chapters of Genesis deal mainly with isolated people, such as the first

---

[131] Hebrews 12:1–2.

people, Adam and Eve and their children. Later came the introduction of other generations who altered the divine purpose through their disobedience. It would be hypothetical, or so it seems to the author, and meandering in asking how history would have run had continuing disobedience not been a factor in the long run of history. Who would deny that with the spread-out deeds of modern history, there has not been a vast amount of human activity displeasing to God? The continued growth of disobedience to God constitutes what one calls sin. To overlook such would be to turn away from the reality of history, the *pleroma* of which is never reached.

Leopold von Ranke made this his ideal in the study of history but here, too, one sees only in part. Von Ranke has been recognized as the father of modern history. God Himself faced human reality undertaking a long purpose to restore creation to its pristine perfection. In the processes of doing so, history would become His chief instrument. Noah was another isolated individual and perhaps one of the most recognizable names of the Bible because of the flood. Archaeological finds of the last two centuries have provided rich insights as to how these Old Testament finds should be interpreted.

Abraham, Isaac, Jacob, and others have historically been identified as the patriarchs. Modern historiography dates their first appearance some two centuries after 2,000 B.C., in the lands of Mesopotamia and Palestine. The most significant thing to note of all this is the deep rootedness of divine providence in human history. In Christ the entire purpose of God is found but it is unveiled through the run of history until its full maturation in Jesus of Nazareth. Most of the material in the Old Testament preceding the choice of Abraham cannot with much certainty be assigned historical dates, and therefore must be listed as pre-historical. Ancient writings, such as the *Epic of Gilgamesh*, betray the human nostalgia for this faraway and distant past, beyond recovery by historians. From ancient of days there has been the human nostalgia for a once golden age now forever lost.

Thanks to the attentive work of fine archaeologists from various regions of the earth we now have more precise and accurate data for the ancient patriarchs of Israel than was the case a century ago. Old Testament scholars have long recognized that there were two traditions regarding the founding father of the Hebrew nation.[132] One looked to Abraham and an earlier time, while the other thought of the deliverance by Moses of the Israelites from Egypt as the inauguration of the nation. That deliverance was so preeminent that one could easily understand how such a tradition might develop. That is not surprising, just as many traditions went into the making of the American narrative of history. It was with the deliverance of Israel from centuries of bondage in Egypt that the sacred name of *Yahweh* was given to Moses, and in time it became the most sacred name for Deity over the older names used by the patriarchs.[133] Moses received the revelation of this name in what undoubtedly constituted one of the most awesome revelations to be found in any religious history. It was here that the tradition of removing one's shoes when standing on such holy ground was commenced, a tradition retained by Muslims in the modern world today.

What a message to mankind when God told Moses that He had seen the affliction of the Israelites in Egypt! Deep affliction of humanity today is often global in scope. Such tribulation once was more localized, such as the Black Death in western and central Europe at the mid-fourteenth century. It was at the occasion of the burning bush that a new name for God was given to Moses; hitherto *Elohim* was the most common name of God used earlier by the patriarchs. "God spoke unto Moses . . . .. I am Yahweh: but I appeared unto Abraham, unto Isaac, and unto Jacob as El Shaddai and by my name Yahweh was not known to them."[134] This particular revelation was so powerful and became so extensive as to spread over many lands where Judaism was to be found. The religion that to an extent succeeded Yahwehism in its early years spread across much of Europe and beyond. There are many points in Yahwehism that were introduced into early Christianity which spread quickly over much of Europe

So sacrosanct was the new name that it was rarely spoken. Consequently, with time, the precise pronunciation grew stale or

---

[132] The author accepts the synthesis of conservative biblical scholarship in bringing these two traditions into one. It appears that there are far more reasons for accepting this than the idea of two unique traditions.
[133] It has become commonplace to note that the name of Yahweh was considered too sacred to pronounce; hence the precise way it was became questionable for later generations.
[134] H. H. Rowley, *The Biblical Doctrine of Election* (London: 1950), p. 21.

unknown. Theologians have long regarded the theophanies to Moses as a high peak of divine revelation. This name (for God) was the highly sacred name of *Yahweh*, so sacred that it was seldom pronounced, leaving a vacuum in which eventually the correct enunciation was no longer retained by the Israelites. God's sight of Israel's bondage in Egypt and resolve to deliver her from bondage was seen by the Israelites as a special act of God, but the creation of the community resulting from the deliverance was to renew this act for long subsequent centuries. The *pleroma* of meaning for this religion of Yahwehism did not reach full maturity before the great eighth century prophets in Israel.[135] The bestowal or largesse of retrospect in history is one of its major properties. Only with that could it be seen that the ancient prophets of history contributed one of the primary planks to the development of Western civilization with its moral and ethical perspective.

The selection of Israel for the accomplishment of Yahweh's purpose in history is a subject that modern scholars have tended to shy away from.[136] "Nowhere is it taught in the Old Testament that God chose Israel because of her inherent greatness; yet there are passages where it is held that Israel's greatness lies in the fact that God chose her."[137]

There has never been a time in history when God did not see the woes of an earthly society. That alone would go a long way in establishing relevance for the Old Testament in the modern world of the twenty-first century. The theophany given to Moses likewise speaks insightfully of the character of the man in his saying, "I will turn aside and see this great sight, why the bush is not burnt."[138] Natural inquisitiveness has been a boon beyond measure to the achievements of humans. Some of the stellar inventions of time were the result of someone's curiosity about nature. William Wordsworth in his warning against the ravages of the eighteenth-century industrial revolution, warned that in turning away from nature: "Little we see in Nature that is ours."

---

[135] The major prophets of the century were Amos, Hosea, Isaiah, and Micah.

[136] Likely one reason for this was an earlier bitter controversy over predestination, especially acute in Calvinistic denominations. This, however, should not be associated with the bountiful place given in both the Old and New Testament to the selection of Israel as God's choice.

[137] Rowley, *The Biblical Doctrine of Election*, pp. 18–19.

[138] Exodus 3:3.

Moses saw the burning bush and became one of the foundational figures of the Old Testament and of God's economy for all time. Someone has pointed out that the revelation came to one who was observant and inquisitive. Moses sought to obey Yahweh and turned aside to see the curiosity of the burning bush. At a time when modernity is struggling to find a place for religion in society, it may be recalled that Moses was the founder of Judaism, which shares a place with Christianity and Islam as one of the great historical world religions. The Old Testament throughout its long, checkered history has been a record of God's revelation of Himself and portrays the divine economy active in the world. The economy of Deity is always a purposeful one, but allowance may be made in the process of history for human delays, setbacks, as well as deliberate resistance to God's will. One of the most intriguing insights in the study of history, however, is to note those thinkers who did appear to find a large place in their thought for God. Many others have not chosen this path, but among the philosophers who helped shape Western thought it may be noted that Descartes, Leibnitz, Spinoza, and to some extent Hegel did allow for the hand of God and a divine purpose in history.

One need not subscribe to extreme views on the freedom allowed by God to human beings to recognize that His purpose may be thwarted or delayed, but never ultimately defeated and destroyed. One of the major teleological concepts of the West is that the hand of God has been at work in human history. Many have staunchly refuted this, but the mainline of western thought has been a positive recognition of this fact and without this, Western historiography would have been quite foreign to what it is. The great prophets of the Old Testament were the first to see this and promote its belief. Not many centuries elapsed before the close of Old Testament prophecy and the appearance of the early Greek philosophers. Plato was primary among those who saw history in this light as did Stoicism and Neo-Platonism. Enough is it to say that God's teleological goal or purpose in history continues to be debated in the West; the prevailing view continues to be that the Divine is active in history.

None of this is to suggest that the concept of the purpose of God cannot be thwarted by the freedom bestowed upon men and women. The accounts of Israel's pursuing false gods in the annals of the Old Testament was surely not Yahweh's will, but His triumph over Hebrew apostasy was a correction of this wayward course.

It would lead one astray to linger long on the revelation God made of Himself in the Old Testament. Surely, however, the messianic poems of Deutero-Isaiah, regarding the suffering of Yahweh's Servant, are one of the summits of His prodigious and awesome economy over so many centuries. Of primary concern, however, is the fact that it was here, perhaps after struggle, that Jesus of Nazareth found His own work and direction in His earthly mission as to what the will of God might be toward the achievement and advancement of the purpose of God. The wilderness temptations, so early on in his ministry, would suggest that Jesus faced real struggle in determining the path His own ministry must follow. The most signal doctrines of Christian faith are that Jesus of Nazareth was the ultimate fulfillment, fruition, and consummation of an eternal purpose of God. Far beyond all mystery is the fact that He was the Lamb of God slain before the foundations of the earth. It was His death that provided the great turnaround for history and set it once more toward the teleological design God originally proposed for it. In theological parlance this is known as redemption of the creation which had gone astray.

All history, accordingly, leads to Jesus of Nazareth; suprahistory leads out from Him. It was Augustine of Hippo who gave a renewed birth to this conception of history that has remained so indomitable throughout much of the history of the West. World War I, and even more so the Second World War, did so much to revive and renovate this ancient view of history; additionally, one might say that with it theology was reborn. World War II proved to be the most destructive in history and there were keen minds on both sides who served in this war. The war produced profound change in the thought of some of these figures; following its upheaval, they produced some of the most thoughtful theology modern centuries have seen. The preceding nineteenth century had developed around the theory that progress was inevitable and could not be thwarted. Since the defeat of Napoleon, this view had steadily gained strength. This view that progress could not be checked proved to be one of the most fallacious interpretations of history ever set forth. As these lines are written, there is increasingly a world fear that lesser hostile governments stand on the verge of becoming nuclear forces.

Through the long tunnels of history, it has been a challenge to humanity to unflaggingly adhere to the Christian philosophy of history, that God is at work undoing the wrong done in the Garden of Eden and pursuing His own purpose in the cosmos. That, however, is perhaps the strongest affirmation the New Testament set forth; and is certainly the pivotal point of the apocalyptic outlook that brings the New Testament to its close. This ancient Christian affirmation, given at a time when the Roman Empire stood on the verge of its highest grandeur, becomes always a contemporary stream of history through which the channel of God's eternal purpose flows to its consummation.

It has been readily recognized that the story of humanity's long historical trek is best read with the backward look; only from such a position does teleological purpose receive much vindication. Perhaps the most clairvoyant perspective for recognizing this is from the unseemly tragic events that came to the people of the Old Testament. Joseph's long individual bondage in Egypt is an early example. From that single act, one would not have concluded that truth wins out. Another example is the fact that in later centuries the bulk of the Israelite population was taken captive to Assyria or absorbed into other ancient Near Eastern cultures to become the Jews of the Diaspora, the majority of whom never returned to their homeland. They were known in history as the "ten lost tribes of Israel;" in God's economy, however, nothing is ever lost in God's providence. Centuries later the Apostle Paul was evangelizing in the Eastern Mediterranean where large numbers of captive Jews had migrated and established new homes. Under the Apostle's ministry, many of them heeded Paul's message and became a vital core in the early Church. Jews of the Diaspora embraced Christianity to compose a significant part of the early Church. This became a trend in the growth of Christianity until after 70 A.D. The destruction of Jerusalem did even more to advance the spread of first century Christianity than had the tragic calamity to Israel and Judah centuries before. Most of the Jews were found living outside of Israel in their wide dispersal. This proved true in both the Near East and the West when large numbers of Jews were found in both the Greek and Roman worlds. It was here that the Apostle Paul and other early evangelists found many of their first converts. Dispersed originally as prisoners of war, these populations proved to be fertile ground for the planting of Christianity. Carried abroad as conquered people, in the later centuries this was no longer the case. For the lure of trade had turned throngs of these people into a class where Christianity found many of its earliest converts. It was there, too, that the synagogues were first founded, as the first Jewish temple erected by Solomon was largely destroyed in 587 B.C.

The synagogue proved useful in the three-year ministry of Jesus in Palestine and pivotal in the missionary experience of Paul and others in the early spread of Christianity. The fact that far more Jews lived outside of Palestine in Jesus' day created a concourse of people who regarded Judea as their real home, but established synagogues far and wide across the eastern Mediterranean. Much of the finest Jewish scholarship, as with Hillel, lay outside the homeland; while a vital part of Judaism's most precious writing occurred on foreign soil, such as the Septuagint. Wherever there were ten Jewish males who had leisure for worship and study of the Torah, a synagogue was found. From these foreign centers of worship, there annually flowed back to Jerusalem the temple tax. Much of the deep sentiment for Judaism was birthed in this foreign environment, but much of the persuasion for Judaism is summarized in the words, "If I forget thee, O Jerusalem. Let my tongue cleave to my mouth, if I do not exalt thee, O Jerusalem, above all else."[139]

It has been seen that the human search for God ended only in futility resulting in idolatry. In like manner it has been observed that in the commonplace, everyday, and prosaic events of history, the God of the ages made Himself known, which is what revelation is all about, making known and advancing the divine purpose. Most often God's purpose has run through the currents of what has been popularized as secular history. God has done this not as a rejoinder to secular history but has chosen this as a chief means of making Himself known. To a degree this may be regarded as incarnational, or the eternal entering the temporal, which is one of the most arresting things about the revelation of God. As has been seen before, the renowned theologian Karl Barth attributed the most far-reaching consequences to the Fall of Man. Other prominent contemporary theologians, such as Emil Brunner, held a more moderate view regarding the Fall of Man, contending that the relation between God and man had not been fully damaged. The

---

[139] Psalm 137:6.

Church once sang, more than it does today, words from the old hymn, "Feelings Lie Buried that Grace Can Restore."

It was through divine revelation that Israel became solid in her monotheist faith that God is One. As early as Mt. Sinai the Oneness of God had become part of her "theology;" even so, for centuries segments of Israelite society repeatedly lapsed into idolatry. This was frequent under the Judges when there was no national unity. Yet in time idolatry became archaic among the Israelites. Approximately a millennium before the birth of Jesus, Israel reached her zenith under the monarchical rule of David and Solomon, and for the first time in her checkered history played a role on the stage of Near East history. Following a time of division into two kingdoms in the wake of David and Solomon, Israel weakened and separated into two kingdoms. These were known as Israel or the Northern Kingdom, and Judah or the Southern Kingdom. Ten tribes composed the Northern Kingdom; while one factor of illimitable value to the south was that Jerusalem lay within its territory. Only the tribe of Judah, and the now-weakened remnant of Benjamin, made up the Southern Kingdom. Lacking Jerusalem and the temple, the Northern Kingdom rapidly fell into paganism, or at best a highly diluted form of Yahweh's religion. The result was the North was overthrown by Assyria around 722 and her people have often been referred to as the "ten lost tribes of Israel." A worldwide fascination has followed as to what happened to them. Doctoral dissertations were written on them at the University of Paris and Duke University. Reference has been made of the fact that these people gradually drifted southward, and still later in time under the ministry of St. Paul became Christian converts.

The Southern Kingdom, now but a petty state, lived on until 586 B.C. when its people were taken to Babylon, and the Jewish temple was burned in Jerusalem. This is known as the Babylonian captivity, an era that lasted about seventy years until some Jews drifted back to Jerusalem. In contrast to those returning to Jerusalem, those remaining in Babylon thrived and many chose to remain in Babylon when permission was officially granted to return home.[140] The restored Jewish community was never militarily strong,

---

[140] They, too, were to play a prominent role in early Christianity, especially while Christianity remained largely Jewish.

but it was during this era that Judaism, as it has been known historically was born.

It becomes necessary to return and note one of the most remarkable things of Western Civilization that began its development even before Israel split as a nation. This was the rise of the prophetic movement that not only stirred Israel but bequeathed to the West a vital element of its own character. The prophets in Israel may be divided into two camps, the non-writing prophets and those who left written material. Obviously, the latter had the greater influence, but pointedly and rich also was the message of the non-writers. Amos was one of the first writing prophets and prophesied not far from the middle of the eighth century. His legacy was of the righteousness of God. Amos has been thought of as a humble keeper of sheep, but his status in life likely was wider, more like an international businessman today. Amos travelled far beyond his home in Tekoa. At any rate, his theme of righteousness, right living and conduct to others in time became a potent concept in Western civilization. Such an understanding of life was first received as a revelation to Amos before it became a message spoken to Israel (the Northern Kingdom). "Surely the Lord God does nothing without revealing his secrets to his servants the prophets."[141]

Hosea was a prophet not distant in time from Amos, but whose experience was unique in that his wife, Gomer, deserted him, apparently to take her place in Baalism. Among the ten northern tribes, Baalism had become an ascendant religion of Yahweh in the days of Elijah the prophet. It was a religion of extreme eroticism; one could go to the many shrines and have sexual intercourse with a temple prostitute. Obviously, one would have to search diligently to find any moral or ethical truth in the religion. When one does, it will be noted that the religion had disappeared in much of the empire giving way to the pagan faith. Earlier on Emperor Augustus had spent considerable money attending the upper class who were familiar with the old morals and what beauty could be found in paganism. Ultimately it had little appeal to the citizens of his day, however.

Micah was yet another eighth century prophet who has the unique distinction of "forth" telling the place of the birth of Jesus of Nazareth. "But you, O Bethlehem Ephrathah, who are little to be

---

[141] Amos 3:7.

among the clans of Judah, from you shall come forth for me one who is to be ruler in Israel."[142] The First Isaiah likewise comes in this time frame, and penned these lines, "For to us a child is born, to us a son is given; and the government will be upon his shoulder, and his name will be called Wonderful Counselor, Mighty God, Everlasting Father, Prince of Peace."[143] It should be noted that the first Isaiah appeared at a time when Assyria was rapidly becoming a world empire and would ultimately conquer the state of Israel (then ten tribes) and carry its people to Assyria as captives.[144]

With the birth of Jesus about 4 B.C., the Roman Empire was still largely pagan, particularly among the upper classes who were familiar with the ancient myths and cults; especially did paganism retain its stronghold on the once-prestigious Senate. Clearly paganism was on the wane as indicated by one emperor's attempt to restore it but in utter failure. When Augustus had fought his way to the throne, he inaugurated a gradual transformation of the once-glorious republic into the empire. Augustus, under whose long rule Jesus was born, spent lavishly from the treasury, attempting to shore up paganism and the old ways of life throughout the Roman Empire. Bithynia was an early example of a Roman province that quickly became a strong Christian enclave. Yet so magnetic was the young Christian faith that it continued to grow rapidly from one province to another. The governor of one important province complained that so many in his territory had become Christians and were no longer buying sacrifices that the economy was being hurt. In other ways Christianity had an impact on the local economy.[145]

As for divine revelation, its summit was reached in the historical ministry of Jesus, which continued for some three years.[146] He was the fulfillment of all the ancient hopes of Israel who believed that God would send a Savior to rescue them from the age-long threats of Gentiles. The historical ministry He carried on was so strikingly unlike Jewish expectations as to have been unimaginable; "God moves in mysterious ways, his wonders to perform. He plants

---

[142] Micah 5:2.
[143] Isaiah 9:8.
[144] The author accepts the thesis that there were two Isaiahs. Isaiah 1–39 was written by the first. The second, who is actually unnamed, is the author of chapters 40–66. Some scholars contend for a third Isaiah, a concept the author rejects.
[145] There were four other provinces, other than Bithynia, whom many scholars believe to have been evangelized by the Apostle Peter early on in Christianity.
[146] Some scholars have placed it at one year, but this appears a fallacy.

his footsteps upon the sea, and rides upon the storm." In the Gospel narratives that relate these things, it was Luke who gave the longest account of the event of the birth of Jesus. "Fear not, for I am with you, be not dismayed, for I am your God; I will strengthen you, I will help you."[147] To know God involves some measure of divine revelation.

Wherever the Christian missionaries commenced work they noted a widespread plurality of gods, but the general attitude was that of their hostility toward those on earth. There was a ubiquitous sense of the need for placation of the gods. This marked not the beginning but the continuation of a need to appease the gods as was seen in much of the Old Testament, and amid all the people surrounding the nation of Israel. Few things have been more intuitive to primitive man than was this. When the modern pioneer missionaries arrived at their appointed stations, few things caught their eye more than the pagan atmosphere of the gods.

Jesus had commissioned His disciples to carry His gospel to all people everywhere; following Pentecost this task was begun with alacrity and enthusiasm. Before the Roman Empire reached its demise in the fifth century, Christianity had spread to an extent that can only be considered remarkable. Even in the second century the Roman governor of the important province of Bithynia was complaining that so many people had turned to Christianity that the economy was being hurt, due to the fact that no longer was there the lucrative trade in the sale of sacrificial animals paganism had traditionally enjoyed.[148]

The Christian religion followed new outlets during the medieval era but following that the geographical discoveries at the beginning of modern times created a new enthusiasm for planting the gospel in hitherto unknown places. With the expansion of the Sahara Desert deeper into Africa, the larger portion of that continent was cut off from Christianity. This, coupled with new discoveries such as the Americas, created a vast new world for the expansion of Christianity. This expansion created something of a return to early Christianity in the ways people came to embrace the Christian faith. In the first two centuries and again in the nineteenth and twentieth centuries most

---

[147] Isaiah 41:10.

[148] A number of emperors blamed Christianity for the empire's decline in its last centuries.

people who embraced Christianity did so on an individual basis rather than through mass conversions to the faith.[149] During the Middle Ages, mass conversions had been common in various parts of Europe.

The rise of the modern missionary movement began with William Carey going to India in 1793 on a Danish ship. This brought to the forefront the question of what should be the attitude of Christians toward such Christian enterprises. It evoked the question of what should be the attitude of Christians toward non-Christian religions of the world. To the mind of the author, it would be futile to deny that there was any revelation of God in the non-Christian faiths. This would be interpreted as general revelation and not reckoned as saving revelation. Long experience from diverse regions would suggest, however, that some of these religions had been tutors to lead people to Christ, to make use of Pauline terminology. Many conservative Christians would reject the idea that there was any connection whatsoever. The author's close association with many African Christians and hearing their comments about their former life leads him to think that there were many who found in paganism a schoolmaster leading them to Christ.[150] For the most part, however, Protestant theologians have insisted on the necessity of this; however, this in itself evoked division within the Christian community as a large segment of Christendom answered this by declaring the necessity for carrying the gospel to others. There was, nevertheless, a large segment that had developed out of fundamentalism, who regarded these as doomed for hell, with the only alternative being to attempt to bring them to Jesus Christ.

During the twentieth century, Karl Barth insisted on the total break between mankind and God as a result of the fall. Many other theologians did not go so far as did Barth, such as Emil Brunner, likewise of wide acclaim. All were in agreement that the damage was sufficient that it was irreparable by humanity and must be repaired by the divine Himself. God's attempt to do this is known as divine revelation and usually regarded as two separate categories,

---

[149] Kenneth Scott Latourette, *A History of the Expansion of Christianity* (London and New York: 1947) p. 487

[150] One will recall that in the ancient world, among the elite, there were slaves whose duty it was to watch over children of the wealthy as they left their homes to attend school and see them safely home. Paul used this to suggest that the Mosaic Law served in such a capacity to lead Jews to Christ.

general and special revelation. General revelation, which need not be saving revelation, was far more common and open. Special revelation was much more restricted and reached its culmination only in Jesus of Nazareth who affirmed, "He that has seen me has seen God." So ingrained in Jewish culture for centuries was the transcendence and otherness of God that this appeared blatantly blasphemous to those Jews who heard Him. Even to the modern Christian, it may prove taxing and imposing on one's faith to maintain a balance between the two concepts. It appears to the author that Americans who believe in God, but have made no personal commitment to Him, err in the tendency to think of God as "the Man upstairs." This marked not the beginning, but the continuation of a need to appease the gods as was seen in much of the Old Testament and in the people surrounding the nation of Israel. Few things have been more intuitive to primitive man than was this necessity of appeasing a deity. When the modern pioneer missionaries arrived at their appointed places of services this attitude appears to have been universally prevalent.

Nothing could have been more incompatible with the nature and character of God than this universal application of fear. When one considers sin from this angle, is there wonder that the Apostle Paul declared all men had sinned and fallen short of the glory of God? Because of this alienation, divine revelation became a prerequisite if there were to be any rapprochement between the Creator and that which He had created. Typically, one of the parties must always take the initiative in bringing such about as seen in history's first railroad accident. At the dedication of a short railroad line at Manchester in 1830, England a huge crowd had gathered for the occasion. On one side of the track stood William Huskisson and on the other the Duke of Wellington. The two men had gone through a political estrangement some years before and had not spoken since that time. Huskisson, motivated by the desire to heal the breach, crossed the track to speak to the Duke. En route back to his station, he was struck by an engine and died a few hours later. The greatest breach ever was between God and man, and it was God who took the initiative in crossing the divide, making apt the words of Isaiah, "By his stripes we are healed."

The sense of alienation was inaugurated in the Garden of Eden after the disobedience. The story itself lies beyond the bounds of anything that could be called history; yet the long, not-yet-ended divine search has been primarily enacted through the channels of history more than anything else. In many and variant ways God has made Himself known, as the author of the Book of Hebrews so eloquently stated in his book's introduction. Of these diverse avenues, perhaps none has been more frequent or personal than in the channels of history itself. It seems an absolute that God has used history in a long and ongoing narrative; on the other hand, there is much that is historical which should not read "written by God." One more recent event was the cutting off of many heads of people in the Near East by Isis.

The Genesis narrative points to at least two significant things; one being that it is God who goes in search of His lost creation. Secondly, creation cannot of itself find its way home to Him. The author fondly recalls an event of his early youth when he and his younger brother were searching for a lost cow. Upon entering on our horse in a heavily wooded area, the younger began to cry and say, "we will never get home again." Perhaps he may have had difficulty, but an older brother who was familiar with the locale was there! God said to His family, "Lo, I am with you always."

The Genesis story relates that when the Fall of Man became an event, God began His search for a creation gone astray through its disobedience to His will. It appears that fallen mankind may early on have begun its search for God, and the evidence for this is seen on every continent. Pioneering anthropologists tended to stress the evolutionary process of this and its Darwinian roots, but a well-known Cambridge Historian, F. W. Maitland, led the way in pointing out this fallacy. More modern studies have stressed that this inclination stems from something much more innate within the human race, and that is the spiritual nature or religious inclination."[151] Religion where revered and embraced has always been a potent dynamic in human society; when rejected a lower form of cult is likely to emerge. Primitive man prayed for such things as the removal of a famine or drought, the protection of his herd, or from attacks by an enemy or pestilence, for his wife not to become barren, and to be saved from the shame of childlessness.[152] These

---

[151] Christopher Dawson, *Progress and Religion: An Historical Enquiry* (Washington DC: 1929) pp. 49–63.
[152] Friedrich Heiler, *Prayer: A Study in the History and Psychology of Religion* (Oxford: 1932) p. 2.

are not unworthy petitions, but neither do they constitute the highest form of prayer.

This is strong evidence, universally observed, that the Fall of Man did not annihilate or obliterate the image of God in man totally. The widespread presence of animism is still another token of this residue. It is impossible to contemplate with any accuracy the time between the transgression of humanity until special revelations of God begin to appear in the Old Testament. The first ten chapters of Genesis reflect the earlier period but are no means a systematized account of this era. As a matter of fact, this is pre-historical. Reflections of God's revelation to mankind do appear in this period, as for example Enoch's walk with God and Noah surviving the flood. Something of a real trauma fell across the Christian world when at another day news of the findings of the story of the Sumerian flood began to circulate in Europe and America. This has come to be known as the Gilgamesh Epic; the comparison of the biblical account of Noah both raised questions and created anxiety about the account of the flood and Noah's salvation. There was a long period of such discoveries, which have not yet run their course. One has but to remember the excitement created by the post-World War II discovery of the Dead Sea Scrolls in 1948.

These things take time for digestion and produce anxiety during that time. The older theology had to be modified by the impact of these finds, just as biblical studies did.

Our knowledge of things about God has been constantly revised in recent centuries, but the crux and core of Christian faith remains unshaken because it is the revelation of an unchanging God. When one thinks of God apart from this revelatory aspect, it is natural to think of Him in philosophical terms, such as His Being, Essence, or the idea that God is indefinable, unknowable, and invisible. While this might have been the bastion of Deism, it is not the faith that created the Church and nurtured its fold since the day of Pentecost. Perhaps the warmest dogma of Christian faith is that God has made Himself known to us in the Person of Jesus of Nazareth. Many of the more elite churches may sing the more stately hymns that do speak of God's transcendence, but more commonly the old hymns that speak of the nearness of God have for generations been loved by the congregations. One such example is, "Just when I need Him, Jesus is near, ready to comfort, ready to cheer." One cannot know who God is without grasping the fact that He is always transcendent and immanent for every individual.

Beginning with chapter ten of Genesis, a family is introduced who became the very vertebrae of the Old Testament, and a long line of special revelation in the Old Testament. The first thing one notes about this long-running revelation is its historicity. Likewise, time itself took on a new meaning. Prior to then, the word *chronology* was apt for describing time, but with the new special activity of God in history it became necessary to think of time as *kairos*, a special time in which God was uniquely at work in the affairs of men. With the coming to Mesopotamia, the Old Testament reached firm historical ground, and from the benefit of archaeological discoveries, dates have become far more precise than even a century ago. Older theologians placed Abraham c. 2500 B.C. and did superb pioneering work in staking out his historical confines. With Abraham, God had inaugurated a new beginning that culminated in Jesus Christ. Oscar Cullman, who was a German prisoner of war during World War II and later became a Christian, made a real contribution to theology by his brilliant analysis in which he declared that all roads led from Abraham to Christ, and from Christ all roads led outward. This makes Jesus of Nazareth the centerpiece of history.

All of this is to say that after the fulfillment of Jesus' ministry on earth there would never be the need for any further revelation of God. That which humanity had been searching for, even before the dawn of history, had now been divinely manifest in the purpose of God. The Holy Spirit would continue to explicate and make real the things of Jesus of Nazareth, but not offer a new or updated revelation. An old hymn put it well, "Showing the things of Christ to me." If this were to be done, a new insight into the purpose of God must be underscored. For example, a deeper insight into the need for sending missionaries far beyond one's homeland, as William Carey made so manifest.

It would necessarily become a long progressive revelation, given to humanity in both a general and special way. The Book of Hebrews, which encountered trouble in being included in the New Testament canon, described God's revelation as "sundry and partial." Until the coming of Jesus of Nazareth there was always something beyond. A child asked, "What is beyond the rainbow?" and mankind longed for that which came next. It appears that the revelation was not always moving forward but proved retrogressive as well. There were times in Israel's history when the face of God was shown less brightly than in previous eras, but in the final analysis the revelation was always progressive. Likely, the norm for many Christian lives follows this flow. Backsliding was a term once heard often in evangelical churches. Though it may be sometimes referred to, it is not used as it was when the writer was a college student just entering the ministry.[153] Initially his plan for life was become a veterinarian, and he had plans to attend Auburn University. A change in college plans became necessary and he withdrew his application to Auburn University in order to attend the Baptist College in Alabama, now Samford University. God's revelation did place him in the ministry of the local church as a pastor, but in time also led him to West Africa. His plan was to continue as a church developer there, but upon arrival was informed by the Mission that he was needed as a teacher in a boy's high school. After more than a dozen years in this ministry, he saw his calling as a college professor in America.

Jesus struggled, or so it appears to the author, as to what form His earthly ministry would take. Most likely, this is what, following His baptism, the desert experience meant for Him. The wildly popular desire was for a Messiah who would deliver Israel from an oppressive foreign rule. It had been roughly a millennium since the nation enjoyed more than a brief respite from foreign rule. In His lonely wilderness struggle Jesus saw something different as God's plan for Israel's Messiah. The resolving of this dilemma was conceivably what the wilderness temptation turned on for Jesus of Nazareth.

New Testament scholars have not been unanimous in their understanding of when Jesus realized that he must go to Jerusalem and there be crucified. Some have seen it as a foregone conclusion that even from His youth, this was known to Jesus. Others, including the author, place it much later in His ministry. Quite possibly, it was a growing issue for Jesus, and there are a number of factors that suggest this. One such was the growing vehemence of the religious leaders of Israel in opposition to His ministry. While the common people of Israel heard Him gladly, increasingly their religious leaders plotted His violent death. The growing hostility of the Scribes and

---

[153] The date for this was July 1944.

Pharisees must have sharpened this reality in Jesus' mind. An increasing disappointment of the commoners was that He would not lead a military campaign against Rome. This as much as anything nurtured the likelihood of Roman taxation, which was high and a constant burden to most of the Israelites. Some older studies suggested that it was beyond forty percent, but it is doubtful if we can pinpoint a precise figure. This coupled with the growing estrangement of the religious leaders, particularly the Pharisees, gave strong evidence to Jesus that the Son of Man must proceed to Jerusalem and there be crucified. There was one smaller group, the Zealots, whose support He might have attracted had Jesus committed to an anti-Roman alliance with them. Likely the most disappointing thing Jesus ever said for the Zealots was, "My kingdom is not of this world." The Zealots were a smaller group than others but believed that if only they provoked war with Rome, Yahweh would intervene in their behalf. The Pharisees were more numerous than the others, but the Sadducees had most to lose in any insurgence against the government in that they came from the wealthier class. Were Jesus to take a stringent stand against Roman rule, it would be likewise the Sadducees who had the most to lose and would be more agreeable to compromise with the Roman government. They were a wealthy caste and followed a policy of appeasement.

All of this is a very clarion case of how the ongoing daily events of history are gathered up and made to fit into God's eternal purpose. It has long been common to speak of sacred and secular events; actually, there is much intermeshing, and God does not separate these into the categories as do finite minds. His purposes are wholistic. Thus, even the mundane things of life find their niche in the eternal, purposeful plan of God.

Chapter 5
To Call His Name Jesus

In what must have been looked upon as a small pedestrian part of a vast geographical area that had but recently been transformed into the Roman Empire, a commoner was born c. 4 B.C. He was given the name Jesus, with the promise that he would save His people from their sin. Many names were to be conferred upon Him. As in the West Africa we knew, names told something about the child. For example, one told the day of the week on which a child was born. At the middle of the last century, a fine English scholar published a book on the names of Jesus based on a series of lectures he had given at Oxford.[154] He divided these into the principal names by which Jesus was known, those that pointed to His messianic and soteriological mission, and the Christological titles.[155] Some names and titles were more common during His own historic ministry in Galilee, Jerusalem, and elsewhere. Others were those frequently used by His followers from 30 to 65 A.D.; the final groups were used more by a second generation and are commonly seen in the later writings of the New Testament.[156] Some would be less known and perhaps obscure to the average reader, while others have become beloved around the globe. Some were used early on in life, while later the Church added other names that are found in later New Testament writings.

The century prior to Jesus' birth was one of internecine wars and foibles of government that witnessed the breakdown of the half-millennium-old Roman Republic. The last century of the Roman Republic was particularly violent and volcanic. The victor in all of this was Octavian, who took as one of his appellations, "Restorer of the Republic," though he did not restore; rather guardedly he created the Empire. It was the naval Battle of Actium in 31 B.C. off the coast of Egypt that brought him to fame, but he sought to downplay his creation of a new all-engulfing empire. "Restorer of the Republic" was his cover-up. Years passed before most Romans realized the extent of Octavian's refashioning and refurbishing of state.

---

[154] Vincent Taylor, *The Names of Jesus* (London: 1956) p. 8.
[155] Ibid., vii–ix.
[156] Ibid, p. 170.

Historical Pursuit of the Purpose of God

A marked and significant feature of the new empire was Rome's dependence upon Egypt for imported grain. Incidentally, the grain vessels were deeply fortunate for the early Christians in their missionary travel. The Apostle Paul, John Mark, and others made use of them in their itineraries. Augustus insisted that the glories of the Republic had been brought back and one of his titles suggested such. He was in the wake of building the most famous empire Europe would ever know. Octavian, who had become Augustus, presided over the empire until his death in 14 A.D., giving him one of the longest reigns in European history. Actium was indeed one of the significant battles of the late era of the classical age. Octavian is better known as Caesar Augustus. Curiously, some of the same things that he did under disguise were aimed against a movement begun by Jesus of Nazareth in the course of His own ministry. Augustus was diligent in seeking to restore paganism. Paganism lasted longer among the senatorial class than any other from its pristine days, Caesar Augustus would know one of the longest reigns of European history prior to his death in 14 A.D. Within two decades, Jesus was proclaiming a Kingdom of God. One may study the two kingdoms, but never find a greater contrast.[157]

Curiously not long into the future, Jesus of Nazareth would be charged with seeking to build another kingdom. With this came the sinister charge that Jesus was preparing to take over the government and establish His own rule. Fallacious ideas have always become deeply planted, and that was something held against Jesus until the very end. The French Revolution, which was launched in 1789, was a war that produced an untold number of false ideas. It is doubtful, however, if any event in history ever evoked as many erring ideas as those that were tossed against the movement of Jesus of Nazareth.

As a child, He was given little consideration, since He was born of peasant stock. Even so, Jesus was to become the focal point of all history and the cornerstone of the Christian Church. His arrival as the Messiah had long been foretold by the great Hebrew prophets—Amos, Hosea, Micah, and first Isaiah. It was upon this single hope of deliverance Israel leaned through some of the most tumultuous years of her long history. In the West, many centuries of

---

[157] Robin Lane Fox, *The Classical World: An Epic History from Homer to Hadrian* (Oxford: 1946) pp. 6–8.

history, extending deep into modernity, would elapse before the stigma of being born a peasant was ended. For centuries to come there were peasant revolts, such as in 1381 and again in the time of Martin Luther, when he lost the support of their estate. Yet has any other person ever done more to lift peasant children from their shackles of squalor and death than did this babe in Bethlehem reckoned a lowborn peasant child?

The writer recalls attending at the age of twenty-six his first meeting of the Nigerian Baptist Convention meeting in Abeokuta, when a rural pastor brought a six-year-old male child to the platform and related the story of how he had heard the baby's cry in the bushes while riding his bicycle to a preaching station. He rescued the child and with his wife reared the child in their home. That day at the convention, the adopted parents brought the child to the platform before a large audience to inform us that the baby had been abandoned because he had begun cutting a tooth earlier than tribal tradition allowed. Without the influence of the Child born in Bethlehem, how many more children would have continued to be sacrificed to a god of the river, killed for cutting a tooth too early, or cast away because of some other taboo that violated tribal mores? The claim that the ethics of Jesus has done more to advance the life of children from squalor and death than any other single factor of civilization is historically justified to its deepest depth.

It was the angelic host and peasant folk of earth who gave the heartiest welcome to the birth of Jesus of Nazareth. This commoner was born in the most humble and unthinkable circumstance, among the animals. Yet he was to be proclaimed as the divine *Logos* who had created the universe, and now entered its mainstream of history.[158] In this claim, one of the most ancient Greek traditions, that of the *Logos* which went back at least as far as Homer, was blended with an ancient Hebraic concept born of God Himself. Despite the birth in such unpretentious circumstances, Jesus was destined to become the most famous man ever born in the Western Hemisphere, or elsewhere. The theology of ancient Judaism had long anticipated the coming of a Messiah, one promised to Israel

---

[158] It was one of His disciples, John, author of the Fourth Gospel, who introduced the concept of the Logos into first century Christianity and wrote the most famous Christological passage in the New Testament as the introduction to his Gospel.

Historical Pursuit of the Purpose of God

from ancient of days;[159] nevertheless, at His birth only a few of the pious recognized its significance. The number in the world who have since learned to revere the birth of Jesus has no parallel in the totality of history; those in the nineteenth century alone who came to such recognition was phenomenal, and as a new factor for the first time in history stemmed from every continent of the earth.

The imperial Roman government, under which Jesus was born, even then was being rapidly transformed from a long and historic Republic into an empire. No other empire has ever caught the imagination of both moralizers and historians as has the Roman Empire into which Jesus was born, but without citizenship, most commonly reserved for only a prized few. The Apostle Paul, who did most in the first century to advance Jesus' message, held Roman citizenship, but not his Master.

Rome's long dominance in temporal history was enacted out in roughly two elongated and somewhat equal eras of time, each approximately a half millennium. Roman power had its unique place in history continued for loosely a thousand years; a millennium enshrined in history as few have ever become in the memory of humanity. Throughout this era, there were other organized states and governments, some, such as Persia in the East, who at times offered serious opposition to Rome. Another such people were the Phoenician states. From their long background emerged religious groups in the Roman Empire that were hostile to Christian faith.

The very dates assigned to the first ruler of the Roman Empire, 37 B.C. to 14 A.D., suggest that something radical had occurred in history. Antiquity made use of many systems for delineating chronology; most common, however, was one in which "before" and "after" were used to designate a historical happening during a ruler's reign. After the birth of Jesus of Nazareth, that gradually became the common measuring rod in the West. Never has the system been seriously altered again.[160] Something like five centuries were to pass ere the Christian calendar became widely established in the West; and not until the eighteenth century was time before Christ denoted as B.C. Oscar Cullman, whose post-

---

[159] It may be that ardent lovers of the Bible have sometimes been too fanciful in interpreting words used in the Bible as a reference to the promised Messiah.

[160] For a brief time during the French Revolution of the eighteenth century, the Christian calendar was abolished in France in favor of a cumbersome and unpopular revolutionary calendar that lasted not more than a decade.

World War writings became widely read in the United States, noted that this development made Jesus the center of history. Is there something ironic in the fact that the eighteenth century is known historically as the most anti-Christian of all the centuries? Yet it set the tone by which modern history is always measured!

The birth of Jesus of Nazareth was within something like a quarter of a century after the beginning of the reign of Octavian, more often referred to as Caesar Augustus.

There could not have been a greater contrast or divergence between these two events. Octavian's reign marked the beginning of a long period of peace known as the *Pax Romana*, following a series of tumultuous wars in the ancient wars in the Roman Republic. Jesus was born in the most humble obscurity, with the only space available for His birth a stable for animals. The site of His birth, Bethlehem, did have the distinction of being known as "The city of David." One of Israel's pastoral prophets, Micah in the eighth century B.C., even named the place where the Messiah would be born. "But you Bethlehem…the least of the clans of Judah, from you will come for me a future ruler of Israel whose origins go back to the distant past."[161] The time period from promise to fulfillment embraced long centuries, but it was a sustaining and unremitting encouragement to Israel in some of the darkest hours of her long history. Perhaps nothing in Israel's long story grew more gruesome than the attacks upon her faith in the days of the Seleucids and especially Antiochus Epiphanes.[162] From those perilous days, preceding the coming of Jesus Christ, was forged a people prepared for the coming of their Messiah. Contradictory and ambiguous to this, He became the "despised and rejected" of Deutero-Isaiah's great Servant Poems.

Augustus, as the first emperor, made serious attempts to revive the Roman Republic. Because of invasions on the borders of the empire, much of his effort was in seeking to control them, and increasingly over the next two centuries this became the pattern of the day for Rome. Across the globe there were interesting historical comparisons of ancient paganism yielding to Christianity. The history of upper-class support for paganism has been a potent one and nowhere more than in the Roman Senate. Long before the end of the empire, Christianity had spread far beyond Rome's

---

[161] Micah 5:1 (NJB)
[162] Many scholars hold to the view that the Book of Daniel was written as a fortress to Israel's faith in this time frame.

boundaries. Though the emperors made ongoing attempts, the Christian faith had penetrated the walls of the empire far too widely, and this effort was nothing more than abortive attempts. By the end of the century, Christianity had spread beyond the borders of the empire.

Jesus began His public ministry at the age of thirty in Galilee of the Gentiles. Prolonged suffering has the capability to dissipate one's hope and ability to persist, but also it generates the opposite, and some of the most tenacious examples from Israel's long past fell within these times of unsurpassed stress. Such eras vouch for Alexander Pope's famous line, "Hope springs eternal in the human breast," and Israel's hope was for divinely glorious days ahead, none of which could surpass the glory of the fruitful days that the Messianic age would bring. The most abiding thing about this hope was the deep longing for God's intervention in history, and that leads to a vital question for the philosophy of history that will elsewhere be addressed. Jesus began His ministry by being baptized by John the Baptist. The writer is persuaded that Jesus, following His baptism, spent forty days in the wilderness talking with God about the ministry and how it would be carried out. Jesus steadfastly committed His life to that of a suffering servant. At this point one has arrived at the most notable and self-giving possibilities for Jesus.

One is confronted with still another paradox in that the Son of David, born in Bethlehem, came to establish a kingdom without borders, or to use Jesus' own words, a kingdom "Not of this world." To a secularist of that age, the birth of Jesus would have been devoid of any substance in the far-reaching stretch of time. In the sharpest contrast, however, the believing community regarded Jesus' birth as "The fullness of time when God did send His Son."[163] Divergent as have been the interpretations placed upon the nature of the Kingdom of God of which Jesus spoke, His followers have been of one mind in proclaiming that it knows no geographical end or temporal boundaries. By any consideration, the birth of Jesus was reckoned as lacking in significance or import, to all but the tiny minority in Israel who had long sustained, and been sustained, by just such hope.

---

[163] For "fullness," the Apostle Paul in Galatians 4:4 used the term *pleoroma*, an old Greek word for "to fill." It was also used in the sense of "to accompany." The right time always brought the maturation of God's purpose.

The three Synoptic Gospels, of which the earliest was Mark, did not appear for some three decades or more after Jesus had completed His mission on earth. Matthew and Luke convey the infancy material, but Mark includes none of this. Luke appears to have been interested in establishing Jesus' relationship to all humanity and begins His genealogy with Adam and Eve. Matthew, the most Jewish of all the Gospels, is content to limit His forebears to the Jewish line alone. Perhaps the best-known part of Jesus' history is that of His birth, presentation in the temple, and visit to Jerusalem at the age of twelve to become a Son of the Torah (Law). Only Matthew relates the account of Jesus being taken to Egypt to escape the wrath of Herod the Great. From the age of twelve to thirty, nothing is recorded of Jesus; consequently, these eighteen years have been called the silent years. If the child is father to the man, something may be garnered from these years, one being His deep consciousness of the long tradition of the Jewish people and the Judaic place in the annals of mankind. In a scattered or random manner, the Gospels sometimes use Aramaic words or phrases, this being the language Jesus learned to speak as a child. Though the Gospels were written in Koiné Greek, it is debatable as to how much of the Greek language Jesus may have acquired. "Abba" must have been the first word Jesus learned, and the final cry to God from the cross, was "Eloi, Eloi, lama sabachthani." These facts must preserve something for us of His earthly use of words.

Very good tradition asserts that Jesus was thirty years old when he departed from Nazareth and the carpenter shop to inaugurate His mission. Today that would appear late for one in the West to begin ministry. For example, the author was not yet eighteen when he left home to attend college in preparation for this. Many have conjectured as to why Jesus began so late in life, but several things have been suggested, such as that Jesus was helping with younger members of the family. Four brothers are mentioned, James, Joses, Judas, and Simon. In addition, there were at least two sisters, though not mentioned by name. One thing is obvious. Many of the parables, which Jesus was so fond of using, bristle with the common everyday observations He had witnessed among a rural peasant people, and things he had seen His mother do in the common chores of rearing five sons, and at least two daughters. Surely, the years afforded Jesus ample time to climb life's hills and observe much about a rural way of life among commoners.

The apocryphal writings fill in these eighteen silent years with things Jesus supposedly did in the time of growing up. One may be grateful that the Holy Spirit guided the early Church in laying aside these things as part of the valid tradition of Jesus of Nazareth. The great positives of these years for Jesus were acquiring knowledge and a love for nature, the systematic practice of attending the local synagogue, and the close observance of the life of the poor or average person. This involved sowing seed, seeking an item that had gotten lost, kneading dough, the goodness and evil inherent in one's neighbors, children at play, and the necessity of manual labor. Jesus mentions the price of the most common, cheapest food which the majority of His neighbors would have eaten, the houses of rural people and how they were swept, the repair of old garments, mud ovens, moths, and rust along with the use of candles, beds, and bushels.[164] "One is struck with the amount of that unconscious assimilation of experience that we find in his words, and which is in itself an index to his nature."[165] The Christian faith survived and this is but one of the ways God works in history.

It was at the age of thirty that Jesus identified Himself with the magnetic ministry John the Baptist was engaged in at the Jordan River; by submitting to baptism by John. Through the ages much has been made as to why Jesus did this, but throughout His ministry Jesus gave striking evidence that His feet had climbed life's hill, and that he knew what was in man. The baptism was followed by what must have been one of the most anguishing episodes of His ministry; it was the temptation for forty days during which time Jesus was considering the kind of Messiah he would be. This, the human mind cannot peer into, but in the time of temptation in the Judean wilderness Jesus found His soul in the Suffering Servant Poems of Deutero-Isaiah. His ministry of preaching, teaching, and healing the Gospels portray readily; nevertheless, the disciples were inept in grasping the Kingdom of God, the theme of His entire ministry. That riddle has continued through the ages to encumber some of the best minds of theologians. Likely, the safest analysis is a persistent and careful understanding of the parables of Jesus, a theme persistently inviting to scholars.

---

[164] T. R. Glover, *The Jesus of History* (New York: 1916) p. 31.
[165] Ibid. p. 33.

To pray for the coming of the Kingdom of God was one of the most formidable themes Jesus taught His disciples to pray for, and one of the most interpreted of His ideas. Here Jesus spoke of the reign of God. That reign has come, is coming, and has yet to come. Its authenticity was seen in the prayer of Jesus in the Garden of Gethsemane, "Thy will be done," and divinely notarized after submitting to the cross. Near the end, He was able to say, "It is finished." This was a saying with seven such words from the cross.[166] That was an authoritative assurance that the Kingdom would continue to come through the course of human history on earth and in the consummation when God shall bring history to its appointed close. God Himself had entered this stream of history through what Christians have come to know as the Incarnation. He who created the world entered its mainstream of history in the person of One who was born a babe. Within a space of something like thirty-three years, in the life, death, and resurrection of Jesus the cornerstone of all that God would do in history was laid.

If we only had the Gospel of Mark, the conclusion might be offered that Jesus conducted almost the entirety of His mission in Galilee. Elsewhere, however, it becomes clear that both John the Baptist and Jesus had an earlier ministry in the south around Jerusalem. The Gospels convey remnants of ministry elsewhere, as in Perea, and it appears that at least once Jesus went out of Palestine in retreat with the disciples. Unlike the ministry of the Apostle Paul, it was a quite localized ministry, nevertheless justifying His statement of not being sent to any but the house of Israel. New Testament scholars a century and more ago were fond of speaking of "the Galilean springtime," by which they gave emphasis to the positives of the ministry, such as His popularity. Later scholars appear justified in having interpreted the earlier ministry from a different framework. The traditional view has long been that the entirety of His mission was about three years; this is derived from the number of Passovers mentioned in the Gospels. Another more radical view of the ministry is that it lasted little more than one year, which to many seems incompatible with the chronology of His life and work.

It has long been traditional to stress that the ministry was one of teaching, preaching, and healing. Certainly, the Gospels refer

---

[166] There may well have been other words that were passed down. This especially could have been as he weakened, or the words spoken were clear.

more often to His teaching than to preaching. Here, the Gospel of Matthew, the most Jewish in thought of any of the four, becomes illustrious, if for nothing more than the Sermon on the Mount, which may or may not have been delivered at one setting. Luke would suggest that it was not. Nevertheless, the writing has captured incomparable praise and plaudit around the world. Even in the eighteenth century Age of Deism, the Sermon on the Mount was a terrain few dared touch. In early America, both Thomas Jefferson and Daniel Webster offered their highest veneration to this passage from Matthew.[167]

Newcomers to the New Testament are often surprised to learn how sparingly the word "church" (*ecclesia*) is used in the Gospels, and how its use is limited to Matthew. The incipient Church, however, is seen in those original men Jesus selected as His first disciples who struggled mightily to comprehend who this Jesus of Nazareth was. Especially to the end of His ministry were their minds obtuse and dull, and most acutely concerning His teaching that the Messiah promised in the Old Testament must be a suffering one. As this band of men quickly multiplied following the Day of Pentecost into the large and varied first century Church it, too, struggled in the attempt to assimilate what God had done in the past with what He was currently doing. To be true, the very concept of the Church was a major step toward establishing a coherency in all that God had been doing in the past and in the present moment. Through the Church founded by His Son, God united the ancient divine economy with the new developments of the first century. It was a theme never to be forgotten in the *ecclesia* of God and from its rationale developed the Christian philosophy of history.

Particularly acute for Jewish Christians was the relationship between God and Jesus of Nazareth with regard for history. When the Church became, by the end of the first century, predominantly Gentile, basking in Greek philosophy, the problem of the trinity forged to the front. Not so much was it the nature of God and history, but the nature of God Himself. Consideration of the fact that three centuries were required for coming to a satisfactory answer to the trinity is an indication of just how solidly the revelation of God is rooted in the chronicle of history. Those who did not fall

---

[167] Luke offers a shorter version of the sermon, but it has not been singled out with the same paean of praise as that of Matthew.

within this pale were regarded as heretics, but some of these, if living today, would be granted a higher status. The presence of Christianity in the modern world is still one of the great dynamics of history. As these lines are written, one of the chief headlines is that of how Christians in the world today are being killed. There have been several centuries in which this act of barbarism was highlighted; yet the Kingdom of God continues its march through history and time. This persecution continues in the modern world from a highly nationalistic Islam. Christians are likewise killed in parts of Africa, but there will be no better success in decrying the faith than in other centuries of violence when Christians were violently persecuted.

Older theologians spoke of Genesis 3:15 as God's Prolegomena, or the first divine pronouncement to undo the wrong of Adam and Eve. "I will put enmity between you and the woman, and between your seed and her seed; he shall bruise your head, and you shall bruise his heel." Older commentators saw this as making known the explanation of why serpents crawl, and why human beings are hostile to them. Pioneer Christian thinkers saw it as the first hint of a divine plan to reclaim the fallen creation. Horace Bushnell once said that there was a cross in God's heart before the wood was seen at Calvary. If this be the case, the central point of an eternal plan of redemption was reached millennia later, when on a spring morning, likely in the years 29 or 30 A.D.,[168] the Roman governor in Palestine, Pontius Pilate, gave permission for Jesus of Nazareth, to be sent to the cross along with two other men that day.

Seemingly, the governor did not feel that the man Jesus deserved such a cruel death, but with Pilate, saving his political job by placating the Jewish crowd was far more important than this point of conscience. One could speak of a thousand crosses, but none comparable to that of Jesus of Nazareth. There had been thousands of crucifixions across the Mediterranean lands in the past century and more. The Romans began their practice of crucifixion in the time of the Republic, which roughly was the five centuries preceding Christ. The empire that followed was looked upon as enduring forever but claimed only the following five centuries. Jesus, however, spoke of an empire that would endure forever.

It was not the Romans who introduced the barbaric punishment of crucifixion however; that infamy appears to have

---

[168] These are the most commonly used dates, but others place it later.

Historical Pursuit of the Purpose of God

been instigated by the Phoenicians. Crucifixion was something that seems to have originated in ancient Phoenicia (where the old cities of Tyre and Sidon were). When the Romans added that part of the world to their empire, they adopted this brutalizing form of execution, something reserved only for the hardest criminal cases from which citizens of the empire were exempt. Thus, Jesus died as a "hardened criminal."

Rome appears to have adopted this means of death approximately a century before the birth of Jesus. The ruling for Jesus' death in this violent manner meant that He who had gone about doing good would die among those who were reckoned as the worst of society and ostensibly something no Roman citizen would ever have to fear. A few years later, there was a sharp contrast with the Apostle Paul, who initially did so much to abolish Christianity, but at the end had done more than any other to advance its growth. Paul was beheaded in Rome by Nero, precisely because of his privilege as a Roman citizen. No one knows how his father obtained citizenship, but historians have noted that it likely came at a time when Rome was expanding this window of opportunity. Paul's fellow Christian and apostle, Simon Peter, who was not a citizen, died by crucifixion not far from the time Paul died. Tradition has asserted that they died at the same time; studies suggesting several months, perhaps a year, appear to have more foundation. The fact that two major apostles had died in the same city was certainly a factor in Rome gaining the ascendancy over older Christian centers, such as Antioch and Alexandria.

It has been noted that in a series of lectures delivered at Oxford at the middle of the twentieth century, Jesus was known by more than forty names and titles that represented who He was. The name Jesus was given to Him by His parents at birth. By the end of the first Christian century, this name had come to evoke a widespread Christian attitude of veneration and worship. Jesus was the translation of a Greek name used for Joshua, who led the Israelites into the Promised Land. Literally the name meant, "He whose salvation is Yahweh," more briefly, "God's salvation."[169]

Though not original with the Romans, they made ample use of crucifixion in the world of their day. There were times when throngs were crucified on the same occasion at the hand of Roman

---

[169] Taylor, *The Names of Jesus*, p. 6.

authority, occasions that have been carved deeply into the annals of history. Nero's reign is a notorious example of such an age. Instances were also recorded of men lasting even four or five days on a cross before death came. With the coolness of night, often-excruciating pain befell one who had hung there so long. If the Phoenicians introduced crucifixion, the Seleucids and still other Near Eastern groups rapidly made ample use of the practice of crucifixion until its stigma had become widespread. So common, however, had this wanton and heartless practice become with Rome, that three men were crucified the same day as Jesus—but by no means was this a record day for the Romans. Nero, for example, far exceeded this on a single day with the execution of hundreds on a single day. Nor was the brutality limited to Nero, one of the most brutal of emperors.

One thing that underscored the barbarism of crucifixion was the length of time one might conceivably live on a cross. Jesus' death was relatively of short duration in comparison with numerous others, who on a few occasions were known to have lasted the better part of a week. Some able theologians have insisted that His early death came as part of a consciousness of taking sin upon Him; that is, He who knew no sin took the sin of the world upon Him. No other crucified person, however, died bearing the weight of the world's sin upon Him as did Jesus of Nazareth. Though the Mediterranean region had known thousands of crosses, that of Jesus stood solitarily alone regarding the uniqueness and meaning of this death. The New Testament put forth this thesis in the most powerful way by insisting that Jesus became sin by taking it upon Himself once and for all.

Since the era between the World Wars, it has become fashionable to depict history as occurring on two parallel lines, that of the secular and salvation history. Some of this concept is quite Augustinian, but it did receive a new emphasis in the West at the time. Christian theology has long insisted that in Jesus of Nazareth, one who knew no sin became sin, the very embodiment of it, as part of the redemptive purpose of God. The very nature of this death in the first century was sufficient to turn some, who might otherwise have been interested in the religion, away from Christianity. Unlike Greek philosophy, the unique thing about Jesus was not His teaching, meaningful and potent as that was. That would have underscored Plato or Plotinus, but for Jesus of Nazareth the most luminous thing was the meaning of His death, the laying of the sin of all the ages upon Him who knew no sin. The Apostle Paul wrote lucidly of the scandal of the cross in his Corinthian correspondence. Throughout Western Civilization there have been heinous crimes, which long blemished the memory of a family who had experienced such. Such was the thought of the Apostle when he referred to the cross as a scandal.

For years, the author as a young minister sought to find something illustrative of how contradictory to His character was the cross for Jesus of Nazareth. As a young college student of nineteen years old, he once spent a very cold night with a widow woman's family at the little country church where he preached during college days in Hale County, Alabama. On turning the sheets on the bed, he noticed how soiled and dingy they appeared to be. For a moment his thought was, "I can never sleep on that." His mother was an impeccable housekeeper and he had never faced such before.

Because of the cold, unheated room, nevertheless, he jumped into the bed quickly pulling the covering over him. It was, however, an experience altogether foreign to anything he had ever experienced. In Jesus, one who knew no sin became sin in order that He might bring redemption to God's creation. In the cross God's purpose came closer to fulfillment than ever before, and in the resurrection that purpose remained continuous until the kingdoms of this world have become the kingdoms of our Lord. It has been suggested that it was the actual burden-bearing of sin that so quickly brought about Jesus' death in comparison with others who had hung on crosses for a much longer time than the six hours he experienced.

That alone made the death of Jesus of Nazareth unique, and anything unique becomes incomparable, transcendent and beyond interpretation. In addition, it abounded in irony, the righteous dying for the unrighteous, and the non-sinful dying for the sinful. This despised cross has become in history the symbol of an unparalleled uniqueness, and Christianity a distinctiveness other religion could never share. God's Messiah "hung on that cross for six long, lazy, loafing hours, and suffered as no other ever did."[170] In those hours, sin died its dismal death, in that He who knew no sin took upon Himself that of all people past, present, and future. Two other men, one on either side of Him, were crucified that morning. Ere death

---

[170] The author is indebted to his erstwhile seminary president, Dr. Ellis Fuller of Louisville, Kentucky, for this striking alliteration.

came, one man came to see in Jesus of Nazareth something he had never witnessed before and became a believer. Thus, in this trio of men, all of whom were looked upon as criminals, one died for sin; another died from sin; while the third died in his sin.

An early Frankish king, Clovis, upon hearing of the crucifixion of Jesus, was said to remark, "If I had been there with my mighty Franks it would not have happened." Christians, of every age, experience something of the same emotional response, except they refer to it as "Amazing Grace;" as did John Newton of England when he wrote the universally beloved hymn "Amazing Grace," that had called him from an eighteenth-century slave trader to the Christian fold as an Anglican minister.

The Nazarene crucified that morning saw His death as teleological, purposive, and something emanating from the mind and will of God Himself. From time immemorial, it was the crucifixion that elevated Jesus of Nazareth to a cardinal or culminating place, not alone in temporal history but in the eternal realm. In the past century, some of the finest philosophers of the West have given ample thought to the purpose of God through history. One of the most notable of these was W. R. Matthews of Cambridge University, who published several works not far from a century ago. Just when the consciousness of Jesus' mission in the world was fully borne into His mind cannot be pinpointed. This is true because at a more elevated theological position, the New Testament affirmed that the self-realization of the death of Jesus was made imminent before the foundation of the earth. Conservative theology has tended to hold that Jesus was fully sensitive to His mission from childhood. Such a view appears, to the author, unlike that of the Fatherhood of God. More scholars, it would seem, see its consciousness dawning upon Jesus from the time of His temptation in the wilderness at the age of thirty. Still others see it even later and are like the older liberals who pictured a Galilean springtime give way to a turning against Jesus.[171]

Liberals used to refer to an early ministry in Galilee as His Galilean springtime. While the date of the full consciousness of His coming crucifixion is debatable, that He increasingly bore this awareness of the cross is as assured as anything in New Testament scholarship. God's creation had been teleological, so was the new

---

[171] Some modern scholars, such as Vincent Taylor, have suggested the old liberals were right.

creation wrought by the death of Jesus of Nazareth. New Testament theology amply illustrates this concept, that in the death of Jesus of Nazareth devout Christians have never pondered it other than seeing it was vicariously done; nor have the illiterate and unlearned failed to grasp this tone of devotion and commitment.

In November 1952, the author in his first year out of the theological seminary, was blessed in purchasing a book by James Denny. Just leaving the seminary the author found Denny a heavyweight at times. The mission Board required that we get some experience at a full-time church before being given a foreign mission assignment. Denny was one of a long line of well-trained and deeply consecrated ministers of Scotland. The reading of this book buttressed the youth's conviction that he should go to West Africa; there Denny's book had been introduced to West African pastors, as well as pastors in Scotland as well as throughout much of Western Europe. "I am not my own, for I have been bought with a price" for ages has resounded around the earth, is the most exacting explanation of this; God loved the world from the time He created it and found it good. As has been seen, something went awry, and creation transformed out of line, totally foreign to the original purpose. Jesus Christ was God's means of renewing that pristine creation.[172] The early church fathers were fond of asserting that in Christ, God had made a new beginning. The New Testament writings affirmed that in Christ, God was indeed preparing a new heaven and a new earth and with its realization, the old order would give way to the eternal Lordship of Jesus. The New Testament put it graphically in claiming, "God would be all and all things in Him."

What a bizarre thing it would have been had such a person as Jesus of Nazareth had no clarified mission or purpose in the world! To reiterate, that divine purpose was consistently pursued through the temporal course of history. Alternatively, for Jesus to have met His fate accidentally does not harmonize with the mind of God. Rather, it was the most defining and purposive moment in history when all God's eternal purposes became focused on one man and in the cross one historical act, the Christ event. All roads led up to that event, and from it, all roads lead out. That is to say this crucifixion of Jesus of Nazareth, giving the appearance of being like

---

[172] Few who read this book will need to be reminded of this verse, but it is the one that resonated the loudest across the globe. "For God so loved the world that He gave His only begotten Son...."

Historical Pursuit of the Purpose of God

so many others, became the focal point of all history. Perhaps, we owe it more to Oscar Cullman, coming to Christ and subsequently becoming one of the most insightful postwar theologians. Incidentally, this is one of his most eminent points of New Testament theology following World War II because of his impact on twentieth century theology. As a matter of fact, Cullman saw the death of Jesus as more than a historical event; he in brilliant fashion pictured Jesus as the center of history, making the Christ event more than historical. It was both cosmological and eternal in scope.[173]

It is difficult to determine precisely when in the course of His ministry Jesus recognized that He would die on a Roman cross. Some scholars are unwilling to admit any development at all in the thought of Jesus. They regard His vision of the cross as being fully clear at least from His baptism onward. Jesus, they believe, saw His pathway clearly from the beginning.[174] This, however, is a very conservative and die-hard field of vision. Others have supposed that Jesus knew this from the visit to the temple in Jerusalem at the age of twelve and point to the wisdom he displayed in the temple on that occasion. This appears, however, to be an affront to the progressive revelation representative of so much of the Biblical narratives, and discordant with all the evidence of the Gospels. It also appears to be too docetic, making Jesus always so elevated as to have never really been human. Some early Christian thought struggled with this problem of Docetism making Jesus only appear or seem to be that which He was.[175] Periodically, Docetism has attempted to creep back into the Church; however, Nicene Christianity acknowledged that Jesus was fully God and fully man with nothing docetic about the reality of the incarnation.[176]

There were a number of factors weighing upon the mind of Jesus, which without doubt must have given Him a growing comprehension that His ministry would come to a violent end. For one thing, there was the long practice in Israel of her prophets coming to such an end. Jesus Himself sometimes referred to this practice. Closer at hand was the brutal fate of John the Baptist. Jesus

---

[173] Oscar Cullman, *Christ and Time: The Primitive Christian Conception of Time and History* (Philadelphia: 1945) pp. 121–130.
[174] Vincent Taylor, *The Life and Ministry of Jesus* (New York: 1955), p. 82.
[175] The English word "Docetism" comes from a Greek word meaning "to appear or seem."
[176] For greater clarity one should read of the Council of Nicaea in 325 A.D.

likewise recognized the thinning of the crowds who had once followed Him, and asked His disciples if they, too, wished to go away. Likewise, he recognized the growing hostility of the Scribes and Pharisees. Most significantly of all, through the life of prayer and devotion, Jesus had found Himself in the servant poems of Isaiah, especially the last and longest one of all. Hoping to the end that the cup might be removed, His submission to the purpose of God remained absolute and unshakeable.

Many scholars see the ministry of Jesus as having lasted between two to three years, and likely toward the latter.[177] This calculation is based upon the three Passovers mentioned in the Gospels, and thus may have been closer to three years or to two. Jesus knew His Jewish history thoroughly and easily recalled the violent fate of the prophets of old; He knew also the fate of John the Baptist who had baptized Him and was later beheaded by Herod Antipas. Likewise, He recognized the growing antagonism of the religious leaders of His day, particularly the Scribes and Pharisees. Perhaps most significant of all was that in the Jewish Scriptures He loved so well, He found His own soul and mission. There, especially in the servant poems of Deutero-Isaiah, Jesus found His mission on earth. It was among these passages from the prophet of the Babylonian exile, that Jesus realized the type of mission that was to be His. His experience in the wilderness of Temptation must have caused these poems to find a lodging place deep within His soul. They brought Him face to face with the type of ministry He saw as His mission. These precise passages were what the Ethiopian eunuch was reading when Philip, one of the original (charter) deacons (as long has been the interpretation) joined his chariot. From these, the deacon presented to the eunuch the message of Jesus, which he immediately embraced and was baptized. "He was wounded for our transgressions, he was bruised for our iniquities, upon him was the chastisement that made us whole."[178] Again, "All we like sheep have gone astray, we have turned everyone to his own way; and the Lord has laid on Him the iniquity of us all."[179]

---

[177] Some have sought to limit it to a single year, but this view has not been widely adopted.
[178] Isaiah 53:5.
[179] Acts 8. As these lines are written, news has come of the recent death of Christians in Ethiopia, presumably by Isis. From the time of Philip to modern times there has

Human thought clearly lacks sufficient depth to explore or probe the entirety of all that Jesus experienced as the incarnate God living among men of Galilee, observing them pursue their daily living from the rich and populated region surrounding the Sea of Galilee. No wider disparity could be imagined than that between the Incarnate God living among mortal humanity; yet that is precisely the meaning of the Incarnation. It is also more than an accident that the man from Ethiopia found that for which he had been seeking when he invited a perfect stranger to join him in his chariot. The man could have been reading from many points in his manuscript. Instead, he was reading from a passage Christians have always accepted as pointing to Christ and His mission in the world. The passage was from the last of the four servant poems in Deutero-Isaiah, and spoke, as did nothing else, of the suffering Messiah whom the prophet foretold. The writing of the prophet of the exile had but recently been fleshed out by Jesus of Nazareth who represented its ultimate fulfillment. Is it more than a curiosity that one of the earliest non-Jewish converts to Christianity, a man from a distant land on another continent, came to understand Jesus of Nazareth.[180] Nothing more meaningful stemmed from a not-so-long-ago Pentecost than that the gospel would be preached to all nations everywhere.

To return once more to the actual ministry of Jesus, at what point did He see the tidal flow of His own popularity change? This cannot be precisely pointed to in the synoptic Gospels, but there were omens of fluctuation, as for example when Jesus saw the crowds abandon Him and asked the disciples if they likewise wished to go away. The increasing hostility of the Scribes and Pharisees was surely one significant omen of what lay before Him. Still another was the growing resentment of the non-religious populace over His unwillingness to embark on a popular mission against imperial Rome. Of the many grievances the Jews had against Rome, the burden of heavy taxation appears to have been perhaps the most onerous. The practice of their own religion and its teaching in the many synagogues of Palestine does not appear to have been a realistic separation between Rome and Israel as early Christianity was interpreted as a faction within Judaism which Rome had in the past

---

been an unbroken line of Christians there. One may well believe this will be the case long after Isis is a thing of the past.
[180] Acts 8:26–39.

recognized as legal. Those religions within the empire that enjoyed this status as *religio licita* (licensed religion) had little to fear from the early emperors.[181] Rome's official policy allowed ample leadway for legalized religions in the empire to remain unthreatened.

Jesus had looked upon His coming death as both a road to be traveled and a cup to be drunk. "I must walk today, tomorrow, and the day following, for it cannot be that a prophet perishes out of Jerusalem." The disciples were asked, "Are you able to drink from the cup that I drink of?"[182] There is nothing to suggest that Jesus ever thought of His death as an act to placate an angry God. This is completely antithetical to the worldwide paganism of His day where such was the core to any religious practice. It is but one more example of how the living of life was a revelation of God. Jesus' focus was that it was we who needed to be reconciled to God, as St. Paul acknowledged in His admonition, "Be you reconciled to God."[183] Without doubt, Paul saw the death of Christ as the chief focal part of the eternal long purpose of God.

The Gospel narratives would suggest that the most difficult thing the disciples had to comprehend about the ministry of Jesus was the fact of His death on a cross. The twelve had already confessed that Jesus was the Messiah, but there was little in the long Judaic tradition to suggest anything but a glorious day of the Lord for the Messianic age. Uppermost in the mind of the devout were the apocryphal writings. They contained little to suggest anything but the glories of the Messiah who would subdue all of Israel's enemies. They speak of Israel's enemies being smitten by God, while Deutero-Isaiah speaks of the promised Messiah being smitten for our sins. For one thing, the total ignominy attached to the cross simply did not couple with the type of ministry and character Jesus had revealed; and of course, there were the century's long portrait of the Messiah that had been built up in the minds of the populace as to expectations of what He would do. A strong nationalistic character had become deeply rooted and inveterate with many religious practices. Such emotions had become more widespread since

---

[181] For many years, Christianity was looked on as being an integral part of Judaism and escaped persecution. The gradual recognition that this was fallacious reasoning led to the series of violent persecutions.
[182] Luke 13:33, Matthew 21:22
[183] 11 Cor. 5:20. The meaning of reconcile here is to accept God's forgiveness in Christ.

Pompey entered Jerusalem in 63 B.C. and were now part of the national milieu. The increasingly burdensome Roman taxation muster was a powerful factor in the increase of the Zealots who were ready to provoke an open revolt against Rome. Though limited in number, the fanaticism of the Zealots brought great destruction to the people. Some scholars have emphasized this as significant in Judas Iscariot's resentment that Jesus would not identify with such zealotry

The Gospels point to meaningful turning points in the ministry of Jesus; one was His withdrawal for the sole teaching of the Twelve. Many would agree that in the idea of the Suffering Servant and the Servant poems of Deutero-Isaiah the Old Testament reached the pinnacle of God's continuous revelation to Israel. At the human angle, one can only imagine the profound impact of these passages on the mind of Jesus as he pondered them in the solitude of His times of withdrawal for prayer. Some of these, we are told, lasted through the night, a time when the inner self is often most responsive. It was not only that the mind of Jesus was quickened, but the soul was in its most direct contact with God. It is in such times that one is most receptive to the will and purpose of God for one's life. Perhaps it is transparent that when Jesus prayed: "Not my will but thine, O Lord," He was most conscious of pushing forward God's purpose in the universe.[184]

Alexander Whyte was a grand preacher of another day in Scotland, who spent the last hour before divine worship in private prayer. Famous as he was, the church worship attracted many visitors. Following the service on one occasion a lady visitor to the Church said to him, "Dr. Alexander, you appeared as if you had come from the direct presence of God." The modest reply was, "Perhaps I did."[185]

Jesus' self-giving mission has delineated across the ages from great towering peaks of Scripture. Not only so, but lines from such continue to resonate across the ages wherever two or three from the believing community have met together for divine worship.

---

[184] For one to ignore the fact that the death of Jesus was cosmic in scope is to overlook one of the
most meaningful and beautiful things of God's revelation and redemption.
[185] Whyte was born out of wedlock in 1836 and died in 1921, after becoming one of the renowned names in the Scottish Presbyterian Church and most notably in Aberdeen.

Historical Pursuit of the Purpose of God

Perhaps to most modern Christians such thoughts mean little, but historically they have kept the work of God alive. During the War Between the States, the Northern blockade of Southern ports cut off Baptists in the Confederacy from their mission work in Lagos, Nigeria, for close to two decades. Some time later, they were able to return to Lagos and were elated to discover that, during their absence, a Yoruba lady named Mother Harden, with help from the English Methodist mission, had kept the small church in Lagos together. Over the years, this young church grew into the flourishing First Baptist Church of Lagos. Its pastor, Dr. J. T. Ayorinde, was internationally known for the office he held in the Baptist World Alliance.

All the synoptic Gospels devote most of their space to the final week of Jesus' life. Luke's Gospel, soon after the Mountain of Transfiguration experience, stated, "He set His face to go to Jerusalem."[186] The Gospels seem to lead one to believe that there was something sacrosanct and hallowed in the mind of Jesus about dying in Jerusalem.

Certainly, His emotions were deeply alive when thinking of this reality, "O Jerusalem, Jerusalem...How often I would have gathered your children together as a hen gathers her brood."[187] Could it be that Jesus fondly recalled that occasion when as a lad he was taken to Jerusalem, and there He lingered after His parents had departed the city? There must surely have been those memories lodged in His soul, which both "blessed and burned."[188] Obviously, it had been deeply instilled in Him that no prophet could perish but there in the city. Luke's Gospel makes Jesus "take the long way around" to reach Jerusalem, but when He did so was poignantly touched, and musing over the question to Himself, "How often would I have gathered your children together...and you would not."[189] It was history's greatest refusal; reminiscent it was of John's, "and His own people received Him not."[190] The author recalls fondly a young Jewish man who converted to Christianity and enrolled in a fine seminary to prepare for ministry. He often came to our country church, as he was a friend of the pastor, and spoke. The church made

---

[186] Luke 9: 51.
[187] Luke 13:34.
[188] Robert Burns line.
[189] Luke 13:34.
[190] John 1:11.

offerings to him to assist with his studies. The story of how his own well-to-do family from New Jersey had turned their backs on him lodged deeply in the mind of one young lad.

It appears that the practice of crucifixion originated in ancient Phoenicia and was adopted as a form of execution by the Romans when they conquered Phoenicia and added its lands to their empire. It was reserved only for the hardest criminal cases. Thus, Jesus died as a "hardened criminal." Historians believe that following the death of Jesus, crucifixion lasted only about one century before Rome abandoned it. Citizens of the Roman Empire were not crucified but were beheaded (a much more speedy death). Paul was a Roman citizen and Jesus Christ was not. Not everyone born in the Roman Empire, by any means, were citizens. It is likely that Paul's father had been one.

Jesus hung on the cross for about six hours; others did so for several days and nights. There is more than a physical consideration of length of time on the cross here. No one had ever died with the weight of sin upon him as Jesus did. He who knew no sin became sin for the salvation of all sinners. It was a unique weight of sin that only He might carry. While others had died due to the impact of sin in their lives, Jesus became sin so that, through His sacrifice, the impact of sin might be negated. Only He could die vicariously for the sin burden of the ages since the Garden of Eden. The most fundamental tenet of the faith is that Christ Jesus died for our sins, and in doing so reversed the long flow of history. Many modern believers hold to the faith that the unparalleled woe of hurt in the world today is but the prelude to the birth pangs of a new age, to continue that which was dismembered by the mythical act of Adam and Eve at a prehistoric time in the Garden of Eden. Jesus was placed on the cross about nine in the morning, sentenced by Pontius Pilate, and then the Roman governor of Palestine, who knew that Jesus was not guilty of such a death.

The six hours Jesus was on the cross was an amazingly short time in comparison to some crucifixions. It was not uncommon for a man to last three or four days, and there are a few cases of hanging even longer before dying. Remember Jesus was already without sleep, and had been punished, or weakened, already. For example, He carried His own cross for a time before collapsing. There are seven recorded sayings from Him while on the cross those six hours. It is possible that others were spoken which did not come down to us. For example, some may not have been heard or understood. The final saying was, "It is finished." Nothing comparable in all of history could have been more significant, for it was God's great turnaround for a creation He had spoken into existence in divine perfection.

A major theological question has been, how did Jesus see His death? Without question, He saw it as vicarious; not from anything He had done. "He who knew no sin became sin for us." Again, He saw His death as the fulfillment of Old Testament Scripture; in so many of these did He find His own soul. Particularly sensitive was He to the suffering poems of Deutero-Isaiah, the Book of Psalms, and to the great prophets such as Jeremiah. Jesus saw His death at the center of an eternal plan of God. In the New Testament Paul was bold to say that such a plan dated from eternity. This, nevertheless, should not become entangled with the famous matter of predestination. Sixteenth century predestination, stemming from the work of John Calvin, captured much of the mind of large parts of Western Europe and the eastern part of North America. It must be remembered that much of what was placed at Calvin's feet actually arose from later interpretations and followers of Calvin, who have been numerous.

It need be noted that Jesus' death became the central core of what His disciples preached following His ascension into the heavens. This core constituted the main line of early apostolic preaching aimed at evangelism. Skilled and artful New Testament scholars have noted that the immediate disciples of Jesus had a basic core of what they taught new converts to the Christian faith; it was given the name *kerygma* and contained no more than six or eight essential facts about Jesus, which every early follower learned. What they deemed the *kerygma* to be was the essential knowledge about Jesus' life on earth. Following World War II, as part of the new renaissance of Christian theology, the *kerygma* was given enthusiastic attention by theologians from England, Germany, Scotland, Scandinavia, North America, and other nations.

The death of Jesus was as an assured event of history as anything could ever have been. The resurrection was so shocking that even the disciples were amazed at hearing the news of it. After His resurrection, Jesus was not continuously with the disciples but rather made appearances among them. Something short of a dozen of these is mentioned in the New Testament; one of the most moving of these is His appearance to Peter who had in the end denied Him. All of the appearances appear to have been so surprising with natural affinity for the person to whom he appeared. When one reads observantly, the emotion Jesus felt toward the person often becomes strangely apparent. Not all of His appearances were to the disciples but were well balanced among His followers.

Chapter 6
Pioneer of The New Testament Gospels

To a modern mind there is something odd or unmatched about the most famous person who ever lived on earth not having anything authentic written about his life for thirty years after his death. Such, however, was true of Jesus of Nazareth, who died about 33 A.D. Some three decades later a young man, John Mark, who had witnessed Jesus' arrest by Roman soldiers, wrote his eponymous Gospel. He had known Jesus, but not as well as the twelve disciples. Mark's Gospel initially enjoyed only a short-term popularity before fading away in favor of the Gospels of Matthew and Luke. This downturn lasted for centuries; however, in contemporary eras this Gospel has enjoyed a remarkable and steady renewal. The occasion for its writing was the reign of Nero (54-68) as the emperor of the Roman Empire. Nero had the apostles Peter and Paul put to death.

The former, according to traditional records, was crucified with his head facing downward, while the latter was given a more honorable death by beheading due to his status as a Roman citizen. Hitherto, for a few decades Christians had been free from persecution under the guise that the religion was a branch of Judaism, a faith legalized by the Roman government. Whatever the truth, the story of Nero's blaming a great fire in Rome on the Christians has been repeated for two millennia. With the recognition that Christianity was not a *licena religio* Nero began an open persecution, which claimed the deaths of two of the most preeminent of the Apostles, Peter and Paul. While the latter had not been one of the original twelve followers early on, resulting in misgivings on the part of some, Paul was in time recognized as an Apostle. The claim of the latter to be counted as an Apostle was the basis of one of the earliest disputes in early Christianity; while Peter's place among the twelve was assured as one of the original disciples and perhaps the most boisterous of the twelve.

John Mark had grown up in Jerusalem, living in a home of means well beyond that of the average Jerusalem family. His father, perhaps deceased, is unmentioned in the Gospels, while his mother lived in a home sufficiently lavish to entertain Jesus and the entire band of His disciples. She apparently was a woman of some wealth and prestige in Jerusalem; most likely, Jesus and the disciples had been guests in her home on more than one occasion. It was also likely that her son was in the Garden of Gethsemane when Jesus was arrested and was the unnamed young man who lost his garments while fleeing from the Roman soldiers on the night of Jesus' arrest. Nothing more was heard of him until a few years later when Barnabas and Saul of Tarsus were organizing the first missionary itinerary from Antioch of Syria.[191] John Mark, a relative of Barnabas, was chosen to accompany them, not as an equal partner but as a domestic servant. After being commissioned by the Antioch church, the missionaries proceeded to Seleucia, the seaport for Antioch, and sailed to the island of Cyprus. They crossed the island and proceeded to Paphos, where something of supreme importance occurred when the governor of the island embraced the Christian faith. His name was Sergius Paulus and is significant in that he was the first high-ranking Roman official mentioned to have become a Christian. This was something that increasingly became common in the empire for the next three centuries. One of the last of great importance in the government to do this before its rapid decline was Ambrose of Milan, whose influence on Augustine was gargantuan in the fourth century.

It would be taxing to come up with an ancient writing that has had a more dramatic rise in esteem than the little book written by John Mark. Unlike Matthew, the Gospel of Mark had to win its way to acclaim over two other synoptic writings, Matthew and Luke. Before the arrival of biblical and higher criticism a couple of centuries ago, Mark was looked upon as being inferior to the other synoptics. Again, unlike Matthew, Mark did not tap into the long Hebraic roots of the Jewish people in relating his narrative of Jesus' work. He does not have anything to suggest what the relationship of Jesus toward the Law of Moses had been, nor is there any genealogy as both of the other synoptics (Matthew and Luke) have. Early tradition had it that Matthew was originally written in Hebrew, which many scholars are inclined to think was the case. It was only in modern centuries that scholars began to recognize the value of Mark and afford it its pristine place as primary in New Testament studies.

By the time Mark was written, all of the canonical Pauline writings had been penned, and some had been in circulation a dozen

---

[191] This church was flourishing with many Gentiles in its membership and was second only to the Jerusalem Church.

years or so. These writings represented numerically almost half of the future New Testament. The single noteworthy significance of this is that the most primitive Christian congregations had never read any of the Gospels. This, of course, would have been true of the great churches in Antioch and Alexandria where early theological schools developed. Generations were to pass before any Christian could have read all of the four canonical Gospels found in Bibles today. In the modern-day church, the practice is widespread of making use of the Gospels in introducing the Bible to new Christians. Would not curiosity seekers love to be able to point to the first congregation which ever had a complete copy of the New Testament! Lacking what is the standard of modern times; the oral tradition was meticulously guarded and passed on.[192] Certainly fewer things are more established in New Testament scholarship than the care with which the tradition was carefully handed down to the next generation.

The *kerygma*, the designation by which the earliest biblical preaching and tradition was passed on, must have been preached far and wide from Jerusalem by those who had learned it through oral tradition, long before any of its main points could have been garnered from a written page such as the Book of Acts. The *kerygma* stated succinctly some of the most essential facts and information concerning Jesus of Nazareth during His days on earth. In fact, at this point in the first century it was most likely that anyone who had become a Christian had derived their faith directly from the tradition rather than from any writing which in time came to be a part of the New Testament. This would have remained the case for at least two decades after the ascension of Jesus Christ.

One attribute of this handed-down legacy was that the earliest churches were well aware of the rift that cropped up between John Mark and Paul early on their first missionary tour. There was a time in modern theology when it was widely accepted among New Testament scholars that there had been a great first century breach between Peter and Paul. Much was made of this, particularly in European critical studies of the New Testament. More recent studies, however, regard this assumed scholarly fray as much ado about nothing. One of the most distinguished modern church historians, Adolph von Harnack, was the great architect of this

---

[192] The tradition here is not commensurate with the *kerygma* of earlier times.

thesis. He was born in 1851 in Estonia but destined to do his great life work in Germany. Like him, his father had also been a professor. There was much in Harnack that is highly laudable to any mellowed follower of Christ, for instance the diligence with which he pursued an answer to his question, "How can I become his [Jesus'] disciple?" Harnack was deeply influenced by not only Ritschl, but also Hegel. However, it has been said that Harnack replaced Hegel's philosophical reason with history, which he considered provided a more solid foundation for the faith. Harnack taught in a number of distinguished German universities where he attracted some of the ablest minds not only from Germany but also around the world.

The impact of this hypothesized rupture between these two outstanding apostolic leaders, Peter and Paul, was well known and widely accepted, but the center of it was always in the German universities where Harnack taught. It must be recalled that these were the early years of critical biblical scholarship when many emerging scholars showed a strong impetus to embrace the new and innovative. At the same time, Germany was moving rapidly toward political consolidation; the Italian states had virtually completed that task on their peninsula; the United States was implementing its decade-long occupation of the Confederacy; Great Britain was enjoying the splendor of its Victorian Age; and abroad generally there was the concept of an unstoppable progress. Scientific advancement was enjoying one of its remarkable eras. Perhaps it was inevitable that theology would be caught up into this whirlwind of change. In this realm it was Germany and Harnack who led the way.

Contention between Paul and John Mark, however transitory it may have been, was an actuality with enduring, but positive results for the advance of the faith. Had there, in the first century, existed the cleavage between Paul and Peter, which nineteenth century Christian scholarship so much reveled in, John Mark would evidently have been caught in the middle in that he had close associations with both Peter and Paul. That there was for a season at least a serious estrangement between Paul and John Mark, the New Testament makes abundantly clear. In time, their rift was beautifully healed, just as the New Testament assuredly made clear all such feuds between Christians should be. For many decades during the younger years of the United States, churches made it their practice to assure that such disruptions did not long continue amongst its members. This is a beautiful chapter of the inner working of American society and church history, which to this writer's knowledge has not received adequate serious study. The exception may be occasional notes or references in a master's thesis, or doctoral dissertation, some of which he has not pursued.

Likewise, the impact of this fading practice among Christians is something that the modern-day church might do well to address. There can be no sustainable denial that the contemporary practice of turning the eye away represents a sharp turn from not only a centuries-old polity, but from the unquestioned teaching of Jesus. Correspondingly, the new mode is far less kin to the historic church than one might imagine. The practice of confronting one who had erred reached even to the apex of society. No one need imagine that the hinges of history will ever be such that a Holy Roman Emperor of Germany might be compelled to stand in the snow begging to see a prelate of the Church. This was the case when Henry IV stood in the snow at the dead of winter at Canossa in 1077 begging to see Pope Gregory VII. Nevertheless, the need of reconciliation in the modern world is too much called for to go perpetually unheeded by the Christian Church who first inaugurated this ethic into western society so long ago.

In turning back, a thousand years to Mark's dispute with the Apostle Paul, it strikes one beyond question that the fissure between him and the apostle had a significant impact on the Christian community and its historical advancement. Without it conceivably the Gospel of Mark would not have been written, but if so, with an entirely different format. Had Mark long remained with Paul, he would have been involved in further forays into Asia Minor advancing the gospel there. Highly probably is it that this would have closed any opportunity for him to come to know Peter, who was likely then at Rome. Most New Testament scholars hold to the view that Mark's Gospel followed quite closely the sermons and traditions he had heard from Peter. If this reasoning merits sanction, then it is another instance of the truth of Paul's, didactic axiom, "We know that in everything God works for good with those who love him, who are called according to his purpose."[193] Mark's seemingly abrupt departure from the mission team resulted in strained relations between him and the Apostle Paul. Perhaps Barnabas, being Mark's

---

[193] Romans 8: 28. The Apostle Paul likely did not intend to limit this to individuals but saw it axiomatic in the general run of history.

relative, understood his reasons for doing so. Mark was yet with the team when they left Cyprus, but upon arriving at Perga tension arose, and scholars have espoused various reasons for the cause of this breakup.

William M. Ramsey held to the view that here Paul proposed a revision to their original plan for the missionary tour which called for the crossing of the Taurus mountain range into new territory where the church would face new ventures hitherto not tested. New Testament scholars have also made something of the notice that earlier in Acts it was Barnabas and Paul, and only later for Paul to be listed first. Ramsay referred to a later observation originating with the natives of this region in which Paul is depicted as having greater importance than Barnabas.

Ramsay's well-earned renown as an excellent pioneer British scholar appeared to show a slight bias in favor of John Mark, which, however, is a value judgment based on slim information for an event more than a millennium and half-removed from his day. Mark has often received, however, negative evaluation and been perceived as failing. Without much support, or so it appears to the author. Mark has been seen as cowardly; perhaps not unlike that which the author did in his missionary career from his first-term failure to tackle the needs in Tamale, Gold Coast. To demonstrate this, one turns away to illustrate this in the author's experience in Africa.

In 1952, my wife and I sailed to Lagos, Nigeria, on a Norwegian freighter as quite young Baptist missionaries. We were both twenty-four and newly out of the theological seminary. Not long before our departure, and after our goods had been shipped to Nigeria, we received a letter stating that our assignment would be in Tamale, Gold Coast. The Nigerian mission was regarded as an old and strong one, and it had sent a token force to the Gold Coast to minister to Nigerian Yoruba churches that had been planted there. Its objective was to minister to the many Nigerians who had gone there as traders but was not committed to the indigenous people of the British colony of the Gold Coast.

Upon arriving in Lagos in March, we were staying at the Baptist Hostel, which was a clean and comfortable place used by its own missionaries and those from many missions for its people en route to various places in Africa. We were to remain there until arrangements were made for our travel to Tamale. While at the hostel an older, highly respected, and much experienced missionary,

Historical Pursuit of the Purpose of God

Miss Ethel Harmon, was also a guest. She had recently spent time in the Gold Coast working with pastors on organizing Sunday Schools. Miss Harmon was adamant in expressing her feeling that it would not be a wise thing for a first term missionary to be sent to Tamale.[194] She pointed out that the mission house had not been built; but only a small structure destined to become a storage place. Whoever went there would need to know something about building, of which the newly arrived missionary knew nothing. The language used in Tamale was Dagomba, which we had not studied. I knew nothing about blueprints, with skills limited to having occasionally used a hammer! When the executive committee met in April, true to her word, she recommended that we be relocated.

We were then assigned to become teachers at the old highly respected Baptist Academy in Lagos, which was planning on moving from its downtown location to a new spacious one adequate for an enlarged academy. In the classroom at the academy, I soon knew that through Miss Ethel Harmon, whom I had never met before, I had found my niche in life.[195] My subjects were English and Bible, with much emphasis on student reading the great books and writing papers. At the end of the year I received a letter from the Nigerian national department of education, then administered by the British, stating that my students had come out near the top on their national exams. A few missionaries appeared to become estranged over this unusual action of changing an assignment, just as Paul and Barnabas once were. Nevertheless, there is a divine providence that sometimes overrides the decision of good and well-intentioned people. Divine providence was something that simply came into the author's life with no preconceived plan to court or pursue it. (Certainly, one should sincerely seek God's hand in one life.) The experience of John Mark with Paul and Barnabas was one clarion case.

The human mind can see but little that is ahead, but both Christian faith and Christian thought have asserted that things are teleological. John Henry Newman expressed this in radiant Christian faith in 1833 when he wrote the beloved hymn, "Lead Kindly Light," with the words "The distant scene I do not see, one step enough for me." It is important to learn to visualize that sight which is not restricted to the straightaway or close range. Incidentally, only one

---

[194] This had been recently tried before with a first term missionary and his wife. They were early on forced to return home because of a breakdown.
[195] I would teach the remainder of my active days.

who learns to do this and look at the long-running landscape in history is apt to discern a token mark but growing sense of God's ongoing ways in human history.

The source of the break between John Mark and Paul stemmed from the fact that on Paul's first missionary journey, well before some of the most crucial events had taken place, Mark abandoned the mission. The New Testament never alludes nor offers a cause for this separation. The breach between the older and younger man was for a time sufficiently wide that Mark found himself *persona non grata* to Paul, who did not trust him to accompany the party on a later second missionary journey. Paul desired Barnabas to go with him but was adamant in his unwillingness to include Mark. One of the most powerful and astoundingly beautiful things about Christianity, after all, has been the astonishing way it has brought about reconciliation as it has plowed its way through more than two millennia of human history. The power to accomplish this has been demonstrated at every level from the individual to larger groups and even nations.[196] Instances could likewise be cited of the exhibition of this power on every continent amid an untold diversity of people and circumstances.

At a later time in the New Testament, Paul and John Mark were reconciled, and Paul wanted Mark with him.[197] Is it too bold a claim to assert that the rectification between two early Christians was embryonic of what would follow in subsequent centuries all over the earth through the rugged application of the Christian faith? The central core of Christian dogma is that "God was in Christ, reconciling the world unto Him.[198] Perhaps it would not be exotic to suggest that, as these lines are written, the citizens of the United States stand in greater need of reconciliation than at any time in its history since 1861. America, as elsewhere, stands face to face with one of its greatest challenges of the last two centuries. Happily, it has gone through a half century in which Christian denominations have moved impressively toward reconciliation. Its current call of the hour is to a nation, once deeply proud of its Christian patrimony, to

---

[196] An example is the prevention of war between Argentina and Chile early on in the twentieth century when a cross was erected to symbolize this commitment to peace rather than war.

[197] II Corinthians 5:19. It is highly likely that Paul wrote these lines at a time in his life when he was attempting to reconcile factions within the Corinthian Church.

[198] II Corinthians 5:19.

Historical Pursuit of the Purpose of God

rise to the occasion of being reconciled among its component parts. Surely, it is one of the hallmarks of Christians perpetually to act as ministers of reconciliation.[199]

Exemplified by the individual and personal reconciliation of Paul and Mark, through the centuries, Christianity gained the power to reconcile larger groups. Historians of that field are almost unanimous in acknowledging that the Christian religion did more than anything else to homogenize the warring heptarchy of Anglo-Saxon Britain into one people. In parts of modern Africa, one sees a similar thing in weakening tribalism in favor of a unified national state.[200] Nothing would ever have brought the Fanti of the Gold Coast, and the Ashanti of the interior together had early Christian missionaries, mainly from Britain and the Continent, not have introduced so effectively Christianity among them.

From this same consummate and classical text of what the Christian religion is, we are instructed that likewise it is the function of all who are in Christ to pursue the goal of reconciliation. Once again, the writer is unmindful of any historical monograph that has dealt with this theme directly, but ample grounds there are for this; such as the impact Christianity had in forging unity among the previously hostile Anglo-Saxon tribes, eventually bestowing the name of England upon much of that island. The potency of the religion to accomplish this has been demonstrated on several continents. Thus, there is something innate and intrinsic within the Christian faith about this plausibility to which adherents of Christianity have been commissioned.

The substance and significance of the renewed harmony between Mark and Paul is detected at a later point in life when Paul desired the presence of Mark on another missionary venture. "Bring Mark for he is profitable for me,"[201] wrote Paul to another of his young confederates or comrades. Paul's summon was furthermore his recognition of Mark's worth and usefulness in potentially turning the Mediterranean into a Christian realm. His comment on him was, "Very useful in serving me." Seeing the spectacular success of the

---

[199] The ongoing division over our President is clearly an example of this.
[200] Modern Ghana of West Africa, created from the Gold Coast, is an example par excellence. In the first half of the nineteenth century the Fanti and Ashanti people were not unlike the states of the heptarchy. The Basle Mission and English Methodism did much to pave the way for a future coming together as one nation.
[201] II Timothy 4:11

spread of Christianity in the East and cherishing his deeply held desire to go west to Rome, there was little reason to suspect that similar success might not be realized in the West. Paul did sense that his eastern ministry was over. Whether Paul envisioned the use of John Mark in such a mission of advance in the West must remain mute.

The impact of the Apostle Paul on first century Christianity is immeasurable; this is true although his personality at times must have been polarizing, as for example in Corinth. There, party spirit developed within the congregation that had been founded by the Apostle Paul. One party claimed to be counted as being in Paul's conclave, while several other cabals identified themselves as belonging to another Christian leader. The New Testament leaves no doubt of the persuasiveness and weightiness of Paul's character. These Scriptures make mention of several individuals who are hardly known beyond the shadow of Paul. John Mark is one of these, for his own Gospel is not highly revelatory of his selfhood; nor does it suggest much of Mark's uniqueness, as does Matthew's having been a Roman tax gatherer or Luke a physician in earlier life. The first non-biblical mention of Mark is from Papias (c. 60-130), who served as Bishop of Hierapolis. Both he and the much better-known Irenaeus (c. 130-200) attested to the fact that Mark served as an interpreter for Peter. Papias took pride in the fact that he sought the best traditions for his information, claiming that he then treasured this in his memory. He said that he made it a point to learn what Andrew, Peter, Philip, Thomas, James, John, Matthew, or other disciples had said. This information Papias collected with considerable enthusiasm and care. He was regarded by some in the early church as being eccentric, perhaps from his strong chiliastic and millenarian ideas. Eusebius in his history of the church seemed not to like him and did not think that he had a great mind. Elsewhere he seems to express conflicting views of Papias. He was also a friend of the aged and beloved Polycarp, and it is possible that both had seen the Apostle John.

For various reasons, early students of sacred writing long gave Matthew the chief seat among the Gospels. One reason for this is undoubtedly the fact that he quoted the Old Testament more often than did any other New Testament writer. According to an early tradition Matthew was first written in Hebrew, and it would not be before the early second century that the church became predominantly gentile. One need not be far advanced in New Testament scholarship to note Matthew's hefty penchant for quoting the Old Testament. This featured far more with him than any other New Testament writing; by reason of this it has been alleged, particularly from conservative scholars, that Matthew is, in spite of chronological consideration, the most appropriate bridge from the Old Testament to the New. Not surprising that the Ebionites, a conservative Jewish group of the second century, accepted only Matthew as an authentic Gospel. They rejected Mark and Luke. The rise of this second century sect bearing the appellation "poor men," was witness to the lingering hold of Judaism in the church and the hearts of many. Jerusalem had fallen to the might of Rome in 70 A.D., and with that the twilight of Judaism set in. The disastrous event reached its full culmination in 135 with the ill-fated Bar Cochba uprising. After this upheaval, Christianity swiftly became dominantly Gentile. According to Irenaeus, the Ebionites accepted only the Gospel of Matthew. Jerusalem fell in the siege of the Romans under Titus in 70 A.D., and with that the twilight of Jewish Christianity set in. This, however, was not the same at the near eclipse that came after 135 and the Bar Cochba disaster.

Perhaps the Gospel of Mark had to earn recognition by reason of a number of things. It is the shortest of the four Gospels; furthermore, it omits an appreciable amount of the data for which the Gospels have become so heartily admired at the popular level. Noticeably, it has no Sermon on the Mount. This omission was precisely the most admirable attraction eighteenth century Deism found in the New Testament. Such a ravenous student as Thomas Jefferson expunged most of the New Testament but showered great accolades on the Sermon on the Mount. Daniel Webster also gave strong expression of his admiration for the Sermon on the Mount. In general, Deists, and others touched by this movement but not in line with their classical stance generally paid lip service to this part of the Gospels.

Mark narrates none of the beautiful and beloved parables frequently seen in the Gospel of Luke, such as the Prodigal Son, peasant folk searching tediously for a lost sheep or a vanished coin. Neither does this earliest Gospel relate the master story in which Matthew poignantly compares two builders, one of whom built his house on sand. Nor is it to Mark that millions annually turn to hear the Christmas story, in that he chronicled nothing of the birth or youth of Jesus. Jesus is thirty years of age when he appears on the scene in that Gospel.

Mark displays one peculiarity that might have some unique appeal for modern folk in his sense of time and exigency. At least sixteen times this is seen in his use of a Greek word *euthus*, usually translated "immediately or straightway." Mark's use of this word began at the Baptism of Jesus, which inaugurated his ministry at the age of thirty. Is his attitude of "without delay" representative of youth? John Mark was not one of the original twelve disciples of Jesus Christ, but as a youth his home knew personal connections to the spirited activity of Jesus, which he delineates in the shortest of the Gospels. In the last week of Jesus' life Mark witnessed his mother's home become a gathering place for Jesus with His disciples. It was a practice possibly followed by His disciples after the crucifixion. Some of the happenings of the last week of Jesus' life on earth in Jerusalem became well etched in the mind of the young man whose mother was matron there. This advantage of youthful proximity to Jesus and His disciples must have had some impact on Mark. Many scholars have conjectured that the one identified by Mark as "a young man," who in the Garden of Gethsemane escaped from being seized by the Roman soldiers because his clothes fell from him, was none other than Mark. If not he, what better explanation is there that no other Gospel writer bears an account of this awkward little episode?

Is it fanciful to suggest that the narrow escape from being seized on that Thursday night in the Garden of Gethsemane must have left a robust aftermath upon this young man? Was it a factor in Mark's purpose in the writing of his Gospel to devote so large a part to the events of that last week of Jesus' life in Jerusalem?

It is improbable that any other religious person on earth ever left a more far-reaching and intimate influence on a single youth than did Jesus of Nazareth upon John Mark. The New Testament conveys no account of commitment to discipleship, no story of a call such as was given to others, and there is no challenging command to follow Jesus. How direct that influence may have been cannot be known. Were there any greetings between this acknowledged Rabbi and Mark as Jesus entered the home? Was Mark only an incidental witness to the activities of Jesus and His disciples when late that Thursday night they left the home to proceed to the Garden of Gethsemane? Be that as it may, Matthew followed Mark in reporting that Jesus and His disciples sang a hymn before leaving the upper room and proceeding to the Garden of Gethsemane. Mark must have been a very keen and close observer of life, as his Gospel has been singled out for often single details that the other Gospel writers omit. The hymn Mark said that they sung before leaving his home for the Mount of Olives likely was a part of the Hallel.

This delineation of John Mark is a clear-cut antithesis to that of another young man who was drawn to Jesus Christ but found himself unable to sever the cord with which his wealth enfolded him. Could it be that Mark wrote with poignancy as he related the account of this young man and the conclusion he came to about life and his wealth?[202] He was unknown to posterity by name; only his wealth characterized him as he so often has been referred to as the "rich young ruler."

Early, as well as strong, tradition credits Mark with being the founder of the influential church in the great city of Alexandria (Egypt), where he became its patron saint. After the destruction of Jerusalem in A.D. 70, Antioch became the chief center of Jewish life and culture. Later it became an outstanding center of the Christian faith and theological center long before Rome rose to its ecclesiastical primacy. It was in Egypt that the famous translation of the Jewish Scriptures from Hebrew to Greek was done.

For various reasons, early students of sacred writ gave Matthew the chief seat among the Gospels. According to an early tradition Matthew was first written in Hebrew, and it would not be before the early second century that the Church became predominantly gentile. One need not be far advanced in New Testament scholarship to note Matthew's hefty penchant for quoting the Old Testament; He does this sometimes loosely. In spite of chronology of the Gospels, it might be argued that Matthew is an appropriate bridge from the Old Testament to the New because of his strong propensity for quoting the Old Testament. It is not surprising that the Jewish sect known as the Ebionites, a conservative Jewish group of the first and second century accepted only Matthew as an authentic Gospel. They rejected Mark, Luke and John. The rise of this second century sect, bearing the appellation "poor men" was witness to the lingering hold of Judaism in the church and the hearts of many. Jerusalem fell to a Roman siege under

---

[202] Mark 10:1–7.

Titus in A.D. 70, and with it came the twilight of Jewish-dominated Christianity. This declining Jewish influence reached its culmination in A.D. 135 with the ill-fated Bar Cochba uprising. After this upheaval, Christianity swiftly became predominantly Gentile.

In a flight of imagination, could it be that something similar might have developed in the life of the youth who chose wealth over discipleship with Jesus of Nazareth? Nothing is known of this young man after his departure from Jesus of Nazareth. One phenomenon is deeply entrenched in the history of Christianity; namely,
its annals that are replete with the names of both men and women who would have remained obscure, if not for their part in advancing the gospel early on. Some of these have won real renown with cities, streets, and schools named for them. One thinks instantaneously of David Livingstone, Mary Slessor, Adoniram Judson, and Aggrey of Africa. Henry Francis Lyte, born in Scotland in 1793 and buried in France in 1847, may have put to verse the sentiment of a vast unnumbered assemblage of Christians who felt that they had found real life only in Jesus Christ. In his exquisite and engaging hymn, "Jesus, I My Cross Have Taken," Lyte spoke of letting his own ambitions perish, yet finding himself in a rich condition. Was there a sense of lack in the heart of this young man who could not break with his wealth? Even when the wealth seemed to multiply, did he experience an emptiness that nothing had ever filled? Over the long centuries from many parts of the earth, the attestation has come that there is an imperishable part of us, placed there by none other than God Himself, which cannot be assuaged through anything material. Those untold throngs have experienced this; perhaps it was left for Augustine to express it best in a line that has become classic: "Thou hast made us for thyself, O Lord, and our hearts are restless until they find their rest in Thee."[203]

Modern people should be able to empathize profoundly with the rich young ruler's feeling of being pulled in disparate directions. The problem may be as ancient as humanity, but since the commencement of the industrial revolution of the eighteenth century the steadily increasing complexity of society has exacerbated it by reason of the labyrinthine affairs with which people are confronted. Colloquially, this dilemma is expressed in the saying "being pulled in two directions." This aptly describes the position

---

[203] Augustine, *Confessions*.

the rich young ruler found himself in through the summons to discipleship Jesus made to him. It does not appear likely that this young man understood the enormity and expanse of his choice; to one reading the account it seems apparent that it was a choice of the temporal versus the eternal. Little could he have known that across the centuries and countries, though never identified by name, he would be known as the young man who prized wealth over One whom the young Christian Church saw as nothing less than God come in the flesh.

Because mankind is what it is, God's creation made in His own image, he has been endowed with dimensions that look beyond the temporal and the immediate present. Not only has God endowed mankind with the propensity to yearn for a more gratifying fulfillment of him in the future, but equally marked is his bestowal on him with an affinity for delving deeply into his past. The former displays the aspiration to know from whence we came; the other to know our past. One of these longings creates theology; the other the source of the study of history. The two are indissolubly intertwined in that it was through history God primarily chose to reveal Himself. This becomes the widest crevice between the varying world religions. There are religions that are historical and those that are antithetical to the very concept of history. Christianity is more solidly rooted in history than all others. The Bible fully accepts the reality of history; the Bible is the record of how God displayed His arm in the field of history.

This is precisely what John Mark set out to narrate, the most recent and the fullest revelation of Jesus that God had yet given. It was the consummate and absolute revelation in Jesus of Nazareth. In narrating this revelation, another characteristic of Mark's youth is manifested. Everywhere in the story there is activity, achievement, movement, and energy. New Testament scholars have loved to depict the Gospel of Mark as the gospel in action. The Gospel of Mark pictures Christ in action with a minimum of discourse and a maximum of deed. To the author the very fact that he omitted some of the things which may be inclined to the more mystical is an indication of Mark's strong sense of the historical. It was once common to speak of a Proto-Luke, one that did not exist. It has been contended that Mark has little theology. If, as a young man, Mark lacked a mature sense of history, in modern times his Gospel is looked upon as highly favorable to those who take the four Gospels seriously.

It may have been Sam Higginbotham, British-born missionary to India under the auspices of the American Presbyterian Church, who popularized among English speaking evangelicals the idea that "history is His-story." Whether or not this may have originated with the highly esteemed missionary who did much to educate young Indians in the skills of agriculture, this definition appears inadequate. My own seminary professor in the philosophy of history would have said that God makes known His story in history, but in itself history is far from being God's story. The professor argued that the theme of history lay not with individuals but with groups. At the same time, we should give due place to human freedom and personal decision. It is free beings who with their ideals and aspirations form the raw material out of which history is built. To hold to the once popular concept that history is God's story, does analytically make it different to argue that God is not one of the tributaries of evil. Likewise, it does nothing to buttress the biblical concept of the freedom of mankind which the creation narratives so beautifully set forth in pictorial parlance. That within the realm of linear history, God found arenas for the revelation of Himself is a fundamental piling of Christian theology. This concept became much more conspicuous as classical culture, especially its Greek aspect, gave way in the early Christian centuries to the Christian concept of time. It is implausible that any book of the New Testament contributed more to this concept of time than did the Gospel of Mark.

Mark characterized his narrative of good news, written from Rome, as "The beginning of the Gospel of Jesus Christ." Gospel is a fine old English word, which means "God-story or "good story." In longer historical perspective, Mark's narrative was not in actuality the beginning of the "good news" God had for His creation. Rather Mark was alluding to a particular time and place in history with the incarnation of Deity as the *ne plus ultra* of long centuries of a self-given divine revelation. This unveiling came in a progressive approach. Mainline Christian theology, for the most part, holds to the concept that a general revelation of God had been given to mankind generically through such things as nature. It is in past history that God so abundantly revealed Himself through such great prophets as Amos, Hosea, the first Isaiah (Isaiah 1-40) and Micah.

Not all scholars accept the idea of a second Isaiah, but a large number do, as does the writer. The first forty chapters of Isaiah are generally assigned to first Isaiah.[204]

This paper moves now to note some musings from Mark with regard to notes for sermon preparation. It would be quixotic to conceive of Mark envisioning the things that did happen in later centuries with his good news written on parchment in the common language of the day, Koiné Greek. He could not have known what impact his Gospel would make in the world of his day. Centuries later in the great monasteries of Europe monks-turned-scribes would meticulously copy repeatedly from one parchment to a new one. This it would contribute to the rise of a new science, that of textual criticism, comparing various renditions of Mark's Gospel. People in lands that were quite pagan and tribal in Mark's time would centuries later embrace the One of whom he wrote; from those lands arose great Christian scholars such as Bernard Weiss, Heinrich Holtzmann, Johannes Weiss, J. B. Lightfoot, B. F. Westcott, Hort, and numerous others who would disseminate their learning across lands never known in John Mark's day. There would arise an international community of great scholars who would help popularize the Gospel of Mark as the foundation to understanding the life and ministry of Jesus of Nazareth.

Unlike the two other synoptic Gospels, Mark offered only a limited introduction before plummeting into his account of the baptism of Jesus, so soon followed by Jesus' preaching and the call of disciples to His cause. The powerful introduction Mark used for the ministry of Jesus came after the arrest of John the Baptist, His forerunner. "Jesus came into Galilee, preaching the gospel of God, and saying, 'The time is fulfilled, and the kingdom of God is at hand; repent, and believe in the gospel.'"[205] It would be difficult to think of a more pregnant and far-reaching lead-off to any book ever written than this one. Mark's use of terms such as time (*kairos*), gospel (*euagégelion*), and kingdom (*basiléia*) have evoked an untold number of monographs, dissertations, and scholarly volumes. Schools of varying theological reflection have been born from the interpretation and implication of these words.

---

[204] They adhere to the belief that chapters 40–66 of Isaiah were written by more than one author.
[205] Mark 1:14–15.

God has given us this revelation of Himself. It was always a thoughtful disclosure, one that was grasped as if seen through a glass darkly. By no means should one think that God was continually revealing Himself, other than general revelation, which is more ongoing. As the Scripture asserted, it was given at sundry times. Nor were His purposes or teleological intents always seen with clarity. Even now, people attribute many erroneous things to "God's will," when it was never such. However, the apex of revelation, usually referenced as special revelation, was necessary for fullness of clarity. This was given to the Jewish people through the channels of history that witnessed the development of Judaism as one of the world's distinct historical religions. The means by which this historical pinnacle was reached has never been more sublimely stated than that given by the unknown author of the Book of Hebrews. "In many and various ways God spoke of old to our fathers by the prophets; but in these last days he has spoken to us by a Son." This revelation speaks volumes in itself about the nature of God in that it was He who inaugurated and sustained this escalating revelation of Himself. In the long sweep and march of history there have been periods of time more pregnant with meaning than others. Similarly, in the historical revelation God was making of Himself there were times in Israel's history when productiveness was more superlative and transcendent beyond other times. One such era of transcendence was the eighth century B.C., which saw great prophets who ushered in a new ethical hue to Israel's faith.[206] Prior to this, one might cite the time of Israel's exodus from Egypt, likely in the thirteen century B.C.

God's self-revelation tells us that it is His desire, an eternal purpose it is, that we should know Him. This characterization of God was portrayed superbly, in a form never surpassed in the annals of literature, by Jesus Himself in that beautiful cluster of parables related in Luke's Gospel. This Gospel, after Mark, is generally reckoned the second of the four Gospels. In Luke, Jesus related movingly of a shepherd seeking a lost sheep; it was followed by an account of a peasant woman searching tirelessly for a lost piece of money. The spiritual and ethical intent of such parables reached their summit only in Jesus of Nazareth. The story recalls to the writer a time when he had just left seminary to go to his first full time church in Kentucky.[207] A faithful member of the congregation and her only daughter invited him and his wife to dinner. It was there for the first time that she related to him how her only son had left home one morning, seventeen years before, and had never been heard from since.

In the case of the father in Jesus' parable, who was awaiting the return of a prodigal whose way of life had not only dissipated a considerable portion of family fortune, but whose conduct had stripped the family of some of its erstwhile respect. In the mid-years of the twentieth century there seems to have been a rise in the number of American sons and daughters reared in good homes who abandoned them to live the life of a hippy. Many of them turned to drugs. Some of us were witness to the continuing love mothers and fathers showed for their decadent children. Perhaps they had a deeper understanding of the father of the prodigal than did families whose children never took this step. It was a forcible, deeply moving, and tender story Jesus used to illustrate how much God loved His fallen creation. In his own account, the father never went so far as to leave home in search of the lost son; Christian theology advocates notably that it was always God who planned and advanced the idea of regaining His lost creation.

Historical theology has sometime erred noticeably in seeking to blueprint in minutiae how God achieved this feat of redemption of mankind in the cross. From a modern point of view some of these theories of ransom that appeared in medieval theology were farcical to ludicrous. However, they were heartfelt and unfeigned attempts to unravel the greatest mystery about God, that of the depth of His love for His creation which He had spoken into being.

The options of God were not narrowly limited in what to do about the predicament of fallen man. They were wide-ranging. In fact, God could have annihilated the universe he had begun. Theologians, and philosophers, have struggled with the idea of God's creation *ex nihilo*. He could have restored His handiwork to this pre-condition; rather he chose to redeem it. As noted earlier, Christian scholars referred to Genesis 3:15 as the Prolegomena. Some saw in this a rather pronounced assurance that a Savior would

---

211 Lewisport Baptist Church was in a suburb of Owensboro.

come to do just this. In my thinking, this read too much of a later Christian revelation into this text. The Genesis account of Noah, which had its antecedent in the Sumerian flood stories, is a jog to our memory that this was one of God's potentialities.[208] While God could have chosen the way of annihilation of His creation, alternatively he fixed on the long path of redemption. Had he opted for the first, it is difficult to conceive of theology ever having become a reality.

Some of the early church fathers, such as Clement of Alexandria in the second century and Origen in the third, ruminated on such a situation as what God was before He created the universe. Both of these men were highly intellectual, but both were ante-Nicene. That is to say, they lived well before the great council of Nicaea in 325 had taken a gigantic step in defining the Christian faith. This was particularly true with the Church in its long struggle with Arianism over the question of the Trinity. Nicaea was one of the great watersheds of theological history. Because both Clement and Origen lived before this gigantic settlement, both were at times accused of teaching those things heretical to the faith. For example, Clement is said by some historians to have held views that were Arian in their theological tone. He had spent much of his life in Greece, and was accused by Photius, Patriarch of Constantinople, of heresy. Clement had lived in Athens for perhaps as long as twenty years before his emergence on the Christian scene in Alexandria. He had the fortune to live in second century Athens at a time when that city had been largely restored to its earlier grandeur by the Emperor Hadrian. Hadrian was a great builder, perhaps best known in the West for the famous defensive wall in northern Britain that bears his name. This second century emperor, who ruled at the time the empire was reaching its apogee, showed great respect for the city of Athens. Prior to becoming emperor, Hadrian spent a year in that city. He showed deep fascination with Greek culture and in his sexual life openly displayed the same affinity for males that had long been prevalent in classical Greece. He took special pride in the restoration from which young Clement benefited. Clement's Christianity showed all the hallmarks of a classical upbringing. He wished to enrich Christian faith with the mixture Hebrew background could bring to Christianity. Especially was this apparent

---

212 Genesis 5–8.

in his understanding of the Logos for a proper interpretation of Christianity.

Certainly, one of the beloved teachers of the famous Christian school in Alexandria has been much disputed. R. B. Tollinton, an Oxford professor in ecclesiastical history, was fair and balanced in his assessment of Clement. It was his final conclusion that the charges against Clement were unfounded. He was a more modern historian of the twentieth century, born in 1930, was long recognized as a foremost historian of the patristic age. Like Clement, Origen never was recognized as a saint. The paramount thing, it seems to me, is to place both these remarkable intellectuals in their historical context, which was a time when Christian doctrine was yet rudimentary and many great doctrines, especially regarding the Trinity, were in an inchoate stage.

There were many reasons why the charges against Origen developed, and why they became as weighty as they did. To begin with, in the early church it took many decades, even a few centuries, for the churches to use the same Bible. There were churches in parts of the Roman Empire that accepted as canonical books that other congregations did not. A number of writers, such as Origen, regarded the Book of Hebrews as the work of Paul. In the long centuries of the Church far more scholars have refused to note this book as a Pauline writing.

Such diversity could lead to variations in theological emphasis, as well as offer a natural propensity to question other doctrinal assertions and interpretations. Still another substantive matter providing fertile ground for differentiate views was the widespread Gnostic doctrines that developed in the early Christian period. It was a time of strong Gnostic sentiment at issue with diverse Christian patterns, much of which can be pointed to the wide incorporation of Christianity among the congregations. One has to linger on this diversity to gain a complete understanding and appreciation for the degree of unity the Council of Nicaea brought to the Church where there was abounding diverseness. It is this property in mankind that gave birth to religion. Natural religion is mankind seeking God. Christianity is God revealing Himself to mankind.

Because mankind is what it is, the creation of an eternal God, it has been endowed with a dimension that could never be content within the orbit in which he lives and carries out daily activity. Rational human beings have the compass that compels them to look backward to a time when they were not, and likewise to a time when once again they shall not be on the earth. It is out of these innate propensities that both history and religion are born. History deals with the recognition that one is endowed with roots, and the quest to know something of them. It begins the search for the origin of that which once was but now is not. It is in seeking to answer such instincts as this that history was born.

It is when normal and lucid human beings recognize that reality, authenticity, and truth are not in the present, the evanescent, and in the fleeting, that ground is laid for the development of religion. It is in the recognition that the moment at hand is ephemeral, momentary, and transitory that religion is born. With this realization the quest to find God has begun. Religion may be thought of as man's search for the Deity. Divine revelation may be viewed as God's answer and response to this search. In the course of this long search, God revealed Himself over a long span of time in a piecemeal, sketchy, and fragmentary manner. Such a broken and intermittent revelation on His part must surely have come in response to man's ability to receive it. Some of this came in the domain of nature and other ways, but the bulk of it was historical. The fullness and completeness of this divine revelation came only in the person of Jesus Christ, and with that we have come full circle back to John Mark and the other Gospels.

Whatever framework or reference the authors might have wished to assign the Gospels or any genre later writers sought to place them, they were confident that in the lowly-born Jesus of Nazareth, the eternal God had laid bare His arm and made Himself known in His person. In Jesus of Nazareth God had become flesh and incarnate on earth. Revelation had come to its climax and could never move beyond that given in Jesus of Nazareth, who is its historical apex. Historical progress would be constantly made in the interpretation of that which he had revealed, but there could be no eclipsing of the revelation given in Jesus.

One additional aspect of history may be noted at this point. It is when that which is has become the past that the most clarion view of history may be seen. Of all things, written history can least tolerate the myopic and short-sighted panorama. Even the need for it does not seem to manifest itself at the moment. One of the best examples of this is the Gospels themselves. Only with the rapid

Historical Pursuit of the Purpose of God

passing of those who had been eyewitnesses was the need for written narratives actually felt. With that came a reinterpretation of the event and happening. While Jesus was on earth, the prevalent contemporary view must surely have been that Jesus would "restore the kingdom at this time." Even after His exit, it was widely understood that His return was imminent. Far-seeing indeed would have been the disciple who could have grasped that history would be long extended, during which the risen Jesus would continue His work in regions and realms first generation Christians were not knowledgeable of. Only nineteen centuries later would historical writing reach its maturity, and with that the term "revisionism" crept into the work vocabulary of historians.

> Only where Jesus enters history and is made in all points like unto His brethren, yet without sin, does history become fully real. At this point we have an event which, although in this world, belongs also to the eternal world and thus transcends all that has preceded it.[209]

Revisionism of history can never negate the ancient longing to find God. In it one finds much that resembles something of mankind's long historical quest for Him. Mature human souls look beyond the immediate present. There is the affinity for delving deeply into His past. This is the deep desire to know one's past, the recognition that one person is more than the moment, and has kinship with what was, and now is not. In Shakespeare's *Macbeth*, Macduff is made to say after learning that his castle has been destroyed, "I cannot but remember such things were that were most precious to me." Then there is the deeply rooted longing to know what is ahead, where providence is leading, in the childish question "What is beyond the rainbow?" It is these properties in the human race that gave birth to religion. Natural religion is mankind seeking God and nothing is more innate than this. Christianity is God revealing Himself to mankind. The realm of religion is born when mankind showed the same innate longing to know where God is going. Thus, mankind has the fundamental desire to know something of the world about him, something of the past, and an

---

[209] Rust, *The Christian Understanding of History*, p. 175.

eternal longing of the gospel, which is essentially the way the Bible itself opened, "In the beginning God." Here the word for *beginning* carries with it the idea of first principle, in Mark it is likely more directed at what is considered a historical beginning. This was not the beginning of God's purpose to redeem the fallen creation. This had been underway long before Jesus of Nazareth had revealed Himself in ancient Palestine. God had made known His age-long purpose in general revelation, as theologians have long designated such things as nature, events in history, and other forms of providence. More specifically He had used special revelation, which is through a person sent by God into the world to perform a specific mission, such as Abraham to found the Hebrew people. It may be through a particular prophet to lay down a specific message from God. From Isaiah it was the holiness of God, from Hosea the *chesed* love of God, or from Amos God's righteousness and justice.

The writing of Mark's script was the first legitimate written historical account of the Gospels. It represents the final (*pleroma* or fullness) of God's revelation. It was the apex of God calling Abraham out of Ur. The fulfillment of the long-promised Savior represented the judgment of human evil, and rebellion that had ushered in the estrangement of His creation. The fact that this was the expressed purpose of Mark's writing accounts for a noticeable literary feature of the book. It is more about action, the meeting of close-at-hand human needs such as feeding the hungry and healing the diseased, as well as other pragmatic things of life; other Gospels are more given to provide emphasis on the less didactic instruction, as Matthew is heavy with. A broader humanitarian approach to life is portrayed with Luke, such as the Parable of the Good Samaritan. The fourth Gospel presents a more mystical interpretation of that truth which is theological and oriented toward the divine realm than anything Mark approaches. It should be understood that none of the Gospels are exclusively this with no teaching. One very fine conservative study argues that Mark contains a great deal of substantive teaching, pointing to the several parables in chapter four.[210] This is true, but not by comparison with the other Gospels. This has been well expressed by someone who said that his Gospel

---

[210] I. Howard Marshall, *New Testament Theology* (Intervarsity Press, 2007), p 76.

placed much more emphasis on the messenger than it did the message.[211]

Mark may not have known of an early Christian document that long remained hidden to the scholarly world. It has been given the name "Q," standing for the German *quell*. Another enigma for scholars has been the question of what Papias, one of the earliest Christians after the Apostles, had reference to when he said that Matthew originally wrote his Gospel in Hebrew. T. W. Manson, one of the most astute New Testament scholars of a generation recently passed in Britain, believed that "Q" may have been the document Papias was referring to.[212] It was in at least limited circulation likely well before A.D. 50; much of his life was spent far removed from Jerusalem and eastern Christianity with the possibility that he never knew the document. Q is heavy on the sayings and teachings of Jesus, precisely as has been noted, something lacking in his Gospel. To be certain, Papias refers to this document as *at logia*. He certainly never saw the Gospel of Matthew, best known for its Sermon on the Mount and other teachings of the Master Teacher.

The Gospel of Mark describes another incident that has captured the fascination of commentators; it is the notice he gives of a young man on the night of Jesus' arrest whose clothing fell down. One superb New Testament scholar offered the suggestion that Mark had gone to the Garden of Gethsemane to warn Jesus that the Roman soldiers were nearby. While fleeing from the Roman posse, Mark's linen cloth fell, leaving him half naked. Mark alone relates this little incident in his account of Jesus. "This verse would then be his modest signature. In the corner of his Gospel, his quiet way of saying, "I was there."[213]

Plenteous and substantial developments occurred in the next fifteen years or so before John Mark was heard again. One would, so it seems, seek in vain for a more meaningful and pregnant similar period of time in all of human history than were these years. The resurrection, Pentecost, and the rapid growth of the early churches characterized the years. The same era witnessed some

---

[211] The author has been unable to document the origin of this observation.
[212] T. W. Manson, *The Teaching of Jesus* (Cambridge: 1931), p. 26–27. The author discusses the possibility of Q having this Semitic origin. In that case, he argues, it is on a comparison with Mark.
[213] Archibald M. Hunter, *Introducing the New Testament* (3rd ed., Philadelphia: 1972), p. 38.

stabilizing of the Roman Empire, still early on in its first century after the dying of the Republic. The Roman legions were on the verge of adding parts of the island of Britain to its far-flung dominions. Christianity had itself penetrated somewhat beyond the confines of the empire. John Mark reappears when Barnabas and the Apostle Paul decide to take him with them on their first missionary tour. Following the chronology of A. M. Hunter, Mark would have been seventeen years older than when he lost his clothes.

Mark was a relative of Barnabas, who was then looked upon by many in the infant church as a full partner of Paul. So esteemed was Barnabas that many believers regarded him as the superior of the two.[214] In the great church at Antioch, Syria, there was conspicuously strong evidence of the Holy Spirit at work in the church. The narrative here is reminiscent of the sense of awe and expectation prevalent in the Jerusalem church at the Day of Pentecost. It was the Spirit who directed the Antioch church to send out its first missionary team in the person of Barnabas, Paul, and John Mark, who did not hold the same rank that the other two. The English translations describe him as "assistant." However, the great Greek scholar, A. T. Robertson, said that the word did not really give a clear definition of what Mark's responsibilities were to be, but the baptism of new converts was likely one. Robertson proposed that it was because Mark was a cousin of Barnabas that he was chosen. It was also his belief that that the use of one word in the Greek text allowed room to suppose that Mark sometimes preached.[215] If the choice of Mark had an affix to his kinship with Barnabas, it might point to the status Barnabas had in the trio at the inauguration of the mission. The team's commission was "To do the work for which I have called them."[216] That defines what Christian ministry really is. It should never have been consigned to the more narrow concepts that it has come to know, such as to preach, administer the sacraments, and baptize. Especially in young mission fields, the tasks at hand most needing fulfillment may be far from this. Otherwise some of the most effective missionaries the author ever encountered never did ministry at all!

---

[214] The argument, which appears weak to this writer, stems from the fact that in the early treatises of Acts dealing with the two, Barnabas is listed ahead of Paul.
[215] Archibald Thomas Robertson, *Word Pictures in the New Testament* (Nashville: 1930), III. p.179.
[216] Acts 21:32.

The mission's itinerary took these pioneering missionaries from Seleucia, the port of the great Christian center, Antioch across to the island of Cyprus, and over the island from Salamis to Paphos. Being in Seleucia must have reminded them of how it derived its name—as a result of the death of Alexander the Great in 323 going to Seleucia and Egypt falling into the hands of a longtime friend, Ptolemy.[217] Other parts of the empire fell into various hands that lie outside our interest here. For centuries to come, both regions cited here would be the scene of major developments in the Christian Church, and from each rival catechetical schools would arise lending support to varying interpretations of the faith that would remain pivotal for the next few centuries.

Any experience the young Mark would derive from this mission tour with Barnabas and Paul would be largely limited to the Island of Cyprus, to which they sailed from Seleucia. In traversing the island from Salamis to Paphos, east to west, Mark witnessed two impressive happenings. First was the encounter with Elymas, reputed to be a magician or sorcerer, who opposed the work of the mission team, with whom Paul grappled face-to-face in one of the most invective charges of the New Testament. This appears to be the first reported case of the young church taking on the embodiment of evil, which had so recently been a discernible part of the ministry of Jesus on earth. Out of this came the conversion of Sergius Paulus, the proconsul, the highest-ranking Roman official on the island of Cyprus.[218] This exhilarating moment had occurred at Paphos from whence the missionaries shortly sailed for Asia, landing at Perga in the Roman province of Pamphylia.

Paphos was the capital city of the island of Cyprus, and it was here that the Roman authorities had their seat of power. This was the new Paphos, some eight miles from the site of the old city famous for its worship of Venus. A fine Roman road led to the new city.[219] It was not centrally located but lay on the extreme western part of the island. Rome, however, did not consider this a primary factor in locating the seat of government. The Roman Empire's well-known excellent road system was well under way and would continue toward its peak for well more than another century. The

---

[217] Lane Fox, *The Classical World: An Epic History from Homer to Hadrian*, pp. 235–36.
[218] Acts 13: 4–12.
[219] Robertson, Ibid.

Historical Pursuit of the Purpose of God

Roman means of communication between one outpost and others was one of the marvels of her ancient civilization.

After the missionaries sailed from the island and reached the Roman province of Pamphylia at Perga, the nadir of this first missionary journey occurred. This was the desertion of John Mark from the team and his subsequent return to Jerusalem. The assumptions and guesswork on this have been many, but they must be left as just this. W. M. Ramsay, longtime earlier English scholar in this area of the ancient world, clung to the argument that Paul made a change in the original plans in deciding to move in another direction, and that Mark was in fundamental disagreement with this. Others have made the assessment that Mark was unhappy with the way Paul had emerged as the leader over Barnabas. This, too, appears circumstantial. The writer would offer this minor consideration: In studying the history of strong-minded missionaries, and his on-the-field observation of them, the case can be made for the fact that that they often appear inflexible and uncompromising.[220]

---

[220] In 1954, the writer was reassigned to the Gold Coast rather than returning to Nigeria. Both countries were anticipating their independence from the British Empire. His commission was to work with the indigenous people there rather than with the Nigerians who had heretofore been the focus. The latter had gone there as traders and many were transient. Dr. George W. Sadler, at the Foreign Mission Board in Richmond, strongly insisted that if additional missionaries were to be assigned to the Gold Coast, they must work with the indigenous people rather than Nigerians, who already had two couples committed to them. The new work was initially directed toward educational missions. This was what the writer had precisely done during his first term in Nigeria, and under the direction of another missionary. He was eager to accept this new assignment in which he would be in charge. With great anticipation he and his wife returned to Kumasi where negotiations were well under way for the land on which the school would be located. The institution had an impressive launching, having been named Sadler Baptist College in recognition of the fact that Dr. Sadler had long advocated expanding the work to the indigenes. Amid this excellent beginning significant developments soon occurred. Dr. Sadler soon retired and was succeeded by the writer's old seminary professor, Dr. Cornell Goerner. Likewise, the Gold Coast on receiving its independence, March 6, 1957, officially changed its name to Ghana. A new wave of pride and nationalism swept the country as the first in West Africa to achieve independence. The writer found it necessary to change policies at the school to provide more Ghanaian teachers rather than Nigerians. At the time he was the only missionary assigned to work with the indigenous people, while there were three couples assigned to working primarily with Nigerians who had moved there. Dr. Goerner in his new enthusiasm pumped large sums of money into erecting beautiful new buildings on the campus. This aroused deep animosity from the three other couples, who resented receiving smaller sums aimed at the Nigerian work. In mission meetings he often found

Ramsay suggested that Mark may have been ill at the time he deserted Paul. Paul was himself a sick man, which likely contributed to his difficulty in quickly forgiving Mark. "At the moment the defection of Mark was keenly felt by Paul; and for years he retained a distrust of Mark."[221] With the return of Mark to his hometown of Jerusalem a gap now arises in our knowledge of Mark and his activities. Ramsay put the date for Mark's departure at A.D. 46.

If the Gospel of Mark was written somewhere between A.D. 65 and 67, this would leave approximately two decades in which Mark is unaccounted for. It is known that after he left Paul at some point, he became associated with the Apostle Peter. At just what point this development took place cannot be dated. Peter makes mention of Mark in his first Epistle. It is unlikely that Mark would have been with Peter during the entire era since his break with Paul; rather it appears likely that there is a considerable span of time in which his presence and activity is not accounted for.

A tradition in the ancient church made the claim that the church in Alexandria, Egypt was founded by John Mark. The gap in Mark's itinerary does allow ample time for him to have been involved in some work of considerable duration. All of this, to be

---

himself isolated and standing alone. From his side he made every effort to be conciliatory and to involve the others in the public acclaim that was being given to Sadler Baptist College. His first term was singularly distinguished, with great gains being made through the students of establishing other indigenous churches. The school won the applause and appreciation from older and more distinguished similar schools in the area. To add to all of this, the senior missionary and his wife were on furlough in America when the institution was named after Dr. Sadler. It was not the policy of the Foreign Mission Board to consult missionaries at home in America as to policies and developments on the field. The unanimous decision of those on the field was to name the institution after Dr. Sadler. At that time the intensity of the feeling between these missionaries and Dr. Sadler was not realized, but there was something of a personal feud. The misunderstanding arose from the fact that they wanted more missionaries assigned to the Gold Coast; his retort was, if this is to be the case, they must be assigned to the indigenous population. He argued that the Nigerians were well taken care of and additional personnel could not be assigned without an expansion of the mission goal. To this writer that appeared factual and reasonable.

[221] William Mitchell Ramsay, *Pictures of the Apostolic Church: Its Life and Thought* (Philadelphia: 1910), p. 140. This was a reprint of a work originally published in 1923; a tremendous achievement has been the
republishing of so many of these fine old books from an earlier day.

true, is very much an argument from silence. To that tradition we now turn.

The Gospel of Mark may be said to have profited greatly from this historical shift. For one thing, much of it was reckoned authentic, with the closing verses clearly proven to be a later addition. Mark's priority among the Gospels had won its rightful standing. Among numerous laypeople this has never been realized.

One thing that made college teaching so enjoyable was the task of integrating in some rational manner the diverse things that were taking place at the same time for even a small segment of history, for example, the French Revolution. That was the way they took place, but not the way a professor could lecture to the class. God does that with divine finesse for the universe as a whole. To gain greater clairvoyance enabling human beings to interpret history it was necessary to dissect, analyze, and categorize historical events. For that reason, periodization, which is highly artificial, crept in. Highly artificial nevertheless, it became enormously useful in getting a handle on history. The novice must realize that this is not the way history unfolded. Since the seventeenth century, western civilization has closely followed the system of Christoph Keller, a German classical scholar who died in 1707, of dividing history into ancient times, medieval, and new period.

To bring God into the temporal, God has ever been active in every realm of creation since the universe began. This activity can only be described as simultaneous, but a historian must bi-sect historical data to deal with it. At this point historical fortune was favorable to the historian in that reliable material has come down to us from the Apostle John, Papias, and Polycarp. The latter had heard the Apostle John preach, and Papias is reported to have known many others who had seen and heard Jesus. He is best known for the many fragments he wrote of early Christian development. He had heard the Apostle John preach and was a friend of Polycarp. Papias is reported to have known many others who had seen and heard Jesus Christ. He is best known for the fragments he wrote of early Christian development; which have been referred to as crumbs from the Christian table. Papias is said to have been a very learned man well acquainted with the Scriptures. In his first Epistle, Peter made mention of Mark being with him. Eusebius reported that when Peter learned of the Gospel of Mark being written, he authorized the churches to read it in their worship.

Historical Pursuit of the Purpose of God

It is time to turn now from Mark's Gospel to more of Mark himself. Perhaps other than his Gospel, he is known best in New Testament circles as one who deserted Barnabas and Paul on their first missionary journey after arriving at Perga. This must have occurred a very few years prior to the middle of the first century. As to why Mark deserted Paul, a perusal at New Testament historiography indicates they have been many. The focus momentarily, however, is how in the providence of God this separation brought such far-reaching results to the Christian Church. In the most theological of all his epistles, Paul himself affirmed this truth when he wrote to the Roman Christians, "We know that in everything God works for Good for those who love him and are called according to his purpose."[222] It appears that far-reaching good things did derive from this breach of association. For one thing, had Mark long continued with Paul, it is highly improbable that he would have developed the fraternal alliance he did with the Apostle Peter. Peter and Paul were both executed in Rome at perhaps approximately the same time. With Paul's active and brisk itineraries, it is not likely that there would ever have been a slot for Peter. That scenario would have represented a huge thing itself in that New Testament scholars hold to a strong consensus that Mark's Gospel follows closely the teaching and sermons he had heard from Peter. Early Church tradition asserted that Mark served as Peter's interpreter. In his First Epistle, Peter refers to Mark as a son.[223] The tradition of the Church also has it that Mark served as the interpreter for Peter. This author understands quite well how valuable this relationship can be. While in one area of West Africa he had an excellent young man very fluent in the language who served as his interpreter. Such a partnership did establish a genuine bond between them.

The New Testament does not seek to camouflage the cleavage between Paul and John Mark. It was genuine and apparently for a time had left Paul befuddled to the extent that he was unwilling for Mark to accompany him and Barnabas on a second mission tour. Disagreement and division that has occurred in Christian ranks across the centuries cannot be disclaimed. It has ranged from individuals, churches, ecclesiastical organizations, and most

---

[222] Romans 8:28.
[223] I Peter 5: 13.

outstandingly in the entire Church, with Martin Luther and those who followed in his path. This is not inherently evil itself. Jesus clearly experienced bitter disputes with the religious leaders in Palestine. This was inclusive of both the Pharisees and Sadducees. To look fully into this would divert us from our course, but a few pertinent points it may be wise to consider. For one thing, when one embraces the Christian faith and becomes Christian, they are not removed from the human race, and the human race has been at war with itself since the earliest days of Genesis. A brother killed a brother in the case of Cain and Abel. On the other hand, no force in history has been more powerful in bringing about reconciliation than has Christianity. Some historic examples of that may be cited.

At any given time in history, there are multitudes of Christians who are at various levels of growing into the mind of Christ. Some are quite immature and others far advanced in this divine growth. Another factor may be noted in that the Christian religion is constantly promoting this pattern of life among its adherents. Jesus taught forgiveness, absence of quick retaliation, and acquiescence in some things pending God's settlement of the issue, and the necessity of non-nurturing of wrongs one has received. These are noble, superlative concepts that the finest ethical teachers of the ancient world never excelled. Neither classical Greek philosophy, nor Stoicism, nor Rome's most sensitive ethical and moral thinkers went beyond these. They are teleological in the sense that this is the ultimate goal. Christianity depicts, however, a people on the move. Numerous are the times when Christian philosophy, hymnody, and its choicest ethics have reminded us that life is a pilgrimage in which the struggle to reach the good is constant. No one ever expressed this sentiment more eloquently than did the eighth century prophet Micah. "He has showed you, O man, what is good; and what does the Lord require but to do justice, and to love kindness, and to walk humbly with your God?"[224] With such a transcendent and unparalleled ethic, is it a wonder, however, that history has experienced its lapses?

The strength in attaining to such heights may now be noted. One attribute of the ancient churches was their ability to know what was going on in other places. More than one congregation would have soon come to know that Mark and Paul were no longer

---

[224] Micah 6:8.

together as a team. There have been times in the history of Christianity when a supposed schism between Christians forces were concocted which had never existed. One of the most historic and famous of these was the supposed breach between Peter and Paul put forth by the distinguished German historian Adolph Harnack in the nineteenth century. To look into this in any detail here would prove highly excursive other than to point out that conflicts between prominent leaders are seldom confined to inner circles but gather a wider circle. Another consequence of such conflicts is that they lend color to the writing of future historiography. One has only to make a casual look at European critical theological study in its young days to see how far off such a compass may point. There was much in Harnack that is highly laudable to any mellowed follower of Christ. Likewise, much in his system had to be dismantled. Who could not admire the genuineness and steadfastness with which he pursued the answer to his question, "How can I become his [Jesus'] disciple?"[225]

---

[225] G. Wayne Glick, *The Reality of Christianity: A Study of Adolph von Harnack as Historian and Theologian* (New York: 1967) p. 6–7.

Chapter 7
Cornerstone of A Christian West

In the first century A.D., the Apostle Peter spoke before the Jewish Sanhedrin, declaring, "This is the stone [Jesus of Nazareth] which was rejected by you builders, but which has become the head of the corner."[226] In this vast purpose of carrying the gospel to the western portion of the Mediterranean, the Apostle Paul boldly set forth the claim that Jesus Christ is, "The cornerstone in which the whole structure is joined together."[227] The joining of which the apostle spoke endured until 1054, when the Eastern and Western Church officially separated. Though having drifted earlier, the official split came only then.

As far as the Middle Ages are concerned, this division was the most decisive formulation to develop, but it had been building a long time. Many things had accrued laying the foundation for this historic event, such as the Bogomile movement, and the nature of Christ where the Eastern and Western churches had long faced differences over Christology. The great ensuing emphasis of the Eastern Church became orthodoxy, while that of the West was the Catholic Church.[228] This estrangement has never been healed. The great councils such as Nicaea in A.D. 325 and Chalcedon in A.D. 451 had vital issues in which there had long been differences in theological thought in the East and West.

Pope Gregory the Great (A.D. 590-604) had earlier dispatched a group of Benedictine monks to Kent in 597 (Island of Britain) with the intent of converting them to the faith. This mission proved to be something of an enduring foundation for Christianity in the West. Gregory proved to be a powerful hand in the development of the ascendancy of the western pope following the growing separation of the East and West Church. Out of trepidation, the Benedictines who were sent to Kent sought to abandon the mission, but at the order of Gregory the venture was completed. The conversion of Kent to Christianity, with King Ethelbert leading the way, became one of the best-known and beloved narratives of

---

[226] Acts 4:11.
[227] Ephesians 3:20.
[228] Walter F. Adeney, *The Greek and Eastern Churches* (Clifton, New Jersey: 1965) pp. 230–235.

English history, and one of the most significant developments of the first millennium of the Church. Tertullian had mentioned the presence of Christians in England possibly as early as A.D. 200. An older view that it was British troops early who first brought Christianity to the island has been questioned; however, the fact that Christianity did early appear on the island is quite substantial. Centuries later, Great Britain would lead the way in widespread international evangelism when William Carey went to India as a Baptist missionary. This became recognized as the birth of the modern missionary movement. It would not be until two decades later that American Congregationalists would send Adoniram Judson and his wife to the Orient.[229]

Without doubt, the English-speaking countries have done more to advance Christianity to the status of a modern world religion than any other in modern time. The early American missionaries surprisingly earlier turned from their Congregational denomination to become Baptists.[230] This was a shocker to everyone and at the time changed the Baptist denomination in America vastly, where it brought divisions between Baptists who wished to support the missionary cause and those who opposed it.

It is unquestionable that Christianity became the predominant religion on the European continent, and in the nineteenth century age of empires, such as the scramble for Africa, a number of major European nations were home for missionaries who carried the gospel of Jesus Christ to Africa, Asia, and elsewhere. Missionaries going to a colony under the rule of their own homeland felt secure enough to labor there and plant strong church, educational, and medical facilities over vast parts of the earth. Many continue to function in the modern world as paragons of excellent institutions even after colonialism has faded away. Thus, it is a bona fide claim that the Christian religion played a vital part in the building of the West. It proved applicable as the cornerstone of Western civilization in Europe, North America, and in the Orient and Africa, which the west colonized.[231]

---

[229] They went as Congregationalists but changed to Baptist upon arrival in the Orient.
[230] Hitherto Baptists had shown no evidence of becoming a great missionary denomination.
[231] In most of these places, strong indigenous churches continue to operate long after becoming independent.

Another factor, difficult to evaluate, was the powerful impact of British commerce and trade in the nineteenth century. British trading companies often sent some of their best colonial employees to England for advanced study. At the time religion was a powerful factor in England and her possessions. The long, distant centuries would witness the West introducing Christianity to the Far East in such vital places as India, Japan, the Philippines, and China. This same impetus likewise planted Christianity in Africa south of the Sahara, something impractical for North African Christianity earlier to have attempted because of the Sahara Desert. This latter region of North Africa produced great Christians, such as Tertullian, Cyprian, Augustine, and distinguished martyrs. All three of these men produced early Christian writings that are still studied by Christians of the West. It was only in the third century, however, after the camel was introduced into North Africa that the making of long treks across the Sahara Desert proved feasible.[232] Not long afterward, however, an equal hindrance was the rise of Islam and its gradual spread southward, which created a formidable barrier against the spread of the Christian faith from the North. Only in the late Middle Ages did European vessels begin exploring the African Coast, a task undertaken with considerable trepidation by the Portuguese. Even so, steady advances were made down the Western Coast.

In retrospect the claim may be made that one of the most elongated events of English history was the decision of Pope Gregory the Great to send a band of Benedictine monks to convert the island of Britain. This well-known pearl of English history must again be viewed with brevity. By the time the Benedictine missionaries departed on their mission of conversion, the Western part of the Roman Empire had no longer existed for well over a century. Again, divine providence may be seen at work; this thesis, the author accepts, and is one long held by many fine historians both in Europe and America.[233]

No book in the entire Bible offers a more panoramic or extended view of God's vast universe and of His purpose to establish the Kingdom of God upon it than does the Book of Ephesians.

---

[232] Still later the Sahara seemed to move at unsteady measures, and Islam was stronger and more centralized.
[233] Obviously, not all historians allow for the existence of providence in Western history.

However, in recent years, though frequently questioned, a majority of English-speaking scholars still accept Pauline authorship for this book. This has sustained a long academic tradition, which though questioned in modern scholarship yet commands a major following. The Apostle Paul could have known nothing of West Africa and the planting of Christianity there; even so, the arrival of Christianity and what ensued there is very Pauline in its nature and outcome. What happened there, as slavery was pulled down and Christianity planted in fertile soil, is precisely what Paul envisioned as taking place all over the earth. His wide-ranging perspective is inaugurated with the stately words, "Before the foundations of the earth," and reaches its apex only when all things have been reunited in God.[234] In a chock full and magnificent statement, the Apostle Paul declared that God's purpose was "To sum up all things in Christ." The inauguration and completeness of God's purpose represents nothing less to Paul than the fullness of the times. In modern times, its authorship has been questioned by some.[235] Paul was in prison while writing this magnificent work, but as a Roman citizen he enjoyed citizenship of the Empire. He enjoyed better circumstances and freedom in Rome and was not confined to a dungeon; but lived in his own hired house in Rome for two years. Undoubtedly, his education and status as a Roman citizen had volumes to do with this reduced mild treatment.

Pliny, a well-known Roman governor in Asia Minor, as has been noted, indicated to his authorities in Rome that Christianity had made such rapid progress by the year A.D. 112 that it had become disruptive to the old primitive religious work in his province. The governor's letter to the authorities was aimed at warning them of the threat of Christianity to the silversmiths, who saw so many turning to Christianity that an old established trade had reached a slowdown.[236] The reality of the threat is seen in the fact that Paul planted churches in as many as four centers of an area that had become favorites of Rome.[237] His view of history is unsurpassed by

---

[234] Ephesians 1:10. Here the writer uses one of the longest words in the entire Greek New Testament, *anakephalaiosas thai*. It is translated "to head up," "to sum up." One of the most distinguished Greek scholars of modern times, A. T. Robertson, put it this way, "To head up all things in Christ."
[235] The arguments against a Pauline authorship appear unconvincing to the present writer and offer no compelling reason to reject the traditional view.
[236] W. M. Baker, *The Church in the Roman Empire Before A.D. 170* (Grand Rapids: 1954) pp. 146–148.
[237] Ibid.

any other New Testament writer. Some modern scholarship has asserted that the thought of Ephesians seemed too advanced to have been written by him. This is unfounded and appears untenable; the traditional view of Ephesians still bears valid support among prime biblical scholars. It is with Ephesians that one sees the Bible's most comprehensible pageant of history, or the eternal panorama of time. Paul's writing proceeds from the pre-temporal, and the beginning of time, to eons when time shall be no more. Always, however, its outlook and vista are solidly rooted in temporal history. It must be acknowledged that Paul's early expectation of the end of the world, so evident in his earlier letters to Thessalonica, was vastly toned down from that in Ephesians. Previously he had stressed to the Thessalonians, in one of his earliest writings, that the end of time was imminent. Early fathers of the Church accepted Paul as the author, including Polycarp, Clement of Alexandria, and Irenaeus, widely recognized as the first theologian against the older view of giving this honor to Origen.

Even more emphatic is that the most noted second century heretic, Marcion, who minimized the New Testament canon drastically and compiled his own canon of about ten New Testament books, attributed Ephesians to Paul. Not before the time of F. C. Baur, who headed the Tubingen School of theology in Germany prior to his death in 1860, was this tradition questioned.[238] In evaluating the traditional view of Pauline authorship, it should be observed that the older view of his being the author was based on strong ancient tradition. Buttressing from such sources has long been an honorable practice in the discussions of biblical scholarship. A great deal of what is now considered established fact was originally based on tradition. Incidentally, studies on West African tradition to a laudatory degree were proven accurate as African history and have gradually gained a growing respectability in the last half of the twentieth century.

There is strong confidence for explicitly supposing that the Ephesian letter may have been intended for other churches than Ephesus alone. The great pioneer English New Testament scholar J. B. Lightfoot considered the evidence for this as strong, and argued that the name Ephesus became attached to this letter because it was the great metropolis of Asia through which it would travel as a

---

[238] Peter O'Brien, *The Letter to the Ephesians* (Leicester, England: 1999) p. 4.

Historical Pursuit of the Purpose of God

circular letter.[239] Paul did have a more extended stay in Ephesus than any other city, and of the importance of this city in the first century there can be no quibbling. All scholars recognize the similarity of Ephesians and Colossians, with most holding to Colossians in priority of time. The opinion is widespread that Ephesians was written as a letter intended for circulation among the main churches of Asia Minor. Paul knew the area well and had previously written letters to several the churches in the Near East region. Much has been made of the fact that Ephesians, in contrast to other epistles, does not make personal references. This is something one would hardly expect to find, however, in a generalized letter aimed for several congregations. Weightier for a non-Pauline authorship is the fact of the different content of Ephesians from those other epistles. It should be remembered, however, that in other epistles Paul was addressing a particular congregation.

Seen in this light, many arguments for a different author for the letter to the Colossians (and other Pauline writings) appear weak. The Ephesian letter, as has been seen, most likely was intended for several nearby congregations planted by Paul and his associates. This better explanation for the difference in theology and ecclesiology of the Book of Ephesians from that of the earlier letters is incontrovertible, and readily understood. Without doubt, Ephesians manifested an advanced and evolving theology of what the Church was. There is a simple theological premise here in that Jesus gave the promise that the Holy Spirit would guide the Church into deeper insights. The more mature concepts interpreted the Church as one, holy, apostolic, and emerging closely to what the ancient Church soon came to think of as the Catholic Church. The latter is a fact that has often been overlooked by modern religious denominations seeking to defend their particular ecclesiology as most biblical. In addition, they seek for a literal, verbal likeness to the Church in its most primitive era. Their goal has been to show the early churches as localized congregations, entirely self-governing, and lacking any concept of a universal concept. An historical example of this would have been early seventeenth century Baptists in England who originated at the time of James I. In modern times, the Baptists have increasingly shown tendencies toward a stronger catholic definition. The argument here is, of course, not the Roman Catholic Church

---

[239] J. B. Lightfoot, *St. Paul's Epistle to the Philippians* (London: 1885), pp. 12.

centered at Rome, but the use of the word in its general meaning of universal.[240]

Scholars of the book of Ephesians have pointed out that in Paul's final imprisonment in Rome, from where he wrote the Epistle of Ephesians, he was not confined to a dungeon, but to his own hired house in Rome. All of his life he had enjoyed Roman citizenship. Residing in circumstances that were more commodious, his mind was free to range over the entire world of that day, much of which he had seen in his missionary itineraries. Paul was unlike any other of the original twelve disciples of Jesus in claiming Roman citizenship and placed him among a minority of inhabitants of the Roman Empire.

At the inception of His mission, Jesus Himself had chosen such humble men as a tax gatherer and fishermen for His followers, but when the Christian movement was expanding well beyond its original confines, its best-known spokesman was one who was quite antithetical to these men. Perhaps there are but few religious facts better known than how one who formerly acrimoniously persecuted Christians was converted, through a heavenly vision he witnessed on the Damascus road, and afterward became the faith's chief advocate for the cause he had once persecuted. Paul is not reckoned as one of the early church apologists, such as Aristides or Justin Martyr. Nevertheless, his conversion represented a complete turnaround from the hatred he had vehemently previously shown against Christianity; no voice now became more widely heard in the first Christian century than his, in the defense of this religion newly derived from ancient Judaism.

Saul of Tarsus was well advanced beyond the social status of any of the original fishermen disciples of Jesus, none of whom was a citizen of the Roman Empire. Not only was Paul a Hellenistic Jew, or one who lived outside Palestine, he was also an established figure in the higher circles of the day. Paul was proud of his standing among the Pharisees within Judaism, but at the same time enjoyed Roman citizenship and was recognized for his fluency in Greek, the *lingua franca* of the day.

---

[240] Until the later twentieth century, a number of Protestant churches tended to deny universality at all in the New Testament. The use of the term *Church* was little used by them, in reference to the churches. One notes a widely different, though not universal, trend in these same Protestant churches.

Historical Pursuit of the Purpose of God

What a splendid time it was to be a citizen of an empire, which at its peak extended from the moors of Britain to the inhabited portion of the Sahara Desert, and in the North followed the flow of the Rhine and Danube Rivers. All scholars who have attempted to calculate the number of first century Christians agreed that it was but a small minority of the empire's total inhabitants. In Paul's lifetime, one of the sharp breaks of ancient history had recently occurred and is representative of the relatively few such breaks recognized in the history of the West. The historical headway from the tumultuous last century of the Roman Republic to a more settled transition that gave birth to the Roman Empire under Caesar Augustus was nothing less than one of the sharp breaks, as Rome's most renowned era lay immediately ahead. This is not to deny that its forerunner, the Republic, had known its glorious episodes, but its final century had been one displaying the worst in a once widely-admired Republic. Nor should this observation obscure the fact that the Republic, too, earlier was admired for its distinctive and phenomenal achievements.

One of the established traditions of Western history has been that of the *Pax Romana*. Historians regard the Roman peace as having lasted the better part of the first two centuries of the Empire, and a distinctive contrast to the last century of the Republic. There is much to justify the appellation historians have given to this period of history. Historians have undeniably been bona fide in evaluating the empire's first two centuries as towering above so much of subsequent Western civilization. It has often been observed that nothing comparable in Europe would occur again until the nineteenth century, the era of the Victorian peace. There is a vocal contrast between the bloody internecine wars of the last century of the Roman Republic, and the contrasting era of peace with the rise of the Empire. Yet Augustus sought to camouflage the emerging new era and took as one of his titles, "Restorer of the Republic."

Few things have caught the eye of the later West more than did the Roman Empire. It has been kept alive in sermons and other moral injunctions, the common man's "lessons of history," and in the enormous historiography of the subject. Edward Gibbons is but the better known of these many writers. The best-known post-New Testament Christian figure, Saint Augustine, made the fall of Rome one of the major themes of his *De Civitate Dei* (*The City of God*), a book that in itself borders on a philosophy of history. Other than the Bible, there have been few books read more widely in the West. More than a thousand years after Augustine, an eighteenth-century historian, Edward Gibbon, chronicled the poignant end of the Roman Empire. Like Augustine, Gibbon was widely read among the elite educated class of the West, and his work was regarded as a classic. In Gibbon's time, a majority of educated eighteenth-century people had turned away from historical Christianity to embrace Deism. A fervent Protestantism that had been so widespread since the reformation lapsed into a lightly taken religion, which characterized the social issues of the day. Deism was stronger in Britain than in some parts of Europe, such as among the German states, but the thought of the philosophes overshadowed religion in France during the eighteenth century. Deism demoted the place of religion in every society, which was precisely the opposite of the historic role of Christianity in the West. Its God was distant, remote, and "absent on leave," not in contact with the problems of earth.

Unlike Gibbon, Augustine of Hippo was concerned with the onward march of a divine purpose being enacted in history. Though people have turned from God, "He reveals his power by using their sinfulness to fulfill his purpose, even as he shows his love in sending the Christ as his very incarnation to redeem them."[241] Again, in contrast Gibbon is known for his very critical, crestfallen, and chastened view of the Christian religion, so typical of much of the eighteenth century led by its philosophes. His great work denoted, sometimes eloquently, one of the memorable and historic civilizations of human epochs. Only with adversity could many contemporaries have foreseen in history that which might be more enduring than the Roman Empire had appeared to be, but it had tottered to its decline. Augustine, meanwhile, always very much a seeker, saw Christianity as the blueprint for the future. He was well positioned to think along such lines as he witnessed the fall of his beloved Hippo to the Vandals; thus, not only a witness to the past, but an adumbration of a future that would bring the empire to its demise. What Augustine witnessed God doing on earth was paralleled only by what He was doing in eternity. Augustine's widespread influence on Western civilization would reach far beyond the Middle Ages, already supplanting his own culture. He was one of the key figures across this chasm, and it is difficult to

---

[241] T. Kermit Scott, *Augustine: His Thought in Context* (New York: 1995) p. 16.

imagine how medieval civilization might have turned without the minds of Augustine, Ambrose, Gregory, Anselm, Aquinas, and those of similar mind. Without them, the making of the West would have been unthinkable as such minds stood as lodestars in the making of one of history's great civilizations, the West.[242]

Not only had Augustine's conversion brought him to Christianity, but also to a new vision of the future. Then in his early thirties, the prayers of his mother for his conversion became reality when St. Ambrose baptized him into the Christian Church. Monica had tirelessly prayed for her son's conversion to the Christian faith, yet it was St. Ambrose of Milan who proved to be the immediate spiritual influence in his life. Ambrose led Augustine to the Christian faith; it was he who baptized Augustine into the faith in Milan, then the capital of the waning empire. No longer did Augustine seek his solace in such teachings as Manichaeism, where he remained slightly less than a decade, or a philosophy that had previously attracted him. It was now in the *De Civitate Dei* that his soul found peace. One thing that brought sore disappointment for Augustine was his long link to Manichaeism. The purportedly learned Dr. Faustus, one of the religion's respected spokesmen, proved to be the chief disappointment for Augustine with Manichaeism. Augustine had fondly looked forward to meeting him at one time but grew disquieted over his limited knowledge and obvious lack of depth.

Almost two decades of Augustine's life were devoted to his writing of *The City of God*. It would be difficult to ferret out books that influenced the interpretation of Christianity in its first two millennia more than this long, repetitious classic by Augustine. Perhaps because it was written over such a lengthy period, the book meanders considerably. The Roman government under Augustus sought desperately to restore paganism, but the heart of the people was no longer there,

Ere the Roman Empire reached its final demise, popular belief had long clung to the view that it would endure forever. Enigmatic as it may seem, the Apostle Paul, himself a proud citizen of the empire, widely planted much of the seed that ultimately contributed to its inglorious demise. By the time the *Pax Romana* came to its end, much of the empire had turned to Christianity. The

---

[242] Augustinianism did not really begin to a show a decline in the West until the latter began to show signs of waning following World War II.

Emperor Julian's brief and vain attempt to turn the empire back to paganism in his short reign from A.D. 361–363 ended in futile failure. The vain attempts to restore paganism failed because there was little in it to restore in the wake of the reputation Christianity had gained throughout the empire. No one can say when or how Christianity had reached the island of Britain, though likely its earliest lodgings had come from Roman military personnel stationed there.[243] By the time Julian put forth his vain effort to restore paganism in the empire, the Faith had spread into some of the most remote portions of both Britain and Scotland. His effort to turn back to the past failed because varying cultures across the empire had found this faith to be just what Jesus had claimed it to be. It was the bread of life. There simply was no longer the intellectual and spiritual thirst and satisfaction in classical paganism, that so many had once known. Archaism could never compete with the promise of Jesus, that one who tasted of His living water would never thirst again.

Ironically, it was the fourth century that witnessed Rome's official attempt to restore paganism. In the same century, Christianity witnessed the greatest era of unification it had previously experienced. There is justification for the continuing argument that the fourth century has not yet been surpassed for its achievements. The first two centuries of the faith were highly embryonic and nascent on such things as which sacred books should constitute its canon. Doctrines of the faith were quite inchoate; theologians such as Origen could write many things that later were questioned without being looked upon as heretical.[244] Particularly this applied to Christological and trinitarian dogma. This unsettled doctrinal arena constituted the major thing that brought about the Council of Nicaea in A.D. 325. Prior to Constantine, the Christian faith was sporadically faced with persecutions for three centuries, some of which proved bitter and costly to such an extent that it could little devote thought to the exactness or precision of theological definition. After primarily four fratricidal Christological controversies, they were largely settled through the great councils brought about from Nicaea to the Council of Chalcedon in A.D. 451, which represented the apex of primitive Christianity's move toward unity.

---

[243] In modern times, this has been questioned by some good scholars.
[244] It was later that Origen's writings came to be considered heretical by many Christians.

In sharp contrast to a developing unity in the Church, the Roman Empire had during the same period become decimated on many fronts.[245] For centuries, the Rhine and Danube frontiers were increasingly menaced by threats from the Germans, whose advances steadily widened. Dependent upon a mercenary army as Rome now was, it was not easy to count on their loyalty when an offer for higher pay could woo men from one generation to another. On another front, this one in the West, the Anglo-Saxon heptarchy experienced invasions from the Picts, Scots, and others. Within something close to a century of the collapse of Rome's great North African province, Islam would begin its penetration of the region. This was greatly influenced by the growing use of the camel in the second and third centuries, which allowed for deeper penetration into the Sahara.

The Donatist movement proved to be a major threat to the Catholic Church and distressful to Augustine, its most noted Catholic bishop. It won many of Christian faith from the Catholic Church, resulting in much sectarian strife in North Africa. North Africa was the scene of many rival bishops between Catholics and Donatists. Throughout most of his life as a bishop in North Africa, Augustine found himself contending with Donatism, known for its stricture and opposition to the Catholic Church. North Africa previously produced some of the notable examples of Christian martyrdom, and distinguished thinkers such as Tertullian, and Cyprian of Carthage. The contribution of such stalwarts played a significant role in making Latin the respected Christian language of the West, as Greek had long been in the East. North Africa was also the scene of two of the earliest schisms in the Church, Montanism, and Donatism. Some historians have advanced the thesis that the latter controversy weakened North African Catholic Christianity prior to the coming of Islam. The author, however, finds this unsustainable and of dubious thesis, as too many local properties of North African culture are left unaccounted for. These had long been a divisive factor in North African Christianity.

These historical developments were harbingers of great change in the Christian religion and of its future; fully complementary to that which had moved the faith from its Palestinian Jewish character, to a distinctive Gentile religion before

---

[245] This need not be looked upon as an absolute, as frictions still abounded in the Church. Particularly, there was a growing divide between Eastern and Western Christendom.

the end of the first Christian century. At the same time, new emerging phases of history were to plant Christianity deeply in European soil and complete its evolution from a predominantly Eastern religion to a Western one.[246] It is incontrovertible that the Apostle Paul was the initiator of the gargantuan step that has led to Christianity becoming the most widespread religion ever known on earth. To those predisposed to accept the hand of Providence in what has perhaps erroneously been termed secular history, this is a striking fact.

The Apostle Paul could not have apprehended all that would derive from his daily, local, and thoughtful decision or judgment, as to where his ministry would lead. Every wise parent, however, teaches their children that choices are consequential. Paul's great decision to turn to the Gentiles and the resulting impact undoubtedly contributed to the weight of his insight that Jesus Christ was a cosmic Christ, as shown in his long opening sentence to the Book of Ephesians in which he affirmed that all things are to be summed up in Christ. With great emphasis, the Apostle made it a clarion fact that he was changing his mission from the Jews and turning to the Gentiles. Approximating three quarters of a century ago, one of the foremost New Testament scholars, C. H. Dodd of Cambridge University, saw in this action of Paul the creation of a new philosophy. He called it an "elevated philosophy of history."[247] It was certainly a prognostication of how future centuries would alter religion on the continent of Europe. By this time, the Church had become more Gentile than Jewish; in this historical development the Apostle saw an act of the providence of God who often has adopted history as the channel through which His divine economy would be sanctioned on earth.

In the mind of St. Paul, Judaism as a whole had rejected the Christian faith; yet he did not see this as finality, as shown in some of the classic chapters of his writing to the Roman Church. God, in His *chesed* love, cared for His own people too much to see this rejection as a historical finale or consummation of the ages. In three great missionary itineraries, Paul had witnessed the rejection of the gospel by his Jewish compatriots while the Gentiles received it, sometimes with alacrity. This choice had repeated itself in post after

---

[246] From a theological point of view, Christian faith presumably asserted that it was neither eastern nor western, but the question must be looked at historically as well.
[247] C. H. Dodd, *The Epistle of Paul to the Romans* (London: 1932), p. 186.

post, as this pattern was constantly repeated. This belief was established as one of the strongest tenets of Paul's creed, basic to his philosophy, making it one of the primary eschatological points of Paul's faith. According to this, he believed, one day all things would turn to God making all things become one in Him.[248]

Not without anguish did the first century Church pioneer in the far-reaching steps that culminated only in the second century Church becoming more Gentile than Jewish. How far this movement of God had come is seen in the saying of Jesus, "I was sent only to the lost sheep of the house of Israel."[249] At another time, He also said that He had sheep not in the fold of Israel. It is so alluring to allow localized statements, uttered for the moment, to become durable and fixed tenets of the entire Christian faith. One of the outcomes of this is heavy reliance on prooftexts, and where there is disagreement the resort to division. It is highly comprehensible why only some first century Jewish Christians found it venturesome for a new movement, so deeply rooted in a centuries-old Judaism, to open its doors to Gentile converts to the faith. It is a historical incongruity that this came at a time when the ancient world was experiencing an emptiness of soul from the increasing distrust of much of the old pagan tradition. The popularity of Greek and Roman cynics and their teaching underscores this truth.

When Paul wrote the letter to the Romans, he had come to visualize the providence of God in some of the mysterious and difficult currents of history. He had seen the Jews' rejection of the good news of Jesus Christ in town after town while on his missionary journeys. Here he spoke of the grafting in of the Gentiles and compared this to the grafting of an olive tree. His positive word to the Jewish people was that this did not represent a casting aside of the Jewish people. Here the Apostle lapsed into a somewhat enigmatic puzzle of history in which he saw Jewish indifference to the gospel of Christ not as a final chapter, but the prelude to a time in history when there would be a mass turning to Christ on their part. The two chapters in his epistle to the Church at Rome are not always easy to decipher and interpret, but of the overarching clarity and reality of his belief that this was a future fact of history there can be but minimal doubt.

---

[248] Ibid., pp. 178–188.
[249] Matthew 15:24.

Already the great Apostle to the Gentiles had seen the Gentiles becoming a majority in the Christian fold. In the following century, Clement and Origen continued the process of this interpretation of history.[250] Paul's roots were in the Diaspora of Judaism, which had its beginning centuries before Christ. He knew of the background of the Roman Empire, and perhaps even something of its forerunner, the Republic. By the time he came upon the historical scene, Rome's far-flung ambition embraced much of the ancient world that the patriarchs of Israel had known. Rome's steady growth ushered in the animosity of her ancient enemies along the Rhine River, and among the Persian satrapies. It is easy for Western historians who have any appreciation for the role of Christianity in the West to sense something of the hand of Providence in these historical foreshadows. The fact, however, that some of the major historians of the West have been in this vein of thought, does not nullify the fact that other noteworthy historians have rejected this point of view, as did Edward Gibbon.

With regard to the providence of God in history, there is no scientific way to prove this thesis; nor, is there a similar means of disproving it. Even so, no group of scholars has dealt with the problem of providence and history, as have Christian thinkers.

The kingdom of God, for which we were taught to pray, is both within and beyond history. Jesus Himself recognized this potential delinquency in saying, "My kingdom is not of this world." The statement was made at a time when the Roman government, represented by Pilate, sought to destroy Jesus; this is not to say, however, that the world would have been better had the Roman Empire won this victory. Christian faith has staunchly asserted the providence of God in all history. It believes that there is an "elect" history in which divine purposes and ends are continually being worked out with divine foresightedness; both theologians and philosophers have contributed to this insightful term *teleological*.[251]

The claim may be set forth that in the historiography of the West, the providential occupied high ground throughout the

---

[250] Of course, there were other factors in this transition. It was Paul; however, who earlier pioneered in planting Christianity among the Gentiles in the great cities of the Empire.

[251] It has a very interesting derivation from two Greek words "telos" which means end, and "logia" meaning "words about." What voluminous theology and philosophy have been constructed on this concept!

Historical Pursuit of the Purpose of God

nineteenth century; admittedly, however, following World War I one sees a sharp turn from this in such works as that of Oswald Spengler, *The Decline of the West*. Historians are interpreters of history, but never its judges and umpires. They are not the decision makers on its rules, for in history there are no pre-established rules or "laws of history." This is not to blemish the concept of the purpose of God, but to underscore the freedom He has likewise bestowed on humanity.

It cannot be proven, or disproven, that Rome's universal political goal influenced Paul in his thinking concerning Christianity being the one thing that united all people everywhere. As William M. Ramsay demonstrated, Paul had shown a propensity for introducing the Christian faith to fringe groups in the empire.[252] Ramsay pointed out that it was after John Mark left Paul prematurely, on their first missionary journey, that Paul advanced deeper into Phrygia and more remote regions. It was here, Ramsay claimed, that Paul for the first time made his great affirmation, "We are all equal, all brethren, all alike in the new faith.[253] Similarly, it was soon thereafter that the Apostle made another decisive affirmation, "We turn to the Gentiles." It does not seem too much to claim that his experience as a Roman citizen stirred him to see Jesus Christ as the one through whom a universal harmony would be achieved. Paul was well aware that at the time merchants in Corinth and other eastern cities were already making journeys to India and China.[254] There is, of course, the ancient tradition that one of Jesus' disciples, Bartholomew, carried the gospel to India. Modern writers have in general supported the ancient view that he, and such other men as Pantaneus of Alexandria, did preach and found churches in India.[255]

The writings of the Apostle Paul suggest that he had sometimes pondered the world's past, present, and future, and saw this world through different lenses, in which Gentiles were part of God's age-long purpose, as well as Jews. One of his very earliest New Testament writings, Galatians, spoke in a stirring and stimulating

---

[252] One of Ramsay's many writings was *Pictures of the Apostolic Church: Its Life and Thought*. The book, along with his other works, captured the picture of a religion advancing ever deeply into fringe groups of the day.
[253] Ibid., p. 141.
[254] It was widely believed that Pantaneus, an early well-educated Christian who founded the great theological school in Alexandria, had spent time in India.
[255] Pantaneus served as head of the famous catechetical school in Alexandria, and was followed in that position by Origen, one of the great pre-Nicene theologians of the early Church.

way of this coming world unity of Jew and Gentile in Christ. Jesus Christ, whose followers Paul had once persecuted so predatorily, had become nothing less than the cornerstone of this worldwide edifice, which God was building in history through Him. Never perhaps, has more anxious thought been expended on the problems of the ultimate destiny of mankind than that of Paul in the Book of Ephesians.[256]

Paul's long introduction to the Book of Ephesians is one of the sources for grasping his far-reaching grandiose vision of what God was doing in history to bring all people together.[257] Paul's foresightedness was stated in a single long sentence in Ephesians, which to a modern mind would have constituted many sentences. To the modern, however, it may appear as a long, unwinding, unremitting range of many ideas, lacking original punctuation, which came to its close only at verse fourteen of the first chapter of the letter. Because of this meandering of thought, this passage of the letter has provoked sharp theological differences as to its theological precision and interpretation. This has been notably true since the Protestant Reformation of the sixteenth century. Historical theology has often reflected these differences; as for example between John Calvin and Thomas Arminius in sixteenth century Protestant Reformation thought, and in the development of statements of faith. Arminius saw a far greater freedom given to humankind in the development of its history than has traditionally been attributed to John Calvin.[258]

The extremely long paragraph with which Ephesians opens bespeaks of a mature and advanced theology, which is elsewhere unsurpassed in the New Testament. Some scholars have argued that such advanced theology points to a later disciple of Paul as its author. The supposition, however, appears to lack sufficient evidence, and proved unconvincing to such erstwhile great pioneer scholars as Westcott, Hort, and Lightfoot. The three are at one in seeing a close

---

[256] J. Armitage Robinson, *Commentary on Ephesians* (Grand Rapids: 1979), pp. 10–12.
[257] Because of its advanced views, some have argued for a later date for the Book of Ephesians than the time of Paul. Such a view was unknown until quite modern times, and even here has gained little support. It must be remembered that Ephesians, as one of the later and more mature writings, came after a world of experience and thought about the Roman Empire and the world emerging around it.
[258] Calvin's famous "predestination" has sometimes been preposterously misunderstood and overstated.

thematic relationship of Ephesians and the Epistle of Colossians. Likewise, its tentacles point back to the Epistle of Galatians. Throughout a number of attempts to make another, other than Paul, the author of Ephesians these cannot be said to be convincing.[259] Careful study of each epistle buttresses the opinion that they came from the same hand. Furthermore, unquestionably in Paul's mind the epistles were intended to be decidedly teleological, with emphasis on God's purpose being worked out in history, toward the goal of a new world order. Emphasis on the reality of God's purposes is viewed as being preexistent, even before the earth knew its beginning.

Few, if any, other biblical passages excel the teleological aspect of the understanding of history as Ephesians reflects. After World War II, there emerged a strong vein of theology, which tended to isolate historical happenings into those in which the hand of God was clearly detected toward the fulfillment of His purpose. This came to be known as "salvation history," as opposed to the general course of history. The author sees this as highly useful to a degree, but at the same time appears to embed potential fallacies. There can be no doubt, to a theist, that history is well stocked with events in which God was showing His mighty arm. This appears obvious, if one gives any credence at all to Old Testament narratives, such as is seen with regard to Israel's relations with both the Egyptian Pharaoh and the Assyrian kings. Historical episodes did occur which may have been detected as salvation history. Even so, God is also always at work in all history, even in those events which may not manifest a clarion evidence of such. Perhaps more accurate would it be to say that God's story is depicted, or imbedded, within history. Again, it would require a highly homogenous setting to reach an accord on which event God was at work. Some events that have happened in history and were attributed to God were nothing less than a ludicrous judgment.

The view of history that the Apostle Paul set forth in Ephesians was that in every age God had been moving forward His eternal purpose. History is the anvil on which God does this work. He has worked in the past—the Old Testament is the record of that

---

[259] Scholars have set forth the thesis that the unknown author of Ephesians attempted to do a synthesis of all Paul's writing from the great epistles. This, however, has not gained widespread acceptance, and in reality, raises additional problems.

activity. He was supremely at work in Jesus of Nazareth and prepared the world for His coming in acts of history incomparable to any other time. As one who works in history, God plans. For example, in the beginning of His ministry, Jesus called Andrew, Peter, James, and John to be His workers and propagate the divine plans for the future.

Christians do not look on the various cycles of history as simply phases of a historical process, but as periods of time when the Divine hand is being shown. It does appear that this divine hand has been more stoutly shown at times than at others. For example, the eighteenth century pales in significance for the rule of God in the world in comparison with the nineteenth, when attempts were made to plant the gospel on continents never before viewed as "fields white unto harvest." In contrast, in the eighteenth century England witnessed absentee priests who seldom observed a service at the established church and were oftentimes on the chase for animals during the stated time for worship. In considering the centuries since the Renaissance and Protestant Reformation, the eighteenth century would represent the nadir for the Christian religion in Western Society.

It has been pointed out that no other epistle has the aura of perspective that Ephesians has. As a divine plan in history, Paul most certainly would not have wanted this to be interpreted as everything in history constituting the will of God. Jesus' insistence that the wheat and the tares must be expected to live and grow side by side is an indication of such. Both good and the evil share the same historical soil and often grow so closely together as to become ensnared. This was the warning of Jesus in attempting to uproot suspected tares emerging among the wheat. There could be no more solid thesis in theology or eschatology than that the overarching purpose of God contends for a divine and eternal purpose that will not be ultimately thwarted by the misdeeds of men or from any residue of original evil. Much of the New Testament reverberates this concept, with confident expectation that at the end, "The kingdoms of the world have become the kingdom of our Lord and of his Christ, and he shall reign forever and ever."[260] God's purpose was deeply encrusted in the historical narratives of humanity, but was continually beset by the wiles of men, who have chosen to go

---

[260] Revelation 11:15.

Historical Pursuit of the Purpose of God

against that purpose. Ephesians affirms that this history had its inauguration with the Old Testament pronouncement of creation. Its larger setting is like a John Milton framework in that it allows the freedom of humanity to reject this plan of Deity. Such a range of thought presents an unparalleled awesomeness, by way of its introduction of the great rift, which came about through the rebellion of Adam and Eve in God's heretofore untainted creation of the universe.[261]

To follow the ways of the Christian religion beyond its pristine days of the biblical narratives, and great fathers and leaders of the early church, is nothing less than astonishing. Here was a religion that some of the most powerful men on earth at the time had long sought to eradicate, but it had outlived their empire and penetrated into the future development of the European continent. Within its earliest days, following Pentecost, the religion did show some gravitation to the East, where large numbers became Christians, not only Jews of the Diaspora but Gentiles as well. Ancient kingdoms such as Armenia, Persia, Edessa, and regions such as Bithynia and Pontus were converted to the faith. The eastern advance, nevertheless, did not prove to be the trend of the future; even so, it is riveting and one of the enigmas of time as to how early the Christian religion reached India. There is also the ancient tradition of how the original band of Jesus' disciples split up and ventured into various parts of the world, and of each contributing a line to the creed that bears their name before separating in the spread of the Gospel of Jesus Christ.

Significant as were these pioneering ventures, it was Christianity's later impact in Europe and its derivatives that has left the most enduring impact on world culture. Europe carried the gospel to North America, and in turn, the latter played a major role in planting that same gospel of Jesus Christ in Africa, Asia, and elsewhere. These momentous steps did so much to identify Christianity as the religion of the West, though it had long and strong roots in the East, Christianity came to be recognized as the foremost religion of the West. It should be noted that it was in later centuries with the rising power of the papacy that this became most apparent in Europe.[262]

---

[261] Another chapter deals with this rift, Genesis 3. The reading of the Book of Job from this perspective may also prove useful.
[262] Only in 1054 did the official split occur.

This was precisely the same period in which the Germanic tribes had their greatest impact on the West. The river frontiers of the Rhine and Danube had always been a challenge to Rome's ability to defend them with the goal of stability. Even so, by this time the breaches had become indefensible, with Germanic tribesmen penetrating at will. Added to this was the fact that Rome now depended for defense on mercenary armies who could easily be persuaded to switch sides when greater lucrative agreements could be secured from other bidders. This use of mercenaries for defense was a key factor in the security of many areas of the Roman Empire.

The rise and gradual unification of the Franks, particularly in the fourth and fifth centuries, in retrospect may be interpreted as the laying of one of the most far-reaching and significant stones in the building of the early West. While this was ensuing, the papacy in Rome, from many factors, gained wider recognition and stronger veneration from Christians beyond the boundaries of Italy.

The Old Testament opened with the awesome, "In the beginning God," not a beginning of God, for He knew neither beginning nor ending. One of the most potent items of faith in the West has long been that without this revelation from God, He remains an unknown God. God is the Absolute, and the only ultimate. Lacking divine revelation, this God remains incomprehensible. Those bereft of the knowledge of God turned to gods and to demonism, which evolved into paganism. Great care was often practiced in paganism to be inclusive of all the gods; witness the Apostle Paul's experience at Mars Hill where he encountered an altar dedicated to the unknown god. This is as good a summation of the property of European paganism on the continent at this time to be imagined. The development of Eastern European Christianity had its start earlier than did the West, but it would ultimately be Western European Christianity that made Christianity a world religion. It appears to the writer that this materialized in the late first century due more to the Apostle Paul than any other, though he could not have envisioned what a large part of the earth would eventually be labeled "the West." That had its commencement in the eighteenth century with William Carey who went to India, and with the colonization of the eastern United States, where nothing more was alive than their religion.

Index

A
Abba, 110
Abel, 160
Abeokuta, 106
Aberdeen, 124
ablest minds, 132
abounding diverseness, 149
Abraham, 42, 67–68, 78, 85–87, 101, 152
Abrahamic religions, 13
Abraham's time, 85
absent on leave, 170
Absolute Power, 15
academy, 135
  enlarged, 135
accepted Paul, 166
accident, 28, 57, 62, 122
  first railroad, 98
acclaim, 26, 97, 130
  public, 157
  universal, 51
to accompany, 109
accountability, 27
Accra, 10
accuracy, 24, 100
accustomed thought, 49
acquiescence, 160
Actium, 104–5
activities, long-reaching, 68
actuality, 18, 79, 132, 144
  historical, 72
actualization, 78
adage, old, 36
Adam, 15–17, 33, 40, 46–47, 58, 62–64, 66, 68–72, 78, 80, 82, 86, 110, 114, 126
adamant, 135–36
Adeney, Walter F., 162

adherents, 137, 160
Adolph, 131, 161
Adoniram Judson, 142, 163
adumbration, 170
advancement, 36, 90
  historical, 133
Aegean civilizations, 29
affirmation, 16, 19, 33–34, 36, 48, 91
  ancient Christian, 91
  apogee, 45
  decisive, 177
  great, 177
affliction, 61, 87
afforded Jesus, 110
affront, 35, 59, 120
Africa, 22, 48, 96, 114, 134, 142, 163–64, 181
  modern, 137
  the scramble for, 10
  southern, 33
African avenues, 34
African chieftains, 11
African Christians and hearing, 97
African climate, 20
African Coast, 164
African continent, 10, 22
African father, 20
African history, 166
African lands, 22
African school, 11
African states, 22
age nothing, 79
Age of Science, 13, 26, 39
ages, 22–24, 28, 37, 39, 48, 50, 65–66, 80, 82, 106, 109–11, 116–20, 124, 126, 140

classical, 105
medieval, 76
messianic, 109, 123
new, 126
patristic, 149
prior, 49
Aggrey, 22, 142
agreement, 97
  large, 60
agriculture, 144
Akokoamong, 35, 59
Alabama, 15, 26, 28–29, 102, 117
alacrity, 96, 174
Alexander, 124, 155
Alexandria, 14, 52, 60, 73, 115, 131, 141, 148–49, 157, 166, 177
Alfred North Whitehead, 42, 83–84
alien, 24, 61
alienated humanity, 79
alienation, 25, 72, 98
  age-long, 58
Allah, 13
with all deliberate speed, 70
alliteration, 117
alludes, 39, 136
allurement, 33, 47
Alpha, 11
altar, 182
  large pagan, 35
Amazing Grace, 58, 118
Ambrose, 130, 171
America, 2, 25, 41, 43, 47, 66, 96, 100, 102, 136, 157, 163–64
  early, 113
  modern, 43
American colleges, 48
American college students, 10

American colonies, 78
American Congregationalists, 163
American congregations, 44
American Presbyterian Church, 144
Americans, 98
American society, 133
American sons, 147
American theology, 14
amid, 85, 96, 156
Amos, 88, 94, 105, 144
anakephalaiosas thai, 165
analysis
  brilliant, 101
  final, 102
  safest, 111
  superb evangelical, 69
ancient, 14, 19, 29, 36, 42, 48–49, 68, 86, 90–91, 95, 107, 130, 142, 177
ancient approaches, 60
ancient chieftain, 68
ancient civilization, 156
ancient divine economy, 113
ancient enemies, 176
ancient Greek, 55
ancient Greek mold, 61
ancient Hebraic concept, 106
ancient Hebrew, 37
ancient Israel, 61
ancient Jewish rabbinical interpretation, 63
ancient Judaism, 106, 168
Ancient kingdoms, 10, 181
ancient longing, 151
ancient myths, 95
ancient paganism, 108
ancient Palestine, 152
ancient patriarchs, 86

ancient philosophy, 37
ancient Phoenicia, 115, 126
ancient prophets, 88
ancient Rabbis, 64
ancient story, 29
ancient territory, 10
ancient tradition, 177, 181
　strong, 166
ancient Upanishads, 14
ancient wars, 108
ancient world, 37, 61, 97, 156, 160, 175–76
ancient writings, 86
Andrew, 138, 180
angelic host, 106
angels, 14, 64
　fallen, 63
angle, 20, 98
　cosmological, 67
　human, 124
Anglican clergyman, 26, 50
Anglican minister, 24, 118
Anglican priest, 62
Anglo-Saxon Britain, 137
Anglo-Saxon heptarchy, 173
Anglo-Saxon world, 25
anguishing problem, 81
animism, 23, 100
animosity, 176
　deep, 156
annals, 89, 110, 116, 142, 146
annihilation, 148
anomaly, total, 59
Anselm, 14, 171
antagonism, 74
　growing, 121
antagonistic, 74
ante-bellum days, 28
antedated time, 79
ante-Nicene, 148

Anthony, 14
Anthropic Principle, 41
Anthropologists, 23
anthropomorphic language Johnson, 76
anti-Christian, 108
anticipation, great, 156
Antioch, 115, 130–31, 141, 154–55
Antioch church, 130, 154
Antiochus Epiphanes, 108
antipodal, 79, 84
antiquity, 43, 107
anti-Roman alliance, 103
antithesis, 18, 141
antithetical, 123, 143, 168
anvil, 18, 179
anxiety, 24, 50, 100
　new, 28
　student's, 24
anxious thought, 178
apex, 36, 44, 71, 133, 146, 152, 165, 172
　historical, 150
apocryphal writings, 111, 123
apogee, 80, 148
apologists, early, 73
Apostle, 46, 79, 115, 117, 129, 133, 153, 162, 174–75, 177
　great, 176
Apostle John, 16, 73, 138, 158
Apostle Paul, 46–47, 49, 54, 82, 84–85, 91, 105, 107, 109, 115, 133, 138, 165, 174, 182
Apostle Paul set, 179
Apostle Peter, 95, 129, 157, 159, 162
Apostle's ministry, 91
Apostolic Church, 157, 177
to appear or seem, 120

appease, 96, 98
appeasement, 103
appellations, 104, 139, 141
application, 70, 102
  rugged, 136
  universal, 98
appreciable amount, 139
approximate age, 23
Aquinas, 171
  Thomas, 49
Arabia, 29
Aramaic words, 110
Archaism, 172
Archbishop, 23
Archbishop Ussher, 28
Archibald, 153
Archibald Thomas Robertson, 154
architect, 28
  great, 131
ardent disputes, 24
ardent lovers, 107
areas, new, 23
arenas, 68, 144
  primary, 65
  unsettled doctrinal, 172
Argentina, 136
Arian, 148
Arianism, 148
Aristides, 73, 168
arm, 143, 150
  long continuous, 66
  mighty, 179
Armagh, 23
Armenia, 181
Arminius, 178
  Thomas, 178
Armitage Robinson, 15, 178
arrangements, 134

arrival, 21, 102, 105, 130, 163, 165
artful New Testament scholars, 127
artificer, 31, 61
artistry, great, 28
ascendancy, 115, 162
ascending number, 34
ascension, 127, 131
Ashanti, 21, 137
Ashanti capital, 21
Ashanti land, 22
Ashanti people, 21, 69, 137
Asia, 155, 163, 166, 181
Asia Minor, 133, 165, 167
assertion, 19, 62
  bold, 45
assessment, 149, 156
Assiduous care, 81
assistant, 154
assuagement, 82
  seeking, 35
assuage philosophical thought, 38
assurance, 15, 54, 61, 68, 72
  authoritative, 112
  pronounced, 147
assuredness, 19
Assyria, 91, 93, 95
Assyrian kings, 179
Athanasius, 19–20, 69
  general, 20
atheism, 34, 71
Athenagoras, 60
Athens, 73, 148
Atlantic Ocean, 75
attestation, 142
attractiveness, 33
attributes, 39, 131, 160
  invisible, 54

attunement, 73, 75
Auburn University, 102
Augustine, 53, 62, 69, 76, 78, 90, 130, 142, 164, 170–71, 173
Augustine's conversion, 171
Augustine's life, 171
Augustinian, 116
Augustinianism, 171
Augustus, 32, 95, 105, 108, 169, 171
Austin Henry Layard, 31
authenticity, 15, 30, 38, 77, 112, 150
authorities, 20, 64, 116, 165
  religious, 9
author's fondest years, 22
authorship, 165
  non-Pauline, 167
author's life, 135
author's tenure, 34
avowal, 33, 51
awesomeness, 17–18, 41, 181
axiom, 68
  ancient biblical, 66
  didactic, 133
axioms, great, 19
Ayorinde, 125

B
Baal, 61
Baalism, 94
babe, 106, 112
Babylon, 69, 93
Babylonian captivity, 93
Babylonian creation myths, 61
Babylonian epics, 39
Babylonian exile, 121
Backsliding, 102
backward, 10, 52, 75, 91, 150

Baillie, 60
Baker, 165
balance, 41, 64, 98
banana leaf, large, 22
band, 113, 129, 164
  original, 181
bang, 50
  big, 26
baptism, 102, 109, 111, 140, 145, 154
baptism onward, 120
Baptist, 109, 111–12, 120–21, 125, 145, 163, 167
  early seventeenth century, 167
Baptist denomination, 163
Baptist Girl's School, 57
Baptist missionary, 163
Baptist World Alliance, 125
baptized Augustine, 171
barbarism, 114, 116
Barbour, Ian G., 50, 67
Barclay, William, 70
Bar Cochba, 139
Barnabas, 130, 133–35, 154–56, 159
  deserted, 159
  desired, 136
  status, 154
Barth, 97
  Karl, 18, 69, 80, 97
Barthian concept, 68
Bartholomew, 177
Basil, 38
Basle Mission, 137
battle, single, 54
Baur, 166
beats, 18
  transcendent God, 18
beds, 111, 117

begging, 133
  snow, 133
beginning God, 48
  in the, 17–18, 26, 33, 41, 48, 152, 182
begotten Son, 119
Behr, John, 19–20
being pulled in two directions, 142
Belgium, 10
belief, 13, 17–19, 21, 26, 30, 32–34, 37–39, 44, 51, 55, 60, 71, 145, 154, 175
  buttressed, 51
  deep, 68
  ingrained, 51
  popular, 171
  singular, 32
  solid, 21
  strong, 25
  universal, 34, 39
believers, 13, 43, 50, 71, 118, 154
  modern, 126
  strong, 15
beloved Son, 11
beloved wife, 5
Benedictine missionaries, 164
Benedictine monks, 162, 164
Benedictines, 162
benefits Jesus Christ, 58
Benjamin, 93
bereft, 80, 182
Bertwhistle, 22
bestowal, 88, 143
bestowing, 62, 137
Beth, 5
Bethlehem, 106, 108–9
Bethlehem Ephrathah, 94

Bible, 17, 19–20, 23–24, 28, 36, 42, 46–48, 68, 70–71, 74, 80–81, 85–86, 107, 131, 143
Bible's opening words, 48
biblical, 19, 39, 64–65, 70, 81, 130, 167
  basic, 48
biblical account, 9, 63, 100
biblical affirmation, 37
biblical assertion, 60
biblical avowal, 50
biblical concept, 144
biblical criticism, 65
biblical doctrine, 36, 39, 87–88
biblical literalism, 25
biblical narratives, 120, 181
biblical outlook, 75
biblical passages excel, 179
biblical portrayal, 74
biblical prooftexts, 74
biblical references, 63
biblical rejoinder, 15
biblical revelation, 77
biblical scholars, 166
  early, 65
biblical scholarship, 166
  conservative, 87
  critical, 132
biblical story, 47
biblical studies, 100
biblical text, 23
biblical theology, 61
biblical theophany, 64
biblical thought, 31, 59
biblical truth, 38
  earlier, 38
biblical understanding, 73
biblical writers, 48–49, 61
Binkley, Olin, 62

biographies, 48
birds, 36, 40
Birmingham, 15, 26
birth, 15, 17, 23, 30, 42, 69, 76, 93–96, 106–10, 115, 139, 149, 151, 163, 169
  brilliant, 48
  renewed, 90
birth pangs, 126
bishop, 72–73, 138, 173
  noted Catholic, 173
Bithynia, 95–96, 181
bitter, 46, 172
bitter controversy, earlier, 88
bitter disputes, 23
  experienced, 160
bitter ferocious persecution, 11
bitter separations, experienced, 25
Black Death, 87
Blake, Calvin, 31
Blandina, 73
blasphemous, 98
blemish, 45, 59, 177
blessed and burned, 125
block history tidily, 67
blood, 67, 82
blueprints, 135, 147, 170
boastfulness, 70
Bogomile movement, 162
bona fide claim, 163
bondage, 43, 87–88, 91
book meanders, 171
Book of Acts, 131
Book of Genesis, 28, 36, 42, 47, 64
Book of Psalms, 127
borders, 108–9, 169
  religious, 78

boundaries, 109, 182
  temporal, 109
bounds, 47, 78, 98
  life's, 72
Box, Hubert S., 19, 41, 83
Boyle Lectures, 49, 54
boys, 22, 102
Brahman, 14
branches, 28, 129
Brazil, 5
bread, 32, 172
breakdown, 104, 135
Breasted, 43
brethren, 151, 177
bridge, 76, 139, 141
Britain, 137, 153–54, 162, 164, 169–70, 172
  northern, 148
British-born missionary, 144
British colony, 134
British commerce, 164
British Empire, 156
British encroachments, 21
British Gold Coast, 21
British government, 10
British historian, 18
British monk, 62
British rule, 22
British scholar, 134
British trading companies, 164
British troops, 163
brother, 5, 38, 110, 160
  older, 99
bruise, 114
Brunner, Emil, 80, 92, 97
builder, great, 148
builders, 139, 162
bulk, 91, 150
bushes, 88, 106

burning, 42–43, 87, 89
Bushnell, Horace, 47, 114
Butterfield, 25
   Herbert, 25, 50
Buttressing, 166

C

Caesar Augustus, 105, 108, 169
Cain, 160
calamity, 58
   tragic, 91
calculation, 75, 121
calleth, deep, 19
call grace, 58
Calvary, 114
Calvin, 78, 127, 178
   John, 48, 127, 178
Calvinism, 42, 47, 78–79
Calvinistic denominations, 88
Calvinists, 42
Calvin's influence, 78
Cambridge, 24–25, 28, 37, 50, 62, 65, 77, 153
Cambridge Historian, 99
Cambridge scholar, modern, 26
Cambridge University, 13, 25, 39, 118, 174
camel, 164, 173
camouflage, 159, 169
camps, 38, 94
campus, 28, 57, 156
canon, 16, 166, 172
canonical Pauline writings, 130
canonization, 78
Canossa, 133
Canterbury, 14
capability, 51, 109

capacity, 63, 97
capital, 10, 171
captivating, 20
captives, 91, 95
Carey, William, 97, 101, 163, 182
Carmel, 61
carpenter shop, 110
Carthage, 173
cast, 63, 74, 106
castle, 63, 151
catastrophic events, 40
Catholic Church, 27, 162, 167, 173
catholic definition, 167
Catholics, 173
ceaseless line, 54
centerpiece, 36
centuries, 16, 23, 25–30, 36–37, 45, 49–50, 52–53, 85–92, 104–9, 112–15, 129–30, 136–37, 145–46, 163–64, 172–74
   beginning, 176
   distant, 164
   early, 60
   final, 169
   following, 27, 176
   fourth, 9, 30, 37, 78, 130, 172
   influential, 50
   last, 50, 96, 104, 169
   living, 45
   long, 70, 108, 142, 144, 149
   mid-fourteenth, 87
   modern, 90, 130
   past, 24, 114, 118
   sixteenth, 30, 42, 78–79, 178
   twenty-first, 33, 88
centuries segments, 93

century age, 163
century anthropologists, 59
century Christian scholarship, 132
century conflict, 24
century missionary explorer, 33
century poem, 70
century prophet Micah, 160
century prophets, 88, 94
Cerf, 2
cessation, eternal, 32, 61
chain, long, 66
Chalcedon, 162, 172
channels, 27, 42, 91, 174
chaos, 27, 50, 56, 77
characterization, 76, 146
character Jesus, 123
chariot, 121–22
Charlemagne, 32
chasm, 69–70, 170
chastisement, 121
chief arena, 82
chief disappointment, 171
chief headlines, 114
chief instrument, 86
chief jewel, 19
chief propensities, 81
chief seat, 138, 141
chief vehicle, 28
child, 28, 59, 69, 72, 95, 101, 104–6, 110
  lowborn peasant, 106
  male, 106
  young, 17, 41
childlessness, 99
children, 10, 86, 97, 106, 111, 125, 147, 174
  decadent, 147
  lift peasant, 106

Chile, 136
chiliastic, strong, 138
China, 164, 177
Chinese science, 29
choice, 9, 15, 55, 57, 62, 64, 81, 86, 88, 143, 154, 174
  erroneous, 62
chores, common, 110
Christ, 13, 15–16, 67–69, 73, 83, 86, 97, 101, 119–20, 122–23, 136–37, 160–62, 174–76, 178, 180
  Jesus, 9, 11, 16, 43–46, 59–60, 79, 97, 101, 140–42, 144, 158, 162–63, 174–75, 177–78, 181
Christendom, 28, 58, 97
Christ event, 119–20
Christ God, 58
Christian apologetics, 44
Christian attitude of veneration and worship, 115
Christian belief, 79
  early, 37
  stringent, 62
Christian calendar, 107
Christian centers, older, 115
Christian centuries, early, 144
Christian century
  first, 46, 52, 115, 168, 174
  second, 72
Christian character, 79
Christian Church, 30, 105, 133, 155, 159, 171
  young, 9, 52, 143
Christian circles, 51
Christian communions, 50
Christian communities, conservative, 50
Christian community, 97, 133

Christian concept of time, 144
Christian congregations, 23
    primitive, 131
Christian Deity, 58
Christian denominations, 136
Christian development, early, 158
Christian Doctrine, 14–15, 73, 75, 149
    primitive, 38
Christian dogma, 31, 37, 60, 136
Christian enclave, strong, 95
Christian enterprises, 97
Christian Era, 32, 37
Christian faith, 13–15, 29–32, 34, 54–55, 96, 100, 107, 109, 111, 127, 130, 135–37, 141, 160, 171–77
Christian faith and science, 32
Christian fold, 118, 176
Christian God, 50, 53, 66
Christian groups, 43
Christian idea of creation, 74
Christian interpretations, 32
Christianity, 13, 22–23, 58–59, 73–74, 76, 91–93, 95–97, 108–9, 114–17, 122–23, 136–39, 148–49, 160–65, 170–72, 181–82
    blamed, 96
    early, 87, 93, 96, 122, 129
    evangelical, 35, 59, 67, 80
    first century, 27, 91, 106, 138
    greatest threat, 45
    historical, 170
    history of, 142, 161
    impact, 137
    mainline, 43
    plant, 174
    planted, 164
    planting, 176
    reputation, 172
    ways, 95
    weakened North African Catholic, 173
Christianity depicts, 160
Christian leader, 138
Christian life, 35
Christian martyrdom, 173
Christian ministers, 65
Christian ministry, 154
Christian missionaries, 96
    early, 137
Christian movement, 80, 168
Christian patrimony, 136
Christian patterns, 149
Christian people, 43
Christian period, early, 149
Christian Philosophy, 49, 54, 160
Christian philosophy of history, 91, 113
Christian practice, 11
    early, 32
Christian ranks, 159
Christian rationale of ex nihilo, 53
Christian regions in West Africa, 22
Christian religion, 9, 11, 32, 45, 60–61, 96, 137, 160, 163, 170, 173, 181
Christian religion in Western Society, 180
Christian religion set, 64
Christian religion to ethics and morals, 60

Christian representatives, early, 73
Christian revelation, 45, 148
Christians, 14, 44–45, 48–49, 52, 57–58, 73–74, 97, 101–2, 114, 121–22, 129–33, 137, 160, 163–64, 180–82
  conservative, 97
  decades, 129
  devout, 23, 25, 50
  earliest, 153
  early, 14–15, 60, 105, 136
  minor, 51
  moderate, 50
  modern, 98, 125
  new, 131
  passage, 122
  persecuted, 168
Christians call grace, 58
Christian scene, 148
Christian scholars, 147
  great, 145
Christian schools in West Africa, 10
Christians forces, 161
Christian spokesman, 22
Christian student, 31
Christian table, 158
Christian terminology, 67
  early, 37
Christian theism, 13
Christian theologians, 67
  noted early, 14
Christian theology, 16, 18, 49–50, 53, 60, 69–73, 75, 116, 127, 144, 147
Christian thinkers, 67, 176
Christian thinking, 60
Christian thought, 41, 45, 52, 59, 61, 72, 83, 135
  early, 49, 54, 72–73, 120
Christian Understanding of History, 18, 78, 151
Christian village in West Africa, 58
Christian West, 7, 59, 162
Christian world, 100
Christian writings, 45
  produced early, 164
Christ Jesus, 45, 126
Christmas story, 139
Christological and trinitarian dogma, 172
Christological titles, 104
Christology, 162
Christoph Barth, 38
Christoph Keller, 158
chronicled nothing, 139
chronicles, 16, 113
chronology, 112, 141, 154
  delineating, 107
Chrysostom, 65
  John, 18
church, 9, 17, 26–27, 35, 38, 73–74, 113, 124–25, 130–34, 138–39, 141, 148–49, 157–60, 165–68, 173–75
  admired, 45
  ancient, 157, 160, 167
  conservative, 23
  country, 117, 125
  earliest, 131
  early, 27, 38, 73, 84, 91, 111, 138, 149, 153, 167, 177, 181
  elite, 100
  established, 180
  evangelical, 102
  full-time, 119
  great, 131, 154
  historic, 133

incipient, 113
infant, 154
influential, 141
local, 102
planted, 165
small, 125
strong, 163
young, 125, 155
church attendance, 71
church developer, 102
church fathers, 37–38, 52, 64–65
  early, 14, 18–19, 47, 69, 79, 119, 148
  pre-Nicene, 30
church history, 30, 53, 61, 133
church worship, 124
circles
  higher, 168
  inner, 161
  religious, 25, 78
  theological, 25
  university, 28
circulation, 130, 167
  least limited, 153
citizens, 94, 115, 126, 136, 168–69
  proud, 171
citizenship, 107, 115
  enjoyed, 165
city, 82, 115, 125, 142, 148, 167
  the bloody, 21
  capital, 155
  eastern, 177
  great, 141, 176
  new, 155
  old, 115, 155
the city of David, 108
City of God, 169, 171

civilization, 33, 80, 106
  characterized human, 9
  medieval, 171
  modern, 49
civilizations, great, 171
Civitate, 169, 171
claim, 16–17, 27, 37, 43, 45, 53, 57, 74, 106, 129, 136, 157, 162, 164, 176–77
  fundamental, 45
  justifiable, 85
claiming Roman citizenship, 168
clairvoyance, 158
clans, 68, 95, 108
clarion case, 103, 135
class, 24, 92, 158
  educated, 170
  senatorial, 105
  wealthier, 103
classes, upper, 60, 94–95
Classical Greek thought, 37
classical text, 137
classical upbringing, 148
classical world, 19, 105, 155
classic chapters, 174
cleavage, 38, 55, 81, 132, 159
Clement, 73, 148–49, 166, 176
Clement's Christianity, 148
Clifton, 162
climax, 16, 150
close-at-hand, 152
clothes, 14, 53, 140, 154
Clovis, 118
clung, 156
  long, 171
cluster, beautiful, 146
coin, lost, 72, 80
college, 24, 28, 110

College, Baptist, 102
College, Howard, 26
college class, 26
college days, 117
college housemate, 5
colleges, influential, 78
college student, 102
   young, 117
colonial employees, best, 164
colonialism, 163
colonies, gained, 10
colonization, 182
colony, 21, 163
color, 41, 161
Colossians, 167, 179
Columbus, 75
Come unto me, 58
comfort, 100
   emotional, 74
comfortable place, 134
commands, 47, 70, 85, 140, 165
commencement, 19, 142, 182
Commentary, 15, 178
commentators, 153
commission, 156
   team's, 154
commitment, 11, 119, 136, 140
   personal, 98
commoners, 103–4, 106, 110
commonplace, 87, 92
community, 76–77, 88
   believing, 109, 124
   international, 145
   restored Jewish, 93
compass, 150, 161
   human, 75
compatibility, 25
complaining, 96

complementary, 173
completeness, 150, 165
completion, 10, 75
complexity, increasing, 142
complex system, 54
comprehensible pageant, 166
comprehension, 54
   growing, 120
   human, 75
concept, 33–34, 52–53, 57, 60, 64, 73, 75, 95, 98, 113, 116, 119, 143–44, 176–77, 180
   frightful, 58
   lofty, 33
   popular, 144
   potent, 94
   problematical, 40
   superlative, 160
   teleological, 89
   universal, 167
concerted efforts, 33
conciliatory, 157
Confederacy, 24, 125, 132
Confessions, 3, 142
confident, 58, 150
confident expectation, 180
conflict, 24–25, 32, 48, 161
   bitter, 24
   centuries-long, 50
conglomeration, 45
Congregational, 14
Congregational denomination, 163
Congregationalists, 163
congregations, 35, 100, 138, 147, 149, 160, 167
   first, 131
   localized, 167
connection, 65, 97

close, 22
conquered people, 91
conquered Phoenicia, 126
consciousness, 116, 118
   deep, 68, 110
consciousness dawning, 118
consensus, 17, 49, 53
   strong, 159
conservatives, 24, 38
Conservative theology, 118
Constantine, 172
Constantinople, 148
consummate, 137, 143
consummation, 65, 90–91, 112, 174
contact, 170
   direct, 124
contemporaries, 24, 170
contending, 82, 92, 173
content, 7, 69, 85, 110, 149, 167
contention, 23, 132
context, 50, 170
   historical, 149
continent, 21, 96, 99, 107, 122, 137, 174, 180, 182
continent amid, 136
continuance, 77
continuation, 46, 96, 98
continuity, 16, 36
contrast, 43, 53, 58, 63–64, 93, 105, 108, 167, 180
   distinctive, 169
   sharp, 115, 173
   sharpest, 109
   total, 32, 61
   vocal, 169
contrast Gibbon, 170
contribution, 60, 173
   real, 65, 101

contributions, large, 31
contributors, primary, 51
control, 26, 108
controversy, latter, 173
conversion, 155, 162, 164, 168, 171
   religious, 44
   son's, 171
Copernicus, 54
Copleston, Frederick, 19
copy, 145
   complete, 131
Cor, 123
Corinth, 138, 177
Corinthian Church, 136
Corinthian correspondence, 117
Corinthians, 20, 51, 84–85
corner, 153, 162
cornerstone, 7, 54, 61, 105, 112, 162–63, 178
cosmic Christ, 174
cosmic disaster, 40
cosmic drama, 67
cosmological, 120
cosmopolitan act, 70
cosmos, 13, 31, 36–37, 39, 53, 55, 91
Cotton Mather, 25
Council, 30, 38, 53, 69, 120, 149, 172
councils, great, 148, 162, 172
countries, 10, 22, 143, 156
couples, 35, 62, 68, 123, 130, 156
   first, 17
   hidden, 68
   primeval, 47
   young, 69
Covenant, 67

cow, lost, 99
craving, 34
  deep, 47
creation, 7, 9–10, 15–24, 26–28, 30–31, 33–41, 46, 48–57, 59–64, 66–67, 69, 72–78, 80–82, 117–19, 147–49
  dated, 23
  day-by-day, 17, 55
  divine, 7, 13, 19–20, 24, 28
  doctrine of, 75
  earthly, 19, 85
  elevate, 39
  erring, 76
  fallen, 66, 68, 79, 114, 147, 152
  highest, 9, 62
  human, 82
  lost, 99, 147
  lower, 76
  miraculous, 13
  perfect, 57, 63
  praiseworthy, 75
  pristine, 119
  progressive, 74
  restore, 72, 86
  retained, 73
  the, 50
  untainted, 181
creation earth, 41
creation God, 57
creation groaning, 40
creation narratives, 144
creation parallels, 74
creation stories, 31
creative action, 65
creative life, 11
creative word, spoken, 61
creativity, 9

creator, 13, 17, 19, 31, 39, 49, 54, 59, 61, 75, 98
  direct, 53
  nature's, 13
Creator God, 18, 74
creatures, 28
  finite, 55
creedal usage, 38
crept, 158
  revisionism, 151
crestfallen, 170
crests, new, 24
cries, 61
  daily, 61
crimes, 71
  heinous, 117
Critias, 49, 54
critical approach, early, 65
critical methodology, applying, 65
crosses, 114, 116–17
crowds, 98, 121–22
  large, 9
crucifixion, 114–16, 118–19, 126, 140
  coming, 118
  practice of, 114, 116, 126
cruel death, 114
cruel sufferings, 14
crux, 65, 100
Cullman, 120
  Oscar, 101, 107, 120
culmination, 52, 98, 139, 142
cults, 95, 99
culture, 48, 78, 141, 170, 172
  classical, 144
cup, 121, 123
curiosity, 88–89, 122
currents, 92
  difficult, 175

cycles, 180
  unborn, 11
Cyprian, 164, 173
Cyprus, 130, 155
  left, 134

D
Dagomba, 135
damage, 68, 97
Damascus road, 168
Daniel, 108
Danish ship, 97
Dante, 80
Danube, 182
Danube frontiers, 173
Danube Rivers, 169
Dark Continent, 21
darkness, 37, 61, 82
  empty, 16
Darton, 2
Darwinian roots, 99
Darwinism, 24
daughters, 25, 110, 147
David, 93, 109
dawn, 82, 101
Dawson, Christopher, 99
day dawns, 77
day Ghana, 22
deacons, 121
dead matter, 15
Dead Sea Scrolls, 100
death, 57, 73, 76, 90, 105–6, 112, 115–21, 123–24, 126–27, 129, 155, 166
  coming, 123
  dismal, 117
  early, 116
  honorable, 129
  speedy, 126
Decalogue, 42

Decian persecution, 53
decipherment, 31
declension, deep, 64
dedication, 5, 98
Deep affliction, 87
defenders, 25
  strong, 13
defense, 168, 182
defensive wall, famous, 148
defined Israel, 39
degree, 29, 32, 34–35, 38, 47–48, 59, 68, 74–76, 92, 149, 179
  large, 75
  laudatory, 166
Deism, 100, 113, 170
Deists, 139
deity, 13, 16–18, 24, 27, 32, 34–35, 41, 43, 46, 58–61, 63, 75, 77, 87, 89
delineation, 141
delinquency, potential, 176
deliverance, 87–88
deliverance Israel, 105
delving, 143, 151
denial, 42, 44–45
  sustainable, 133
Denny, 119
  James, 119
Denny's book, 119
denominations, 25
  modern religious, 167
departure, 25, 133–34, 142
depict, 71, 143
depiction, 61
  anthropomorphic, 31, 61
  literal, 63
depravity, total, 42, 47, 80
depth, 22, 63, 122, 147, 171
  deepest, 106
  far-reaching, 72

derivatives, 181
Descartes, 89
  Rene, 33, 51
Descartes' assumption, 19
Descartes philosophical, 51
desegregation cases, famous, 70
deserted Paul, 157, 159
design
  central, 65
  intelligent, 13
designation, 131
despised and rejected, 108
destruction, great, 124
deteriorate, 35
Deutero-Isaiah, 37–39, 66, 90, 108, 111, 122–23, 127
  servant poems of, 121, 124
devastation, 40, 82
devotion, 119, 121
devout, 80, 123
Dialogue, 49
Diaspora, 91, 176, 181
dictums, pragmatic, 36
didactic instruction, 152
differences, 31–33, 57, 59, 72, 76, 162, 167, 178
  pronounced, 76
  provoked sharp theological, 178
dilemma, 102, 142
dimensions, 143, 149
  known, 81
Dirac's Universe, 31
direction, 65, 90, 156
disagreement, 159, 175
  fundamental, 156
disappointment, 53
  increasing, 103
  sore, 171

disapproval, 35, 59
disasters, 57
disastrous event, 139
disciples, 16, 96, 106, 111–12, 121–23, 127–29, 132, 138, 140, 145, 151, 161, 168, 178
  first, 113
  original, 129
  original fishermen, 168
discipleship, 140, 142
discipleship Jesus, 143
disciples sang, 141
discipline, long, 76
discoveries, 31–32, 75, 85, 100
  archaeological, 101
  geographical, 96
  human, 76
  new, 96
discrepancies, 63
disfigurement, 59
disobedience, 9, 15, 17, 30–31, 40, 47, 57, 69–71, 83, 86, 98–99
  great, 31
  mankind's, 19
  tragic, 82
disobedient, 70–72
disobedient Adam, 50
disparate audience, 48
Dispersed, 91
disputes, earliest, 129
disruptions, 132
disseminate, 145
dissertations, 29, 145
distance, 22
distinctiveness, 37, 117
distinguished German historian Adolph Harnack, 161

distress, 61
distrust, 157
　increasing, 175
diverseness, unique, 58
diversity, 149
　untold, 136
divine, 34, 47, 54, 59, 61, 67, 83, 89, 97, 152, 180
divine act, 17
divine activity, 9
divine Artificer, 53
divine attributes, 63
divine care, 31
divine direction, 68
divine economy, 28, 61, 89, 174
divine finesse, 158
divine foresightedness, 176
divine goals, 63
divine growth, 160
divine Logos, 106
divine majesty, 74
divine mind, 26
divine perfection, 127
divine plan, 47, 67, 78, 114, 180
divine power, 19
　self-limited, 40
divine process, 31, 78
divine pronouncement, first, 114
divine providence, 86, 135, 164
divine purpose, 11, 13, 86, 89, 92, 119, 170, 176
　local, 78
divine revelation, 17, 42–45, 57–58, 64, 75–76, 83, 85, 88, 93, 95–98, 150, 182
　self-given, 144

divine revelation bespeaks, 75
divine revelation God, 41, 83
divine search, 99
divine transcendence, 17, 41–42, 83
divine truth, 60, 65
divine warrant, 36
divine worship, 124
Diving Being, 52
Divinity Department, 22
divisions, 37, 93, 137, 159, 162–63, 175
　evoked, 97
　historical, 67
divisive factor, 173
Dixie, 24
Docetism, 120
Doctoral dissertations, 93, 133
doctrinal assertions, 149
Doctrinal Expression, 32
doctrinal volumes, 14
doctrine, 16, 27, 38, 61, 70, 75, 78, 172
　accepted, 26
　great, 149
　religious, 23
　signal, 90
document, 153
　early Christian, 153
document Papias, 153
Dodd, 174
dogma, 27, 38, 52–53, 58, 61, 73, 75
　warmest, 100
domain, 76, 150
dominance, long, 107
Donatism, 173
Donatist movement, 173
Donatists, 173

doors, 45, 175
downtown location, 135
drama, general, 68
drama awake, 63
Duke, 98
Duke University, 93
dungeon, 165, 168
duration, 157
  long, 16
  short, 116
dynamics, great, 114

E
early Christian, famous, 14
early church apologists, 168
Early fathers, 166
Early theologians, 67
Early tradition, 130
early tradition Matthew, 138, 141
earth, 21–24, 44, 47–50, 54–55, 58, 61–64, 66–71, 106–7, 118–19, 140, 150–51, 165, 170, 174, 181–82
  new, 11, 77, 119
earth's place, 41
eastern, 162, 174, 181
Eastern and Western Christendom, 173
Eastern and Western churches, 162
eastern Christianity, 153
Eastern Churches, 39, 162
eastern creation accounts, 49
eastern cultures, 91
Eastern European Christianity, 182
Eastern Mediterranean, 91–92
eastern myths, 31

East history, 93
East region, 167
Ebionites, 139, 141
ecclesia, 113
ecclesiastical organizations, 159
ecclesiastical primacy, 141
ecclesiology, 167
eclipse, 139
  total, 68
ecological imbalance, great, 31
ecology, 30, 59
economy, 38, 65–67, 89–91, 95–96
  eternal, 65
  local, 95
economy of God, 18, 79
Eden, 40, 46, 64, 66, 69, 83, 91, 98, 126
Edersheim, Alfred, 64
Edessa, 181
Edgar Young Mullins, 32
Edinburgh, 13
educated eighteenth-century people, 170
education, 135, 165
Edwards, Jonathan, 78
effort, 64, 108–9, 157, 172
  humanity's, 69
  unfaltering, 79
Egypt, 43, 87–88, 91, 104, 110, 141, 146, 155, 157
Egypt for imported grain, 105
Egyptian bondage, 16
Egyptian dynasty, 43
Egyptian Pharaoh, 179
Egyptologists, 43
eighteenth century, 10, 58, 107–8, 142, 170, 180, 182

early, 10
eighteenth century Age, 113
Eighteenth century Deism, 61, 139
eighteenth century England, 180
eighteenth century pales, 180
eighteenth-century philosophies, radical, 34
election, 78, 87–88
elemental core, 35, 59
elevated Jesus, 118
elevated theological position, 118
Elihu Yale, 25
Elijah, 61, 94
elite, 97, 170
Elohim, 16–17, 42, 78, 87
Eloi, 110
elongated events, 164
El Shaddai, 87
Elymas, 155
emanations, 19, 74
embark, 42, 122
embed potential fallacies, 179
embodiment, 116, 155
emergence, 64, 80, 148
eminent philosopher, 49, 53
emotional beauty, 50
emotion Jesus, 128
emotions, 18, 123, 125
Emperor Augustus, 94
Emperor Constantine, 9
Emperor Hadrian, 148
Emperor Julian, 172
emperors, 95–96, 109, 116, 129, 148
  early, 123
  first, 108
emphatic, 65, 82, 166
empire, 94–96, 104–5, 107–9, 114–15, 123, 126, 130, 148, 154–55, 163, 165, 169–72, 176–77, 181
  new, 105
  new all-engulfing, 104
  waning, 171
empirical proof, 58
empirical reasoning, 29
emptiness, 71, 142, 175
encountered Indian mysticism, 60
endowment, highest, 64
endurance, 20, 22
enduring, 114, 132, 170
enduring axioms, 72
enduring fixity, 65
enduring foundation, 162
enduring impact, 181
energy, 39, 143
English history, 163–64
English Methodism, 22, 137
English Methodist mission, 125
English philosopher, 20
English scholar, 104
  earlier, 156
  reputable, 26
English-speaking countries, 163
English speaking evangelicals, 144
English-speaking scholars, 165
English translations, 154
English word, 120
  old, 144
enigmas, 31, 64, 153, 181
  unfathomable, 63
Enoch, 100

enrich Christian faith, 148
entertain Jesus, 129
enthusiasm, 35, 96, 138
  new, 96, 156
entrancing book, 66
enunciation, correct, 88
eons, 74, 166
ephemeral, 9, 150
Ephesian Letter, 80, 166–67
Ephesians, 15, 36, 79, 82, 162, 165–68, 178–81
  attributed, 166
  book of, 20, 69, 80, 164, 167–68, 174, 178
Ephesus, 166–67
Epic History, 105, 155
Epicureans, 37, 61
episodes, 64, 140
  anguishing, 111
  glorious, 169
  prehistorical, 71
epistle buttresses, 179
Epistle of Colossians, 179
Epistle of Ephesians, 168
Epistle of Galatians, 179
epistles, 159, 167, 174–75, 179–80
  great, 179
Epistles, Pauline, 44
epistles Paul, 167
equivocal interpretation, 81
era, 25, 82, 93–94, 100, 102, 107, 116, 132, 146, 153, 157, 169
  contemporary, 129
  contrasting, 169
  equal, 107
  greatest, 172
  late, 105
  long, 60
  medieval, 96
  primitive, 167
  renowned, 169
  transitional, 17
eras vouch, 109
Ere, 171
Ere death, 117
eroticism, extreme, 94
error, 29, 68
erstwhile president, 80
erstwhile seminary president, 117
escape, 71, 110
  narrow, 140
escape anthropomorphism, 55
eschatology, 180
estate, 106
  fallen, 66
Estonia, 132
estrangement, 132, 152, 162
  growing, 103
  political, 98
Eternal God, 11, 18, 85, 149–50
eternal purpose flows, 91
eternity, 127, 170
eternity's resounding words, 58
Ethelbert, King, 162
ethical code, high, 37
ethical hue, new, 146
ethical intent, 146
ethical system, 60
ethical thought, 37
ethics, 60, 106, 133, 160
  choicest, 160
Ethiopia, 121–22
Ethiopian eunuch, 121
euagégelion, 145

Europe, 24, 77, 87, 97, 100, 163–64, 169–70, 174, 181
  central, 87
  famous empire, 105
European circle, 19
European continent, 163, 181
European critical studies, 131
European educational concepts, 60
European history, 29, 105
European missionaries, 21
European Morals, 32
European mother, 20
European mystics, 44
European nations, 163
European paganism, 182
European soil, 174
European vessels, 164
Europe monks-turned-scribes, 145
Eusebius, 138, 158
evaluation, 66
  negative, 134
evanescent, 77, 150
evangelic message, direct, 20
evangelism, 22–23, 127
  international, 163
evangelists, early, 91
evangelizing, 91
Eve, 17, 33, 40, 46–47, 50, 58, 62–64, 66, 68–72, 78, 80, 82, 86, 110, 114
Eve hid, 70
evening, 9, 36
everlasting, 48
Everlasting Father, 95
everlasting thou, 48
everyday observations, common, 110
evidence
clarion, 179
rational, 58
strong, 100, 103, 154
evil, 9, 20, 53, 71, 79, 81–82, 111, 144, 155, 160
  original, 180
evil conscience, 68, 71–72
evil matter, 53
evolution, 36, 50, 174
evolvements, 40
exaltedness, 66
examination, 44
execution, 115–16, 126
executive committee, 135
Exemplified, 137
exercise, 9, 57, 62, 64
exercise unsound, 62
exhilarating, 155
existence, 13, 15, 18, 31, 34, 36–37, 40, 51, 54, 58, 61, 74, 127, 164
existence of God, 18, 33, 51
ex nihilo, 30, 37, 53, 60, 147
Exodus, 43, 88
expansion, 11, 22, 96–97, 157
expectations, early, 166
experience, 35, 41, 44, 46, 59, 79, 82–83, 94, 111, 117–19, 121, 135, 142, 155, 177–78
  author's, 134
  desert, 102
  human, 17
  missionary, 92
experimentation, 29
exploration, 33
explosions, produced, 57
extent Hegel, 89
extent John Mark, 73, 75
eye-catching, 31
eyewitnesses, 151

F
factors weighing, 120
failure, 11
   first-term, 134
   utter, 95
faith, 9–11, 13, 45, 48, 60, 68–69, 72, 97–98, 100, 126, 129, 131–32, 171–73, 175, 181–82
   historical, 55
   monotheist, 93
   new, 177
   non-Christian, 97
   old, 25
   religious, 50
faith's chief, 168
fallacious, 28, 68, 105
fallacious interpretations, 90
fallacious reasoning, 123
fallacy, 95, 99
Fall of Man, 64, 70
familial closeness, 24
familiarity, 43
family, 99, 101, 110, 117, 147
   average Jerusalem, 129
   well-to-do, 126
   widow woman's, 117
family fortune, 147
famine, 43, 99
Fanti, 21, 137
farcical, 30, 147
Far East, 164
far-flung ambition, 176
far-flung dominions, 154
farmer searching, 80
Far-seeing, 151
fascination, 153
   showed deep, 148
   worldwide, 93
fate, 119, 121
   brutal, 120
Fatherhood, 118
father longing, 72
Father of Christian Theology, 53
fathers, 14, 20, 27, 30, 38, 46, 53, 61, 80, 84–86, 110, 115, 129, 132, 146–47
   earliest Christian, 73
   first Christian, 67
   founding, 86
   great, 181
   minor, 69
   our, 24
Faustus, 53, 171
favorites, 44, 165
feather flock, 36
Federal occupation, 24
Feelings Lie Buried, 93
fellowship, 51, 55, 75–76
   desired, 75
fertile soil, 165
Fervent, 24
to fill, 109
finality, 16, 31, 78, 174
   resounding, 15, 29
findings, 26, 46, 61, 100, 142
finest, 64, 160
finest Jewish scholarship, 92
firmament showeth, 27
First Centuries, 37
first century, 73, 75, 84, 107, 113, 116, 131–32, 154, 159, 162, 167
   great, 131
   late, 182
first century Christians, 169
first century Jewish Christians, 175
First Epistle, 157–59

First Isaiah, 95, 105, 144–45
First Principles, 14, 53, 152
  written, 27
first word Jesus, 110
five centuries, 107, 114
  first, 26
  following, 114
fixation, 26, 36, 76
  static, 16
flamboyant days, 22
flaw, 31, 59, 81
  emerging, 59
flee, 71
fleeing, 70–71, 130, 153
flesh, 82, 143, 150
flippancy, frequent, 43
flood, 86, 100
Florida, 51
flourishing, 130
flourishing First Baptist Church, 125
fluctuation, 122
Flynt, Robert, 13
focal point, 105, 120
fold, 100, 175
folk, modern, 81, 140
followers, 13, 53, 104, 109, 127–29, 168
  early, 127
  mellowed, 132, 161
followers Paul, 178
Following World War II, 120, 127
fondness, fading, 63
food, cheapest, 111
force, 160
  blind, 15
  token, 134
foreign centers, 92
foreign environment, 92
foreign mission assignment, 119
Foreign Mission Board, 156–57
foreign rule, 102
  oppressive, 102
foreign soil, 92
forerunner, 145, 169, 176
forgiveness, 123, 160
forlorn people, 58
form
  aspirations, 144
  brutalizing, 115
  diluted, 93
  highest, 15, 30, 34, 43, 64, 100
  lower, 99
  storied, 81
formidable barrier, 164
formidable support, 42
formidable themes Jesus, 112
fortune, 148
  historical, 158
Fosdick, 24
Fosdick's sermons, 24
foundations, solid, 132
founder, 89, 141
founds joys, new, 48
fountainhead, 50
Fourth Gospel, 73, 75, 106, 152
Fox, Lane, 155
fragments, 158
framework, 15, 30, 33, 51, 112, 150
France, 10, 107, 142, 170
Frank, Erich, 54
Franks, 182
  mighty, 118
fraternal alliance, 159

fratricidal Christological controversies, 172
freedom, 9, 15, 27, 30, 40, 62, 64, 81, 89, 165, 177–78, 181
  divinely-ordained, 15
  human, 144
  ordained, 30
  real, 55
  unbridled, 62
  wide-ranging, 40, 62
freedom of choice, 9, 57, 62, 81
freedom of mankind, 15, 144
Freeman, 20–22
  Thomas, 21–23
Freeman's approach, 23
Freeman set, 22
Freeman's legacy, 22
French Revolution, 105, 107, 158
freshman, 23
  brilliant college, 23
Friedrich Heiler, 99
fruit, forbidden, 47, 69–70
fulfillment, 52, 67–68, 95, 101, 108, 117, 127, 143, 152, 154, 179
  long, 85
Fuller, Ellis, 117
fullest biblical exposition, 46
fullness, 11, 40, 44, 47, 109, 146, 150, 152, 165
  complete, 63
function, 137, 163
fundamentalism, 32, 97
fundamentals, 19
futile, 72, 97
futile failure, 172
futility, 92
  religious, 38

G
Galatians, 109, 177, 179
Galilean Springtime, 9, 118
  the, 112
Galilee, 104, 109, 112, 118, 122, 145
Galileo, 29, 49
gamut ranging, 14
gap, 76, 83, 157
Garden, 40, 46, 64, 66, 69, 83, 91, 98, 112, 126, 130, 140–41, 153
gargantuan step, 174
garments, 130
  old, 111
gathered up, 79
genealogy, 110, 130
general revelation saving revelation, 43
generation Christians, first, 151
generations, 23, 49, 54, 59, 67, 71–72, 86–87, 100, 131, 153, 173
  second, 104
Genesis, 13, 16–19, 26–28, 31, 36–37, 39, 41–42, 47–49, 51, 54–55, 63–64, 69–71, 99, 101, 147–48
  chapters of, 23, 61, 64, 85, 100
  interpreted, 68
Genesis account, 18, 33, 148
Genesis account of creation parallels, 74
Genesis creation, 14, 37
Genesis narratives, 38, 81
Genesis story, 69, 99
genre, 42, 150

gentile entrance, 84
Gentiles, 27, 45, 54, 95, 109, 113, 130, 139, 141–42, 174–78, 181
   we turn to the, 177
genuineness, 161
geographical area, 104
geology, 23–24
George Foot Moore, 37
German classical scholar, 158
Germanic tribes, 182
Germanic tribesmen, 182
German prisoner of war, 101
German quell, 153
Germans, 173
German states, 170
German universities, 132
   distinguished, 132
Germany, 10, 65–66, 127, 132–33, 166
Gethsemane, 112, 130, 140–41, 153
Ghana, 10–11, 21–22, 35, 59, 156
Ghanaian teachers, 156
Gibbon, 170
   Edward, 169–70, 176
Gibbon's time, 170
Gifford Lectures, 50
gift, 25, 40, 62
gigantic step, 148
Gilgamesh, 31, 86
Gilgamesh Epic, 100
glass, 11, 146
Glick, Wayne, 161
globe, 23, 33–34, 41, 48, 59, 79–80, 104, 108, 119
glory, 19, 47, 73, 105, 109, 123
   praise earth's, 48

glory of God, 27, 44, 48, 73–74, 98
Gloucester, 14
Glover, 111
Gnostic doctrines, 149
Gnosticism, 17, 74
   refuted, 45
   second-century, 45, 74
Gnostics, 45, 55, 74
Gnostic thesis, 74
goal, 15, 30, 37, 137, 167, 179, 182
   universal political, 177
God, 2–182
   age, 179
   Amos, 152
   angry, 123
   be you reconciled to, 123
   call, 55
   channeling, 13
   disobeyed, 70
   display, 66
   distant, 24
   elucidate, 41, 82
   event, 179
   false, 89
   fear, 71
   finding, 47
   forward, 124
   freedom, 15, 62
   a general action of, 28
   good news, 144
   indefinable, 50
   inferior, 74
   kingdom of, 11, 105, 109, 111–12, 114, 145, 164, 176
   like, 47
   made by, 26
   maintaining, 30
   narrative, 78

past, 44
perfect, 18
portrayed, 31
relentless, 66
seeking, 149, 151
teleological design, 90
thought, 14
transform, 61
unchanging, 100
unknown, 182
witnessed, 170
written by, 99
God/gods, 34
Godhead, 81
God healing, 83
God is love, 59
God likeness, 69
God longing, 82
God of Genesis, 49, 54
God of theologians place, 67
God on mission, 20
God plans, 180
God saw, 55
God scrutinizing, 31, 61
God set, 16
God slain, 90
God supersedes, 77
Goerner, 156
  Cornell, 156
Gold Coast, 10, 21–22, 35, 59, 134–35, 137, 156–57
  the, 10
golden age, 86
  faded, 63
Golden age of Greek philosophy, 49
golden ages, long-forgotten, 80
Golden Stool, 21
Gomer, 94

Good Book, 19
Good Samaritan, 152
gospel, 73, 75, 96–97, 110, 112–13, 120–22, 129, 131, 138–46, 150, 152–53, 158–59, 162–63, 174–75, 180–81
  authentic, 139, 141
  canonical, 131
  earliest, 139
  eponymous, 129
  first, 73, 75
gospel narratives, 96, 123
Gospel of Mark, 112, 130, 133, 139, 143–45, 153, 157–58
Gospel of Mark pictures Christ in action, 143
Gospels convey remnants of ministry, 112
Gospels depict, 9
Gospels point, 124
Gospels portray, 111
gospel writer, 140
gospel writers omit, 141
government, 9, 11, 22, 95, 103–5, 107, 130, 155
  lesser hostile, 90
  sympathetic, 10
governor, 95, 114, 130
grace, 46, 51, 80
Grace Can Restore, 93
grain vessels, 105
Grand Canyon, 69
grandeur
  earlier, 148
  highest, 91
grand preacher, 124
Grand Rapids, 15, 38, 165, 178
grappled face-to-face, 155

grasping, 101, 111, 178
gratitude, expressed, 47
gravitation, 181
Great Britain, 10, 132, 163
great Christians, produced, 164
great rift, 80, 181
  the, 69
Greece, 45, 148
  classical, 52, 148
Greek, 37, 52, 73, 141, 144, 162, 168, 173
Greek and Roman cynics, 175
Greek and Roman worlds, 91
Greek civilization, 16
Greek concept, 36
Greek contribution, 38
Greek culture, 148
Greek language Jesus, 110
Greek logos, 16
Greek name, 115
Greek New Testament, 165
Greek paganism, 37
Greek philosophers, 52–53, 60
  early, 89
Greek philosophy, 31, 45, 48–49, 52, 59, 72–73, 75, 113, 116
  classical, 27, 37, 160
Greek scholar, great, 154
Greek scholars, distinguished, 165
Greek soldiers, determined, 66
Greek text, 154
Greek thought, 16, 20, 72
Greek word euthus, 140
Greek words, 120, 176
  old, 109
Greek world, 20

Gregory, 38, 162, 171
groaning and travailing in pain, 15
ground, 37, 56, 150
  common, 25
  fertile, 91, 149
  higher, 44
  occupied high, 176
grouping, first, 67
groups, 13, 34, 57, 66, 103, 136–37, 144, 162, 176
  conservative Jewish, 139, 141
  eastern, 116
  emerged religious, 107
  final, 104
  fringe, 177
  small, 14
growth, 32, 45, 86, 91, 115
  brilliant, 71
  potential, 40
  rapid, 153
  steady, 176
guests, 130, 135
guilt, 46, 70
guilty, 71, 126
gulf, 23, 83

H
Hadrian, 105, 148, 155
Hale County, 117
half century, 136
  last, 38
Hallel, 141
hallmarks, 137, 148
handiwork, 26–27, 34, 59, 74–75, 147
  bountiful, 9
  happiest segment, 21
  hardened criminal, 115, 126

hardest criminal cases, 115, 126
Harmon, 135
  Ethel, 135
harmony, 29
  renewed, 137
  universal, 177
Harnack, 131–32, 161
Harry Emerson Fosdick, 24
Harvard, 25
harvest, 10, 12
  fields white unto, 180
hath, 85
  fool, 33, 61
to head up, 165
to head up all things in Christ, 165
healing, 38, 111–12, 152
healing process, 25
healings, partial, 25
heartiest welcome, 106
hearts, 17, 33, 39, 48, 61, 68, 71–72, 76, 82, 114, 139, 141–42, 171
  human, 47
heavens, 15, 21, 27, 44, 47–48, 66, 70, 74, 83, 127
  first, 64
  new, 11, 77, 119
heavyweight, 119
Hebraic, 75
Hebraic biblical expression, 27
Hebraic thought, 72
Hebrew apostasy, 90
Hebrew concept, 72
Hebrew exodus, 43
Hebrew language, 41
Hebrew mind, 43
Hebrew people, 152
Hebrew prophet, 85
Hebrews, 15–16, 30, 43–44, 68, 72, 84–86, 99, 101, 130, 138, 141, 146, 149, 153
heeded Paul's message, 91
heedlessness, 59
Hegel, 132
Hegel's philosophical reason, replaced, 132
he has founded it upon the seas, 13
heights, 44, 160
Heilsgeschichte, 66
Heinrich Holtzmann, 145
heirs, 63, 84
hell, 72, 97
Hellenistic Jew, 168
Hellenistic thought, 74
Henri De Lubac, 14, 53
Henry Francis Lyte, 142
Henry IV, 133
heptarchy, 137
  warring, 137
Heresies, 17, 45, 74
heretical, 30, 53, 148, 172
Herod, 110
Herod Antipas, 121
hesitancy, 42, 81
Hierapolis, 138
Higginbotham, Sam, 22, 144
higher power manifesting, 61
high school days, 66
Hillel, 92
Himself, Jesus, 120, 146, 168, 176
Himself, Son, 51
hindrance, equal, 164
hint, first, 114
Hippo, 3, 53, 79, 90, 170
  beloved, 170

His story in history, 144
by his stripes we are healed, 98
historians, 10, 25, 27, 76, 86, 107, 115, 148–49, 151, 158, 161, 164, 169, 173, 176–77
  appellation, 169
  distinguished modern church, 131
  eighteenth-century, 170
  first-rate, 77
  illimitable, 82
  modern, 149
  western, 60, 68, 176
historical act, 119
historical beginning, 152
historical comparisons, 108
historical criticism, 65
historical data, 158
historical dates, assigned, 86
historical developments, 173–74
Historical Enquiry, 99
Historical episodes, 179
historical events, 65, 120, 158
historical finale, 174
historical foreshadows, 176
historical ground, 64, 85, 101
  solid, 82
historical headway, 169
historical incongruity, 175
historical line, distinct, 67
historical monograph, 137
historical occurrences, 27
Historical progress, 150
Historical Pursuit, 2–182
historical situations, 11
historical soil, 180
historical stream, 11
Historical theology, 147, 178

historic civilizations, 170
historic event, 162
historic examples, 160
historicity, 101
historic role, 170
historiography, 65, 76, 161, 169, 176
history, 14–18, 25–30, 65–68, 77–79, 81–82, 84–92, 97–99, 105–9, 111–14, 116–20, 143–44, 150–51, 158, 169–71, 174–81
  acts of, 68, 180
  adopted, 174
  ancient, 66, 169
  centerpiece of, 11, 101
  channels of, 99, 146
  checkered, 43, 89, 93
  continuous, 66
  critical understanding of, 65
  depict, 116
  earth's, 48
  ecclesiastical, 149
  elect, 176
  elevated philosophy of, 174
  entered, 66
  events in, 105, 152
  human, 15, 86, 89, 112, 136, 153
  influential two-volume, 14
  laws of, 177
  lessons of, 169
  linear, 144
  literal, 82
  long, 18, 105, 108
  magisterial, 22
  mainstream of, 106, 112
  modern, 24, 86, 108
  panorama of, 15, 29
  past, 144

period of, 10, 169
philosophy of, 68, 109, 144, 169
　religious, 27, 87
　salvation, 54, 66, 116, 179
　temporal, 107, 118, 166
　theological, 148
　written, 150
History and Psychology of Religion, 99
history God, 143
　human, 67
history is His-story, 82, 144
History of Christian Doctrine, 15
History of European Morals, 32
History of Philosophy, 19
History of Western Philosophy, 14
history searches, 66
holiness, 43, 152
holy, 39, 167
holy ground, 87
Holy Roman Emperor of Germany, 133
Holy Scripture, 15
Holy Spirit, 101, 111, 154, 167
home, 20, 71, 94, 97, 99, 106, 129–30, 140–41, 147, 157, 163
　established new, 91
　good, 147
　left, 110, 147
　mother's, 140
　real, 92
homeland, 91–92, 101, 163
Homer, 16, 73, 105–6, 155
homilies stemming, 45
Hort, 145, 178

Hosea, 88, 94, 105, 144, 152
Hostel, Baptist, 134
hostility, 9, 96
　growing, 102, 121
　increasing, 122
　vehement, 38
hours, 57, 98, 117, 126, 136
　darkest, 108
　last, 124
　loafing, 117
hours Jesus, 126
house, 111–12, 139, 175
　hired, 165, 168
human activity displeasing, 86
human approach, 68
human beings, 29, 34–35, 44, 59, 63, 68, 89, 114, 150, 158
human breast, 109
human delays, 89
human epochs, 170
human evil, 152
human expression, 41
human frailty, 76
human habitation, 41
Human hands, 48
human inclination, 66
human intellect, 62
humanitarian approach, 152
humanity, 33, 36, 40, 42, 45–47, 58, 62–64, 68, 70, 75–76, 82–84, 87, 91, 100–101, 180–81
humanity's centrality, 36
humanity's violation, 62
humankind, 30, 43, 47, 62, 64, 69, 72, 76, 178
human life, 22, 41
human mind, 13, 62, 111, 135
human nostalgia, 86
human nostalgic, 63

humans, 9, 58, 62–63, 88
  endowed, 62
human soul searches, 72
human thought, 20, 54–55, 80, 122
human unproductiveness, 69
human world, 57
hung, 116–17
hunger, 32–33, 46
Hunter, 153–54
hurt, 95–96, 126
Huskisson, 98
  William, 98
Hyksos, 43
hymn, 141–42
  beloved, 58, 118, 135
  old evangelical, 44
hymn Mark, 141
hymns
  old, 93, 100–101
  stately, 100

I
i am the bread of life, 19
i can never sleep on that, 117
identification, 41, 83
idolatry, 69, 92–93
ignominy, total, 123
II Corinthians, 136
II Timothy, 137
ill-fated Bar Cochba uprising, 139, 142
illimitable value, 93
illustrious, 113
image, 15, 36, 46–47, 68, 76, 100, 143
imagination, 63, 107, 142
immanence, 41, 83
immanent, 41, 83, 101
Immanuel Kant, 16, 36

immediately or straightway, 140
impassable abyss, 72
impeccable housekeeper, 117
imperfection, 80
imperial Rome, 122
implanted thesis, 47
implication, 32, 145
imported grain, 105
impossibility, 61
impregnable thesis, 33
imprisonment, final, 168
In, James I., 167
inauguration, 87, 154, 165, 181
Incarnate God, 122
incarnation, 11, 19–20, 58, 73, 112, 120, 122, 144, 170
incarnational, 92
inchoate, 16, 172
inchoate stage, 149
incident, 23, 153
incompleteness, 84
incongruous, 63
incorporation, 149
indebtedness, 65
independence, 10, 22, 156
India, 14, 22, 60, 97, 144, 163–64, 177, 181–82
  early, 69
Indian, 29
indictments, general, 42
indigenous churches, 157
  strong, 163
indigenous instinct, 80
indigenous people, 134, 156
indigenous population, 157
indisputable doggedness, 62
individuals, 133, 138, 144, 159
  produced great, 32

industrial errors, 57
industrial revolution, 142
  eighteenth-century, 88
industrial world, 57
inevitability, 81
infancy material, 110
infinity, 66, 69
influence
  declining Jewish, 142
  intimate, 140
  potent, 14
  spiritual, 171
  stabilizing, 54
influenced Paul, 177
information storage, 2
ingredient, vital, 64
inhabitants, 168
  total, 169
iniquities, 121
innate idea, 51
innate propensities, 150
innumerable number, 74
inquisitive, 89
inquisitive minds, 28
inscrutable ways, 64
insistence, 31, 34, 37, 81
institution, 25, 156–57
  excellent, 163
  recognized, 26
  religious, 71
  theological, 25
intellectuals, 149
intensity, 69, 157
intermeshing, 103
international businessman, 94
internecine wars, 104
  bloody, 169
interpreted Paul, 15
interpreters, 45, 138, 159, 177
interpretive comebacks, 82

Intervarsity Press, 152
intervention, 109
interwoven, 78
intimidation, experienced, 24
introduction, 48, 54, 84, 86, 106, 181
  book's, 99
  limited, 145
  long, 178
introduction Mark, 145
invasions, 79, 108
  continuous, 66
  experienced, 173
invective charges, 155
invincible tool, 66
invitation, 68, 84
  global, 71
Iran, 81
Irenaeus, 17, 27, 45, 47, 69, 72–74, 139, 166
  better-known, 138
  surpassed, 47
Irenaeus thought, 72
Isaac, 86–87
Isaiah, 3, 37, 39, 43, 66, 85, 88, 95–96, 98, 121, 144–45, 152
Isis, 99, 121–22
Islam, 13, 89, 164, 173
  nationalistic, 114
Islamic fundamentalism, 76
island, 130, 137, 155–56, 163
island of Britain, 154, 162, 164, 172
island of Cyprus, 130, 155
Israel, 16, 42–43, 78, 81, 86–89, 91, 93–96, 98, 102, 106, 108–9, 120, 122, 124, 175–76
Israelite population, 91
Israelites, 87–88, 93, 103, 115
Israelite society, 93

Israel's bondage in Egypt, 88
Israel's enemies, 123
Israel's exodus, 146
Israel's faith, 108, 146
Israel's greatness, 88
Israel's history, 102, 146
Israel's Messiah, 102
Israel's pastoral prophets, 108
Israel split, 94
Israel's relations, 179
Issues Involved, 13
Italian states, 132
Italy, 10, 182
itineraries, 105
   brisk, 159
it is finished, 9, 112, 127
i was there, 153

J
Jacob, 86–87
James, 22, 110, 138, 180
James Weldon Johnson, 50, 76
Japan, 164
   belligerent, 81
jealousy, 49, 54
Jefferson, Thomas, 113, 139
Jeremiah, 127
Jerome, 52
Jerusalem, 73, 92–93, 102–4, 110, 112, 123, 125, 129, 131, 139–41, 156–57
   destruction of, 73, 91, 141
   entered, 124
   the fall of, 72–73, 75
   temple in, 43, 120
Jerusalem and eastern Christianity, 153
Jerusalem Church, 130, 154
Jerusalem temple, 85

Jesus, 9, 11–12, 19–20, 43–45, 71–72, 78–79, 81–83, 90, 92–96, 100–127, 129–33, 140–43, 145–47, 150–53, 160–62
Jesus' arrest, 130, 153
   witnessed, 129
Jesus' birth, 104, 109
Jesus' day, 43, 92
Jesus' death, 115–17, 127
Jesus' disciples, 177
Jesus' disciples split, 181
Jesus' employment of nature, 40
Jesus' focus, 123
Jesus' history, 110
Jesus hung, 126
Jesus' insistence, 180
Jesus' life, 125, 127
Jesus' life in Jerusalem, 140
Jesus' life Mark, 140
Jesus' life on earth in Jerusalem, 140
Jesus' message, 107
Jesus' mind, 103
Jesus' ministry, 101
Jesus' mission, 118
Jesus' preaching, 145
Jesus' work, 130
Jewish, 9, 27, 93, 110, 113, 174–75
   young, 125
Jewish Christianity set, 139
Jewish Christians, 113
Jewish compatriots, 174
Jewish crowd, 114
Jewish culture, 98
Jewish-dominated Christianity, 142
Jewish expectations, 95
Jewish history, 121

Jewish indifference, 175
Jewish life, 141
Jewish line, 110
Jewish males, 92
Jewish people, 43, 110, 130, 146, 175
Jewish Sanhedrin, 162
Jewish Scriptures, 121, 141
Jewish sect, 141
Jewish stamp, 73, 75
Jewish temple, 93
  first, 92
Jews, 43, 91–93, 97–98, 122, 174–75, 177–78, 181
  captive, 91
Job, 46–47, 74, 81, 181
John, 16, 31–32, 36, 61, 80, 84, 106, 109, 111–12, 120–21, 125, 138, 141, 145, 180
John Henry Newman, 135
John Mark's day, 145
John Mark set, 143
John sets, 16
John's Gospel, 16
Jonah, 71
Joseph, 91
Joseph Mary Plunkett, 67
Joses, 110
Joshua, 115
journeys, 59
  making, 177
joy, 44, 85
Judah, 93, 95, 108
Judah centuries, 91
Judaic, 60
Judaic Christian writings, 45
Judaic place, 110
Judaic thought, 73

Judaism, 45, 73, 75, 87, 89, 92, 94, 122–23, 129, 139, 141, 146, 168, 174, 176
  centuries-old, 175
Judaism set, 139
Judas, 110
Judas Iscariot, 124
Judea, 92
Judeans, 13
Judean wilderness Jesus, 111
Judeo-Christian God, 13
Judges, 93
judgment, 23, 152, 174
  classical, 30
  ludicrous, 179
  value, 134
juju, 57–58
justice, 152, 160
justification, 172
Justin, 60

K
kairos, 101, 145
keen, 10, 141
keen minds, 90
keeper, humble, 94
Kelley, Beth, 5
Kenneth Scott Latourette, 22, 97
Kenny A Brief History, 14
Kent, 162
Kentucky, 62, 117, 147
kerygma, 127, 131
Kindle, 13, 26, 28, 31, 39, 47, 50, 64
king, 20, 28
  early Frankish, 118
kingdoms, 11–12, 20, 79, 93, 105, 109, 112, 117, 145, 151, 180

King James Version, 23, 28
kinship, 151, 154
Kletz, Trevor, 57
kneading dough, 111
knowledge, 10, 44, 58, 100, 111, 127, 157, 182
  author's, 47
  creature's, 20
  human, 77
  internal, 83
  limited, 171
  writer's, 133
known Jesus, 129
Koiné Greek, 110, 145
Kumasi, 21–22, 35, 59, 156
Kwame Nkrumah, 22

L
labor, 32, 61, 71–72, 163
  manual, 111
labyrinthine affairs, 142
lad, 80, 125
  young, 126
laden, 71
  heavy, 71–72
lady visitor, 124
Lagos, 57, 125, 134–35
lama sabachthani, 110
Lamb, 90
landmarks, great, 60
lands, 11, 21, 86–87, 126, 145, 156
  native, 78
landscape, long-running, 136
language, 16, 41, 135, 159
  anthropomorphic, 55
  common, 145
  crude, 34
  respected Christian, 173
language groups, 34

language Jesus, 110
late Herbert Butterfield, 77
Latin, making, 173
Latin texts, 52
law, 81, 110, 130
leaders, 65, 156, 161, 181
  apostolic, 132
  noted military, 21
  religious, 102–3, 121, 160
Lead kindly Light, 135
lectures, 13, 26, 104, 115, 158
lecturing, public, 26
Lee, Desmond, 49, 54
left Paul, 157, 159, 177
legacy, 36, 74, 94
  handed-down, 131
legalization, 9
legitimate written historical account, first, 152
Leibnitz, 89
Leicester, 166
lending support, 155
Leopold, 86
Leslie William Barnard, 60
letter, 49, 54–55, 67, 134–35, 166–67, 175, 178
  circular, 167
  generalized, 167
  governor's, 165
letters
  earlier, 166–67
  written, 167
Lewisport Baptist Church, 147
liberal audiences, 26
liberals, 38, 118
  old, 118
  older, 118
life, 9–11, 27–28, 39–41, 51, 94–95, 102–4, 109–12, 120–

21, 123–24, 135–37, 141–42, 147–48, 152–53, 160, 171–73
  earlier, 138
  gentile, 46
  real, 142
  sexual, 148
life and ministry, 120, 145
life Augustine, 53
life's hill, climbed, 111
life's hills, 110
life work, great, 132
lifting words, 18
Lightfoot, 145, 166–67, 178
likelihood, 82, 103
likeness, 44, 46, 51, 68, 75
  verbal, 167
linger, 90, 149
lingua franca, 168
link
  long, 171
  perfect, 73
literal interpretation, 64
literalists, 79
literary feature, 152
Livingstone, David, 33, 142
local events, 78
local interest, 68
Loci Praecipus Theologici, 27–28
lodging place, 121
lodgings, earliest, 172
logia, 153, 176
logo, standard, 28
logos, 16, 36, 38, 45, 73, 75, 106, 149
London, 18–19, 22, 41–42, 49, 53–54, 57, 60, 65, 78, 80, 83, 87, 97, 104, 167
long-dedicated line, 43
long-established date, 23

Long experience, 97
longings, 68–69, 82, 143
  deep, 109
  deepest, 47
  eternal, 152
  implanted, 83
  innate, 151
  modern, 70
  obliterate humanity's, 69
  rooted, 151
Longman & Todd Ltd, 2
long purpose, 66, 86
  eternal, 123
long rule Jesus, 95
long sentence, single, 178
longtime friend, 155
Lord, 3, 10–12, 44, 51, 56, 66, 70, 117, 121, 123–24, 142, 160, 180
Lord God, 94
Lordship, eternal, 119
Louisiana, 10
Louisville, 62, 117
love
  agape, 58
  chesed, 39, 152, 174
  curiosity seekers, 131
  eternal, 82
love kindness, 160
love mothers, 147
lowly-born Jesus, 150
lucrative agreements, 182
Luke, 79–80, 96, 110, 113, 123, 125, 129–30, 138–39, 141, 146, 152
Luke convey, 110
Luke's Gospel, 125, 146
Luther, Martin, 106, 160
Luther's associates, 27
Luther's break, following, 27

Lyons, 72–73
Lyte, 142

M
Macduff, 151
Mackay, 80
  John A., 69, 80
  young, 80
magnetic field, 41
magnetic ministry John, 111
magnus opus, 65
Mainline Christian theology, 144
Maitland, 99
majestic, 33, 48, 51
majesty, 18, 73
  unsurpassable, 39
Maker, 35, 62
making Jesus, 120
malfeasance, 65
Manchester, 98
Mani, 53
Manichaeism, 53, 171
manifest, 13, 101, 150, 179
manifestation, 54
manifesting, 31
mankind, 14–15, 17, 19, 21, 46–48, 51, 57, 83, 85, 87, 100–101, 143–44, 147, 149, 151
  endowed, 143
  fallen, 20, 99
Mankind's error, 68
Manson, 153
the Man upstairs, 41, 98
march, 71, 114, 146
  onward, 170
Marching, 66
march questing, long, 66
Marcion, 166
Marduk, 39

Mark, 110, 112, 130, 133–34, 136–41, 143–46, 152–60
  followed, 140
  forgiving, 157
  John, 105, 129–32, 134–36, 138, 140–41, 150, 153–54, 156–57, 159, 177
  rejected, 139, 141
  tradition credits, 141
  young, 155
Mark approaches, 152
Mark pictures Christ, 143
Mark's departure, 157
Mark's dispute, 133
Mark's Gospel, 129, 133, 145, 159
Mark's itinerary, 157
Mark's linen cloth, 153
Mark's priority, 158
Mark's purpose, 140
Mark's responsibilities, 154
Mark's script, 152
Mark's time, 145
Mark's uniqueness, 138
Mark's youth, 143
Marshall, Howard, 152
Mars Hill, 182
martyr, 14, 53, 73
Martyr, Justin, 60, 67, 73, 168
martyr, second century Christian, 60
martyrdom, 53
  brutal, 73
  instant, 53
martyrs, distinguished, 164
mass, 14, 175
mass conversions, 97
master, 45, 107
masterpiece, 36
master's thesis, 133

Master Teacher, 153
Material Reality, 31
Mathews, 20
Matthew, 41, 49, 53–54, 71–72, 83, 110, 113, 118, 123, 129–30, 138–41, 152–53, 175
Matthew's hefty penchant, 139, 141
Matthews work, 65
maturation, 86, 109
Mature human souls, 151
maturity, 23, 88, 151
  spiritual, 80
McDuff, 63
meandering, 17, 86, 178
measure Ghana, 10
measuring rod, common, 107
medical facilities, 163
medieval thought, 50
medieval world, 29
Mediterranean, 137, 162
Mediterranean Christianity, 73
Mediterranean churches, 16
Mediterranean lands, 114
Mediterranean region, 116
Mediterranean thought, 52
Melanchthon, 27–28
  following, 28
  Philip, 27–28
Melanchthon's opening words, 28
members, 132, 147
memory, 107, 117, 125, 138, 148
Memphis, 35
Memphis church, 35
mercenaries, 182
mercenary armies, 173, 182
merit, 69

real, 31
Mesopotamia, 68, 86, 101
Messiah, 64, 73, 102, 105–6, 108, 111, 113, 117, 122–23
  promised, 107, 123
Messiah's birth, 73
metal roof, 35
method, critical, 65
Methodist, 25
Methodist church, conservative, 25
metropolis, great, 166
Micah, 88, 94–95, 105, 108, 144, 160
Middle Ages, 44, 97, 162, 170
  late, 164
Mighty God, 95
mighty universe, 15
Milan, 130, 171
military campaign, 103
millennia, 15, 68, 71, 85, 114, 129, 136, 171
millennium, 45, 66, 93, 102, 107, 134
  first, 163
  half, 107
Milton, 63, 80
  John, 63, 181
minds obtuse, 113
mingle, 35, 59
ministers, 24, 134, 137
  consecrated, 119
  young, 117
ministry, 16, 24, 90, 92–93, 102, 105, 109–13, 120–25, 140, 145, 154–55, 174, 180
  earlier, 112
  early, 118
  earthly, 9, 102
  eastern, 138

historic, 104
historical, 95
localized, 112
public, 109
ministry Jesus, 111, 120
Minns, Dennis, 47
minority, 109, 168
  small, 169
misapprehension, real, 31
miscalculation, 66
misdemeanor, 64
Miss Ethel Harmon, 135
mission, 102, 110, 112, 118, 121–22, 134, 136, 138, 152, 154, 162, 164, 168, 174
  clarified, 119
  earthly, 90
  educational, 156
  popular, 122
  self-giving, 124
  soteriological, 104
missionaries, 5, 11, 20, 22, 105, 130, 134–35, 155–57, 163
  arrived, 135
  consult, 157
  distinguished English, 22
  earlier, 20
  early American, 163
  effective, 154
  esteemed, 144
  experienced, 134
  first term, 135
  longest-surviving, 21
  pioneering, 33, 155
  sending, 101
  senior, 157
  strong-minded, 156
  transformation Methodist, 22
  white, 21
missionary career, 134
missionary connections, 33
missionary denomination, great, 163
missionary itineraries, 168
  great, 174
missionary itinerary, first, 130
missionary journey
  first, 136, 156, 159, 177
  second, 136
missionary journeys, 175
missionary life, 21
missionary lore, 46
missionary movement, 20
  modern, 97, 163
missionary Thomas Birch Freeman, 20
missionary tour, 134
  first, 131, 154
missionary venture, 137
mission Board, 119
mission enterprise, 33
mission goal, 157
mission house, 135
mission meetings, 156
mission's itinerary, 155
mission team, 133, 155
mission tour, 155
  second, 159
mission work, 23, 125
  foreign, 21
missteps, 17, 78
misunderstood, 178
mixture Hebrew background, 148
mode, new, 133
Modern evidence, 73
Modern Ghana of West Africa, 137

Modern historiography dates, 86
modernity, 33–34, 50, 62, 64, 89, 106
Modern Science, 26
Modern students, 65
Modern writers, 177
Mohammedans, 13
momentous steps, 181
monasteries, great, 145
money, 35, 94, 146, 156
Monica, 79, 171
Montanism, 173
moral effect, 29
moral injunctions, 169
morals, 29, 32, 60
  old, 94
mortal humanity, 122
mortal life, 9
Mosaic Law, 97
Moses, 42–43, 64, 87–89, 130
mother, 53, 79, 110, 117, 129, 140, 171
Mother Harden, 125
mother hid, 14
Mount, 113, 139, 153
mountain peaks, great, 43
mountains, 48, 125
Mount of Olives, 141
movement, 29, 68, 105, 139, 143, 175
  new, 175
  prophetic, 94
Mt, 61, 93
mud ovens, 111
Mullins, 32
multiplicity, 74
multitudinous ways, 84
mundane, 27, 103
musing, 32, 57, 125, 145

Muslims, 87
my Father works, 31
my kingdom is not of this world, 103, 176
mysteries, 57, 62, 64, 71, 78, 90
  deepest, 76
  esoteric, 49
  greatest, 147
  multitudinous, 64
mysterious ways, 95
mystical interpretation, 152
mythical act, 126
mythology, 31, 82
not my will but thine, 124

N
NAACP, 51, 76
nadir, 156, 180
name Ephesus, 166
Name Jesus, 7, 104, 115
name kerygma, 127
names, 16, 22, 25, 30, 34, 42–44, 46, 87–88, 104, 110, 115, 137, 141–43, 153, 155–57
  common, 87
  new, 87
  older, 87
  recognizable, 86
  renowned, 124
name Yahweh, 42, 87
Napoleon, 90
narrative display, 55
narratives, 33, 63
  beloved, 162
  historical, 180
  written, 151
Nashville, 154
National Council, 2
national department, 135

national exams, 135
nationalistic character, strong, 123
national milieu, 124
nations, 3, 78, 85, 87, 94, 96, 98, 102, 122, 127, 136–37
native Egyptians, 43
natives, 21, 134
natural disaster, large, 40
Natural growth, 81
Natural inquisitiveness, 88
natural religion, 17, 55, 68–69, 76, 80, 149, 151
  global, 69
natural world, 40
nature, 17–20, 35–36, 40–44, 46, 54–55, 59, 62, 88, 109, 111, 113, 144, 146, 150, 152
  divine, 54
  harmonious, 26
  invisible, 46
  personal, 55
  spiritual, 99
nature religions, 48, 76
naval Battle, 104
Nazarene, 118
Nazareth, 19–20, 43–45, 58, 78–79, 85–86, 90, 100–102, 105–8, 110–11, 113–14, 116–19, 122, 142–43, 145–46, 150
Nazareth devout Christians, 119
Nazareth God, 45, 150
Nazareth hung, 83
nearer, 49, 54, 59
necessity, 35, 39, 59, 72, 75, 97–98, 111, 160
  absolute, 57
  complete, 57
negotiations, 156

neighbors, 111
  local, 68
Neo-Platonism, 49, 54, 89
Nero, 115–16, 129
  licena religio, 129
Nero's blaming, 129
Nero's reign, 116
Newcomers, 113
new critical methods, adopted, 65
New England, 78
new era, 27
  emerging, 169
New Jersey, 126, 162
New Jerusalem Bible, 2, 45, 47–48, 61
new outlets, followed, 96
New Testament, 15–16, 40, 43–44, 51–52, 71, 73–74, 79, 81, 118–19, 131–32, 136, 138–40, 153–55, 159, 166
New Testament Book of Ephesians, 36
New Testament circles, 159
New Testament Gospels, 7, 129
New Testament Paul, 127
New Testament scholar, popular, 70
New Testament scholars, 102, 112, 131, 133–34, 143, 153, 159, 174
New Testament scholarship, 118, 131, 139, 141
New Testament set, 91
New Testament studies, 130
New Testament Theology, 16, 119–20, 152
New Testament writings, 104, 119

earliest, 177
Newton, 49
John, 58, 118
Newton's Principia, 49
new world picture, 29
New York, 19–20, 24, 26, 31–32, 60, 97, 111, 120, 161, 170
Nicaea, 30, 38, 53, 69, 120, 148–49, 162, 172
Nicene Christianity, 120
Nicene faith, 20
niche, 27, 30, 103, 135
Nigeria, 10, 57, 82, 125, 134, 156
Nigerian Baptist Convention meeting, 106
Nigerian mission, 134
Nigerians, 134–35, 156–57
Nigerian work, 156
Nigerian Yoruba, 134
nights, 70, 126
Nineveh, 71
NJB, 2, 108
Noah, 86, 100, 148
Noah's salvation, 100
non-biblical, first, 138
non-Christian population, 76
non-existent material, 53
non-Jewish, earliest, 122
non-nurturing, 160
nonsensical, 15, 30
non-writers, 94
North Africa, 164, 173
North African Christianity, 164, 173
North African culture, 173
North America, 24, 54, 127, 163, 181
Northern blockade, 125
Northern branches, 25
Northern congregations, 25
northern England, 25
Northern Kingdom, 93–94
North Korea, 81
Northwestern State University in Louisiana, 10
Norwegian freighter, 134
noted second century heretic, 166
nothing docetic, 120
nothingness, 72
not-so-distant, 33
novices, 53, 158
now-weakened remnant, 93
nuclear forces, 90
nuclear weapons, 81
nullify, 69, 176
Nyssa, 38

O
objectives Jesus, 33
obliterate, 27, 50, 56, 80, 100
obliterating, 15
obliteration, 50
  total, 69
O'Brien, Peter, 166
obscure, 104, 142
obscurity, humble, 108
observance, close, 111
observation, 40, 71, 82, 134, 153
  on-the-field, 156
observation obscure, 169
observer, close, 141
observers, produced, 29
occasion, 87, 98, 115–16, 120, 124–25, 129–30, 137
occupation, decade-long, 132
oceans, 36, 59, 67
Octavian, 104–5, 108

Octavian's refashioning, 104
Octavian's reign, 108
office, 23, 65, 125
oftentimes, 21, 180
oftentimes discordant, 57
not of this world, 109
Older commentators, 114
Older theologians, 39, 68, 101, 114
Older theologies, 76
Old Testament, 16–17, 31–33, 38–39, 41–43, 51–52, 71–72, 85–86, 88–91, 96, 98, 100–101, 138–39, 141, 179, 181–82
Old Testament Book of Job, 47
Old Testament revelation sprang, 74
Old Testament scholars, 86
Old Testament Scripture, 127
Old Testament theology, 66
Old Testament writings portray, 38
Old Time Religion, 24
Olives, 141
Omega, 11
omens, 122
omnipresence, 81
oneness, 79, 93
opening page, 23
opening sentence, long, 174
opening words, 16–17, 55
opposition, 53, 102, 107, 173
Orient, 48, 163
Origen, 14–18, 27, 30, 37, 52–53, 73–74, 148–49, 166, 172, 176–77
Origen on First Principles, 14, 53

Origen's death, following, 30
Origen's fame, 30
Origen's noteworthiness, 30
Origen's writings, 172
origin, 9, 17–18, 26, 47–48, 53, 55, 59, 66, 71, 81, 108, 150, 153
orthodox religious beliefs, old, 25
Oswald Spengler, 177
otherness, 66, 98
outlook, 166
  apocalyptic, 91
out of nothing, 28
overarching clarity, 175
overlook, 86, 124
over-towering peak, 63
Owensboro, 147
Oxford, 14, 28, 54, 99, 104–5, 115, 149

P
Padua, 29
pagan atmosphere, 96
pagan conceptualizations, 35, 59
pagan customs, 23
pagan faiths, 21, 94
paganism, 21–22, 35, 52, 58–59, 82, 93–95, 97, 105, 108, 172, 182
  classical, 172
  least advanced, 29
  old traditional, 60
  restore, 105, 171–72
  sacrificial animals, 96
  worldwide, 123
pagan priest, 57
pagans, 21, 46, 57–58, 95, 145
pagan shrine, 35, 59

pagan terminology, 55
pagan village, 21
Page Kelley, 5
pain, often-excruciating, 116
Palestine, 86, 92, 112, 114, 122, 126, 160, 168
Palestinian Jewish character, 173
Pamphylia, 155–56
panorama, 53, 66, 79
   eternal, 166
   short-sighted, 150
panoramic, 164
   rich, 84
Pantaneus, 60, 177
panteth, 34, 68
   hart, 34, 68
pantheism, 18–19, 41, 53, 83
Pantheism's assertion, 75
papacy, 181–82
Paphos, 130, 155
   new, 155
Papias, 138, 153, 158
   information, 138
parables, 72, 110–11, 146, 152
   beloved, 139
   catchy, 72
paradox, 109
   life's strangest, 47
parchment, 145
parent, wise, 174
parents, 115, 125
   adopted, 106
Paris, 28, 93
parlance, 14, 70
   pictorial, 144
   religious, 23, 25
   theological, 90
Parson's Porch Books, 2
parties, 98, 136, 138

partner, 154
   equal, 130
partnership, 159
passages, 88, 113, 121–22, 124, 178
   famous Christological, 106
   magnificent, 40
   precise, 121
pass ere, 107
passing flux, 42, 84
Passovers, 112, 121
pastors, 35, 102, 119, 125, 135
   rural, 106
path, 71, 82, 89–90, 160
   long, 148
pathways, 67, 120
patriarchs, 86–87, 148, 176
Patristic Thought, 65
Patristic writings, 73
Paul, 46, 54, 73, 75, 92, 97, 123, 126, 129, 131–38, 149, 154–57, 159–61, 165–68, 174–80
Pauline, 149, 165
Pauline authorship, 165–66
Pauline terminology, 97
Pauline writings, 167
Paul's admonition, 45
Paul's character, 138
Paul's conclave, 138
Paul's faith, 175
Paul's father, 126
Paul's fellow Christian and apostle, 115
Paul's foresightedness, 178
Paul's lifetime, 169
Paul's mind, 179
Paul's roots, 176
Pax Romana, 108, 169, 171

peace, 44, 58, 95, 108, 136, 169, 171
peasant folk, 106
peasant folk searching, 139
peasant people, rural, 110
peasant revolts, 106
peasant stock, 105
peasant woman searching, 146
pedigree, 73
  long, 25
peer, 20, 111
Pelagian controversy, 62
Pelagius, 62
penetration, 173
Pennsylvania, 71
Pentateuch, 33
Pentecost, 100, 113, 153–54
  following, 96, 181
  not-so-long-ago, 122
people attribute, 146
Perea, 112
perfection, 9, 62, 78, 80
  race's, 47
Perga, 155–56, 159
Perga tension, 134
perhaps i, 124
perilous days, 108
periodization, 28, 67, 158
permission, 2, 35, 93, 114
perpetuation, 25
persecutions, 114, 129, 172
  endured bitter, 73
  escaped, 123
  ferocious, 85
  open, 129
perseverance, 85
Persia, 107, 181
Persian satrapies, 176
persistence, 18

person, 19, 100, 106, 112, 119, 128, 150–52, 154
  average, 111
  crucified, 116
  famous, 129
  religious, 140
personal connections, 140
personal decision, 144
personal feud, 157
personality, 66, 138
personal operation, 17, 55
personal references, 167
perspective, 53, 180–81
  clairvoyant, 91
  ethical, 88
  historical, 144
  unique, 10
  wide-ranging, 165
persuasion, 50, 92
persuasiveness, 138
Peter, 73, 75, 127, 129, 131–33, 138, 157–59, 161, 180
  Simon, 115
Peter's interpreter, 159
Peter's place, 129
petty state, 93
pharaoh, 42–43
Pharisees, 103, 121–22, 160, 168
phases, 180
  new emerging, 174
phenomena, 29, 142
Philadelphia, 32, 55, 120, 153, 157
Philip, 121, 138
Philippi, 45
Philippians, 45, 167
Philippines, 164
philosophers, 16, 36, 41, 55, 65, 82, 89, 147, 176

finest, 118
great classical, 60
renowned, 52
philosophes, 170
Philosophical Understanding and Religious Truth, 54
philosophy, 19, 29, 52, 60, 69, 73, 171, 175–76
  early modern, 19
  false, 18
  moral, 31
  new, 174
Phoenicians, 115–16
Phoenician states, 107
phoenix bird, 29
Photius, 148
photocopying, 2
phrases, 27, 110
  famous, 28
Phrygia, 177
Picts, 173
pictured Jesus, 120
Pictures, 40, 157, 177
Pilate, 114, 176
pilgrimage, 19, 160
piling, fundamental, 144
pinnacle, 37, 124
  historical, 146
  supreme, 44
pioneer, 7, 21, 65, 85, 129
  excellent, 134
  first century Church, 175
Pioneer Christian, 114
pioneer English New Testament scholar, great, 166
pioneer historians, 43, 65
Pioneering anthropologists, 99
pioneering ventures, 181
pioneer missionaries, 23, 48

modern, 96, 98
pioneer scholars, great, 178
pivotal, 92, 155
pivotal point, 91
placate, 24, 123
placating, 57, 114
plagued humanity, 72
plan, 36, 47, 54, 63, 66, 80, 102–3, 127, 181
  college, 102
  eternal, 114, 127
  original, 134, 156
  preconceived, 135
plank, foundational, 80
planks, primary, 88
plant, 44, 95, 163, 180
planting, 91, 96, 165, 181
platform, 53, 106
Plato, 49, 53–54, 80, 89
  primary purpose of, 49, 53
  underscored, 116
Platonic, 60
Platonic thought, 49, 54
Platonist, 60
Plato's philosophy, 49, 54
Plato's Timaeus, 49, 54
plausibility, 137
Plenteous, 153
pleroma, 47, 86, 88, 152
Pliny, 165
Plotinus, 49, 54, 73, 116
plurality, 30, 96
poems, 50, 67, 70, 76, 121, 127
  messianic, 90
poignant, 48, 170
poignant evaluations, 26
polarization, 25
pole, opposite, 37
political consolidation, 132

political job, 114
political posture, 43
polity, centuries-old, 133
Polkinghorne, 26, 39–40, 50, 62
  John, 13, 39, 50, 62, 81
  John C., 26, 62
Polycarp, 73, 158, 166
  beloved, 138
Pompey, 124
Pontius Pilate, 114, 126
Pontus, 181
poor men, 139, 141
Pope, Alexander, 109
Pope Gregory, 162, 164
Pope Gregory VII, 133
populace, 123
  non-religious, 122
popularity, 112, 175
  short-term, 129
popularity change, 122
population, largest, 10
populations, 91
  central African, 33
portrait, long, 123
portrayal, 61, 77, 84
Portugal, 10
Portuguese, 164
positives, 112
  great, 111
possessions, 164
possibility, 16–17, 41, 45, 83, 153
  human, 47, 63
  remote, 42, 84
post, 107, 174–75
  final, 15, 30
posterity, 141
  plagued, 71
post-reformation, 46
post-World War II, 70
post-World War II discovery, 100
post-World War II world, 32
potency, 81, 137
potent, 99, 108, 116
potentialities, 40, 148
potent items, 182
power, 9, 11, 13, 20–21, 34, 43, 59, 62, 64, 70, 82, 136–37, 155, 170, 181
  descriptive, 77
  eternal, 46, 54
  great, 21
  higher, 21, 31
  single, 81
practice
  common, 28
  contemporary, 133
  fading, 133
  heartless, 116
  honorable, 166
  long, 120
  systematic, 111
praise, 61, 113
  captured incomparable, 113
  euphonious, 80
pray, 9, 11, 112, 176
prayer, 50, 79, 99–100, 112, 121, 124, 171
  private, 124
preach, 71, 73, 154, 177
preaching, 35, 111–13, 145
  earliest biblical, 131
  early apostolic, 127
preaching station, 106
Precedence, 66
precious, 63, 92, 151
  things most, 63
precision, 172

theological, 178
precocious signs, 37
pre-condition, 147
predecessors, 52, 75
predestination, 78, 88, 127, 178
predicament, 147
preeminent, 87, 129
preexistent, 179
preexisting matter, 20
prehistorical, 85
prehistoric time, 126
prelude, 126, 175
premise, 76
  theological, 167
preponderant belief, 18
preposterous, 15
Presbyterian denominations, 25
Presbyterian pastor, 14
presentation, 110
Present Time, 80
President, 137
prestige, 65, 129
price, 111, 119
pride, 43, 70, 138, 156
  special, 148
Primitive Christian Conception of Time and History, 120
primitive religious work, old, 165
prince, 32, 95
Princeton Theological Seminary, 80
principalities, 82
Principia, 52–53
principles, 36–37
  basic, 13, 16
  basic long-standing, 16

great, 36
moral, 16, 36
spiritual, 36
strong, 16
a priori thinking, 29
priority, 20, 66, 167
prison, 165
  high security, 71
pristine, 75, 80
pristine beauty, 72
pristine days, 105, 181
pristine perfection, 63, 86
pristine place, 130
pristine time, 15, 30
privilege, 21, 115
  high, 57
probe, 64, 122
process, 28, 30, 78, 86, 89, 176
  creative, 59
  evolutionary, 99
  historical, 180
  long, 66
  never-ending, 77
  systematic, 59
proclaiming, 105, 109
prodigal, 147
productiveness, 146
professional assumptions, 22
proffered decision, 57
profoundness, 62
profundities, 65
prognostication, 174
progressive approach, 144
progressiveness, 16
progressive revelation, 69, 120
  long, 101
Prolegomena, 114, 147
Prologue, 16, 36
promise, 104, 108, 167, 172

Promised Land, 115
pronunciation, precise, 87
prooftexts, 28, 175
propensity, 64, 143, 177
  mankind's, 48
  natural, 149
  strong, 141
properties, 9, 29, 39–40, 43, 88, 149, 151, 182
  local, 173
  long-enduring, 31
prophet Elijah, 84
prophet foretold, 122
prophet perishes, 123
prophets, 61, 84, 88, 94, 120–22, 125, 146, 152
  great, 16, 89, 127, 144, 146
  great Hebrew, 105
propitiation, 34, 59
proposition, 79
prosaic events, 92
prosperous areas, 10
protest, 25
Protestant break, 30
Protestant churches, 168
Protestant denominations, 25
Protestantism, 27
  fervent, 170
  new, 27
Protestant Reformation, 178, 180
Protestants, 28
Protestant sermonizing, 25
Protestant theologians, 97
Proto-Luke, 143
protrusive role, 78
prove taxing, 98
providence, 18, 25, 39, 44, 46, 65, 91, 151–52, 159, 164, 174–76

providential, 176
province, 95–96, 165
  great North African, 173
proximity, youthful, 140
Psalm, 27–28, 34, 37, 39, 48, 61, 74, 92, 127
psalmist, 28, 34, 61
Psalms portrays, 75
Psaltery, 61
psychology, 58, 99
Ptolemy, 155
publishers, 2
pumped large sums, 156
punctuation, original, 178
punishment, 71
  barbaric, 114
purpose
  age-long, 152, 177
  entrenching, 66
  eternal, 18–20, 36, 90, 103, 119, 146, 179–80
  expressed, 152
  original, 17, 119
  overarching, 180
  redemptive, 116
  ultimate, 78
purposive, 74, 118–19
pursuit, 70–71, 76
  human, 68
puzzle, enigmatic, 175

Q
question
  childish, 151
  complex, 40
  earliest, 17, 41
  first, 71
  moot, 52
  raised, 100
  searching, 29

theological, 127
vital, 109
question humankind, 29
quick fix, 66

R
Rabbi, acknowledged, 140
Rabbis, 63
race, 15, 63, 85
  human, 99, 151, 160
  radiant Christian faith, 135
  railroad line, short, 98
Ramsay, 134, 156–57, 177
  William M., 177
Ramsey, John, 29
Ramsey, William M., 134
range, 63, 67, 168, 181
  close, 135
  long, 58
  unremitting, 178
Ranke, 86
rapprochement, 98
rational beauty, 13
Rational human beings, 150
rationality, 34, 64
rationalization, 50
Rawlinson, Henry, 31
raw material, 144
Ray, 24
  John, 24
Ray's calculation, 24
Ray's effort, 24
realization, 119, 150
Real religion, 68
reasons, good, 69
rebellion, 152, 181
recognition, 10, 42, 49, 81, 107, 129, 137, 139, 150–51, 156, 182
  gradual, 123

positive, 89
reconcile factions, 136
reconciliation, 26, 35, 59, 133, 136–37, 160
  personal, 137
reconciling, 136
reconstruction, 74, 76
recovery, 86
resilient, 50
rectification, 136
redeem, 63, 65–66, 77, 147, 152, 170
redemption, 20, 23, 63, 65, 79, 90, 114, 117, 124, 147–48
rediscovery, 31
redoubtable efforts, 79
reeking disaster, 62
reformation, 67, 170
refusal, greatest, 125
regions, 9, 20, 22, 24, 86, 97, 134, 151, 155, 173, 181
  benighted, 20
  latter, 164
  populated, 122
  remote, 177
reign, 12, 108, 112, 129, 180
  ruler's, 107
  short, 172
reigns, longest, 105
rejection, 37–38, 174–75
relationship, 16, 19, 22, 113, 130, 159
  ancient garden, 68
  establishing Jesus,' 110
  personal covenant, 16
  thematic, 179
reliance
  deep, 74
  heavy, 175
religio licita, 123

religion, 17–18, 22–26, 42–44, 48–50, 53, 75–76, 80, 87–89, 94, 99, 116–17, 149–51, 170–71, 174, 181–82
  ascendant, 94
  comparative, 48
  conservative, 50
  distinct historical, 146
  distinctive Gentile, 173
  eastern, 174
  false, 76
  good, 64
  legalized, 123
  licensed, 123
  making, 24
  mystery, 64
  non-Christian, 97
  orthodox, 23
  overshadowed, 170
  popularize, 70
  predominant, 163
religion and science, 23–24, 26, 32, 50
  conflict of, 37, 50, 56
religious facts, 168
religious figures, 44
Religious Ideas, 42
religious inclination, 99
Religious insecurity, 25
religious perception, 68
religious practices, 123
religious thought, 37, 60
  modern, 50
Religious Truth, 54
remainder, 80, 135
remembrance, 36, 63
  re-emerging, 63
Renaissance, 180
renaissance, new, 127
renewal, steady, 129
renown, real, 142
renowned theologian Karl Barth, 92
repetitious, 171
reported case, first, 155
Republic, 105, 114, 154, 169, 176
  historic, 107
republic, once-glorious, 95
Republic, widely-admired, 169
republishing, 157
reputation, 30, 36
rescue, 16, 95
resentment, growing, 122
residue, 47, 100, 180
resistance, 21
  deliberate, 89
respectability, growing, 166
respected Baptist Academy, 135
respected spokesmen, 171
response, 14, 31, 55, 59, 71, 150
  emotional, 118
  humanity's, 46
  mankind's, 48
responsibility, 57, 62, 82
  carried, 62
  human, 82
restless, 76, 82, 142
restoration, 63, 83, 148
Restorer of the Republic, 104, 169
resurrection, 112, 117, 127, 153
retaliation, 160
retardation, 71
retrieval system, 2
retrogressive, 102

retrospect, 74, 88, 164, 182
return, 24–25, 94, 96, 122, 125, 147, 151, 156–57
return home, 93, 135
revelation, 34–35, 43–45, 51–52, 55–56, 63, 65, 67–69, 82–83, 85, 87, 89, 100–102, 143–44, 146, 150
  absolute, 143
  complete, 45
  continuous, 124
  elevated, 31
  escalating, 146
  final, 83
  fullest, 143
  general, 21, 27, 42–44, 46, 49, 54, 67, 97–98, 144, 146, 152
  great, 36
  higher, 43
  intermittent, 150
  long, 41
  long-running, 101
  partial, 16
  saving, 42, 44, 46, 67, 97–98
  single-minded, 85
  updated, 101
revelation God, 90
  historical, 146
revelation of God, 42–43, 52, 83, 85, 92, 97, 101, 113, 123
revelatory, 70, 138
revelatory acts, 46
revelatory character, 65
reverence, 43, 64
Revised Standard Version, 2
revision, 52, 134
Revisionism of history, 151
revival, 9–10
revolt, 81
open, 124
revolution
  experienced, 22
  scientific, 27–29, 49–50, 75
revolutionary, 29
revolutionary calendar, unpopular, 107
revor Kletz, 57
Rhine, 169, 173, 182
Rhine River, 176
Richmond, 156
rift, 79–80, 83, 131–32, 181
righteous, 28, 117
righteousness, 11, 94, 152
Righting Wrong, 7, 78
risen Jesus, 151
Ritschl, 132
rival, great, 37
rival bishops, 173
rival institutions springing, new, 25
River, Jordan, 111
river frontiers, 182
rivers, 67, 106
Riverside Church in New York, 24
rivulets, 67
roads, 79, 101, 119, 123
road system, excellent, 155
Robert Browning, 47
Robert Burns line, 125
Robertson, 154–55, 165
Robin Lane Fox, 105
Roman authorities, 155
Roman Catholic Church, 167
Roman Christians, 159
Roman Church, 174
Roman citizen, 115, 126, 129, 165, 177
Roman citizenship, 107

enjoyed, 168
Roman cynics, 175
Roman Emperor Hadrian, 74
Roman Empire, 9, 91, 95–96, 104, 107, 126, 129, 149, 154–55, 164–65, 168–71, 173, 176, 178, 182
Roman government, 85, 103, 129, 171, 176
  imperial, 107
Roman governor, 96, 114, 126, 165
Roman law, 60
Roman legions, 154
Roman military personnel, 172
Roman peace, 169
Roman posse, 153
Roman power, 107
Roman province, 95, 155–56
Roman Republic, 104, 108, 169
  half-millennium-old, 104
Roman road, 155
Roman rule, 103
Romans, 40, 42, 46, 54, 60, 69, 104, 114–16, 120, 126, 133, 139, 156, 159, 174–75
  first high-ranking, 130
  highest-ranking, 155
Roman Senate, 108
Roman siege, 141
Roman soldiers, 129–30, 140, 153
Roman taxation, 103
Roman taxation muster, 124
Roman tax gatherer, 138
romantic poet, great, 84
Roman worlds, 91

Rome, 103, 107–8, 115–16, 122–24, 126, 129, 138–39, 141, 144, 159–60, 165, 168–69, 173, 175–77, 182
Rome's ability, 182
Rome's dependence, 105
room, 45, 50, 62, 79, 154
  unheated, 117
  upper, 141
rooted assertions, 41
rootedness, deep, 86
roots, 9, 150
  long Hebraic, 130
  strong, 181
  sustaining, 85
  verifiable, 66
route, 55, 98, 134
Rowley, 87–88
RSV, 3
rudimentary, 149
Rufinus, 52
rule
  earthly, 79
  monarchical, 93
  pre-established, 177
ruler, 95, 108
  first, 107
  rich young, 141, 143
rupture, 25
  hypothesized, 132
rural church, small, 28
rust, 18, 78, 111, 151

S
sacred name, 42, 87
sacred writ, 141
sacred writings, 43, 60
sacrifices, 95, 126
sacrosanct, 42, 87, 125
Sadducees, 103, 160

Sadler, 156–57
  George W., 156
Sadler Baptist College, 156–57
safety, viewed, 57
Sahara, 48, 164, 173
Sahara Desert, 96, 164, 169
Saint Athanasius, 19–20
Saint Augustine, 169
saints, 39, 44, 149
  patron, 141
Salamis, 155
salvation, 79, 115, 126
Samford University, 26, 102
Samuel Noah Kramer, 31, 85
Sandars, 31
Sarkiss, 26
Satan, 81
Saul, 130, 168
Savior, 95, 147
  long-promised, 152
sayings, 153
  greatest, 49, 53
  recorded, 126
scaffolding, 48
  old, 50
scandal, 117
Scandinavia, 127
scene, 140, 155, 173
  distant, 135
  historical, 176
schism, supposed, 161
schisms, earliest, 173
Schofield Bible, 54
scholarly fray, 131
scholarly volumes, 145
scholarly world, 153
scholars, 22, 24, 95, 108, 111–12, 118, 120–21, 124, 130, 134, 145, 149, 167–69, 176, 178–79
  conservative, 139
  emerging, 132
  good, 172
  great, 145
  modern, 88, 118
  older, 9
scholars contend, 95
scholarship, modern, 165–66
scholars regret, 14
Scholastic Approach, 19, 41, 83
schoolmaster, 97
schools, 22, 32, 35, 59, 97, 142, 145, 156–57
  agricultural, 22
  best high, 11
  boarding, 11, 59
  discordant, 81
  early theological, 131
  erudite, 52
  famous catechetical, 177
  famous Christian, 149
  high, 35, 59, 102
  rival catechetical, 155
  small missionary, 11
science, 13–14, 18, 23–26, 29, 31–32, 37, 39, 42, 49–50, 56, 84
  new, 145
  new emerging, 23
  renounce, 50
Scientific advancement, 132
scientific discoveries, 26, 29
  great, 23
scientists, 39–40
  brilliant, 50
  distinguished, 13, 26
  erudite, 29

scope, 83, 87, 120, 124
Scotland, 70, 80, 119, 124, 127, 142, 172
Scots, 173
Scott, Kermit, 170
Scottish Presbyterian Church, 124
scramble, 10, 163
Scribes, 102, 121–22
Scripture quotations, 2
Scriptures, 2, 17, 38, 124, 138, 146, 158
scrutiny, 32, 39
sea, 66, 96, 122
search, 26, 46, 48, 50, 68, 70–72, 79, 82–83, 94, 99, 147, 150
  human, 92
  long, 150
seat, 155
Second Apologies, 60
second century, 32, 45, 67, 73, 85, 96, 139, 141, 148
  early, 138, 141
second century Athens, 148
second century Church, 175
second century emperor, 148
second century sect, 139, 141
second Isaiah, 145
Second World War, 90
sectarian strife, 173
secular events, 103
secular history, 67, 92, 174
  latter, 67
secularism, 71
  growing, 34
secular world, 34
security, 26, 182
seduction, 64
seer John, 77
segment

large, 97
predominant, 37
small, 158
selection, 78, 88
Seleucia, 130, 155
Seleucids, 108, 116
self, inner, 124
self-disclosure, 48
  progressive, 83
self-existence, 13
self-existent, 56
self-inflicted wound, 83
self-realization, 118
self-revelation, 44, 48, 55, 146
seminary, 119, 125
  left, 147
  theological, 65, 119, 134
Semitic mind, 33
Semitic origin, 153
Senate, once-prestigious, 95
Seneca, 32–33
sentiment, 11, 32, 76, 142, 160
  deep, 92
  noble, 10
  strong Gnostic, 149
separateness, 83
separation, 37, 122, 136, 159
  growing, 162
Septuagint, 92
Sergius Paulus, 130, 155
Sermon, 22, 113, 133, 139, 153, 159, 169
sermon preparation, 145
serpents crawl, 114
servant poems, 121–22
  great, 108
servants, 94, 109
  domestic, 130
service, 11, 42, 98, 124, 180

lip, 139
student, 35
set, 13, 16, 19, 32, 41, 48, 68, 74, 82, 84–85, 90, 108, 125, 176, 179
  early civilizations, 64
  settlement, 160
  gigantic, 148
  seventeenth, 50
  seventeenth century, 19, 23, 25, 28–29, 39, 50, 63, 74–75, 158
  pregnant, 49
  seventeenth century questions, 49
  seventeenth century syllogism, famous, 33
seventy years, 26, 93
sexual intercourse, 94
sexual relations, 63
Shakespeare, 63
Shakespeare's Macbeth, 151
Shedd, 14–15
sheep, 72, 94, 121, 175
  lost, 80, 139, 146, 175
Shekinah glory, 64
Sheol, 72
shepherd, 72, 146
shift, 29, 73, 75
  historical, 158
shining light, 73
shoes, 64, 87
showed higher elevation, 34
showed strong theological inclination, 78
showered great accolades, 139
shrines, 35, 94
Sidon, 115
silversmiths, 165

Simon, 110
sin, 15, 17, 28, 30, 80, 86, 98, 104, 116–18, 123, 126–27, 151
  impact of, 126
  original, 70, 72, 78
  philosophy of, 15, 30
  world's, 116
Sinai, 93
sinful step, 83
sinister charge, 105
Sir Garnet Wolseley, 21
Sixteenth century predestination, 127
sixteenth century Protestant Reformation thought, 178
sixteenth century reformation, 30
Skilled and artful New Testament scholars, 127
skills, 135, 144
slave girl, 73
slavery, 21, 165
slave trade dealers, 21
slave trader, 58
  eighteenth-century, 118
Slessor, Mary, 142
slim information, 134
small church building, 35
small voice, 85
  a still, 84
Smith, George, 31
smitten, 123
social development, 34
social status, 168
society, 11, 34, 71, 89, 115, 133, 142, 170
  earthly, 88
  human, 31, 66, 99
  modern, 24

secularized, 70
strong missionary, 10
society adhering, 37
sociologists, 23
Softcover, 2
soil, bad, 12
solar system, 41
solitude, 32, 124
Solomon, 92–93
son, 20, 25, 84, 95, 103, 109–10, 113, 130, 146–47, 159
  five, 110
  lost, 80, 147
  prodigal, 72, 139
soul, 14–16, 19, 34, 44, 68, 72, 111, 121, 124–25, 127, 171, 175
Southern Baptist Convention, 25
Southern Kingdom, 93
Southern ministers, 24
Southern ports, 125
Southern Seminary, 62
southward, 164
  drifted, 93
space, 33, 38, 51, 108, 112, 125
spacious, new, 135
spanned Elijah, 85
special activity, new, 101
special revelation, 27, 42–43, 67, 98, 100, 146, 152
  long line of, 68, 101
  reckoned, 44
speculative thought, 36
Spinoza, 89
spirited activity, 140
spirituality, 44
  higher, 44
splendor, 64, 75, 132

split, 25
  official, 162, 181
spokesman, 42, 168
squalor, 106
stability, 182
  economic, 22
stabilizing, 154
Stace, 55
stalwart assertions, 13
St. Ambrose, 171
statement, 38, 45, 84, 112, 176
  highest paradoxical, 60
  magnificent, 165
  oft-repeated, 68
  succinct, 61
states
  distant, 80
  independent, 22
  perfect, 17
stations, appointed, 96
St. Augustine, 3, 79
staunch proclamation, 73
steadfast, 34, 54
steadfastness, 161
stellar inventions, 88
step-by-step, 17
stigma, 106, 116
stirred Israel, 94
St. John, 79
St. Justin Martyr, 60
Stoicism, 31–32, 37, 59–60, 89, 160
Stoic philosophical fraternity, 37
Stoics, 32, 49, 60–61
stones, 162, 182
storage place, 135
story, 20–21, 27, 48, 53, 70, 91, 98, 100, 106, 126, 129, 140, 143–44, 146, 179

good, 144
history is his, 27
long, 108
master, 139
St. Paul, 93, 123, 174
St. Paul's Epistle, 167
straightaway, 135
stranger, perfect, 122
strength, 160
　gained, 90
stress, 31, 99, 112
　unsurpassed, 109
stretch, far-reaching, 109
stronghold, 95
　theological, 36
struck, 98, 111
students, 35, 59, 135, 157
　early, 138, 141
　novice, 55
　ravenous, 139
subject, 25, 27, 49, 53, 88, 135, 169
sublime, 29, 33, 51
sublime mystery, 36
sublimity, 55, 74
substance, 68, 109, 137
successors, 60, 85
Suffering Servant, 124
Suffering Servant Poems of Deutero-Isaiah, 111
Sumerian cosmology, 33, 51
Sumerian flood, 100
Sumerian flood stories, 148
summation, 10, 182
summit, 33, 44, 66, 76, 79, 82, 85, 90, 95, 146
　to sum up, 165
　to sum up all things in Christ, 165
Sunday Schools, 28, 135

sundry and partial, 101
sung, 44, 141
sun shines, 81
superb commentary, 62
superb New Testament scholar, 153
superb pioneering work, 101
superb work, 20
superlative, 146
supersede, 44, 79
superstitious, 14, 29
suppositions, 32, 178
Supreme Being, 55–56
surrender, 19, 33
sweep, long, 146
swept, 111
　nationalism, 156
synagogues, 92, 122
　established, 92
　local, 111
Synoptic Gospels, 110, 122, 125, 145
synoptics, 130
synoptic writings, 130
synthesis, 50, 87, 179
Syria, 130, 154
systematized account, 100

T
tactic, unique, 22
take the long way around, 125
Tamale, 134–35
Tannaim, 37
tares, 81, 180
　suspected, 180
Tarsus, 130, 168
Tatian, 73
Taurus mountain range, 134
taxation, heavy, 122
tax gatherer, 168

Taylor, 115
  Vincent, 104, 118
teachers, 102, 135
  beloved, 149
  esteemed, 53
  ethical, 160
teaching, 21–22, 25, 30–31, 38, 40, 45, 111–13, 116, 122, 124, 148, 152–53, 159, 171, 175
  college, 158
  preceded Greek, 37
  substantive, 152
  unquestioned, 133
team, 134, 156, 161
  first missionary, 154
Tekoa, 94
teleological, 15, 30, 74, 118, 135, 160, 179
teleological activity, 67
teleological goal, 89
teleological intents, 146
teleological plan, 66
teleological purpose, 77, 91
  overarching, 67
teleological vision, 39
telos, 19, 176
temple, 43, 93, 110, 120
temple prostitute, 94
temple tax, 92
temporal world, 44
temptation, 47, 111, 118, 121
  ancient biblical, 47
  tempter's, 33
tenacious examples, 109
tendencies, 62, 167
tender story Jesus, 147
tenets, 39, 175
  fixed, 175
  fundamental, 126

ten lost tribes of Israel, 93
tentacles point, 179
term, 18, 24, 29, 36, 41–43, 65, 102, 145, 151
  first, 156–57
  generic, 15
  older, 42
term Church, 168
term economy, 65
term Elohim, 17, 41
terminology, 66
  direct Greek, 27
  philosophical, 41
term pleoroma, 109
term teleological, 176
terrain, 81, 113
territory, 93, 95
  largest, 10
  new, 134
  prosperous, 10
Tertullian, 163–64, 173
testimony, 33
  beautiful, 61
textual criticism, 145
thanksgiving, 61
thatch roof, 35
thee, 34, 44, 68, 82, 92, 142
  exalt, 92
  fly, 70
theism, 13, 19, 36, 41, 83
theistic, 55
  undiluted, 18
theistic approach, 17, 34, 55
  unabridged, 17
theistic belief, 13
theme, 31, 48, 72, 94, 111, 113, 137, 144, 169
  central, 73
  regal, 74
  theological, 69

then-Gold Coast, 69
theologians, 14, 36, 42–44, 54–55, 65–66, 85, 88, 97, 111, 116, 147, 152, 161, 172, 176
  acute early American, 14
  contemporary, 92
  distinguished American, 32
  first, 52, 166
  first systematic, 27
  great pre-Nicene, 177
  postwar, 120
theologians depicts, 66
theologians place, 67
theological controversies, 26
theological definition, 27, 172
theological disputes, 46
theological emphasis, 149
theological peak, 44
theological point, 174
theological school, 73
  great, 177
  influential, 60
theological thought, 162
theological tone, 148
  highest, 39
Theologici, 28
theology, 27, 32, 47, 50, 52, 69, 75–76, 81, 90, 101, 106, 143, 148, 166–67, 179–80
  advanced, 178
  classic Protestant, 28
  good, 76
  high-church, 67
  medieval, 147
  modern, 131
  older, 100
  voluminous, 176
theophanies, 43, 85, 88
  beautiful, 42
  great, 42, 78

Thessalonians, 166
Thessalonica, 166
thinkers, 19, 33, 49, 51, 89
  baffles, 16
  conservative, 36
  distinguished, 173
  distinguished colonial, 79
  moral, 160
  theological, 60
thinking, 29, 33, 39, 41, 50–51, 83, 125, 148, 177
  religious, 54, 58
  theological, 27, 40
the thinking reed of humanity, 26
thirst, 172
  intense, 48
  spiritual, 172
thirties, early, 171
Thomas, 138
Thomas Birch Freeman, 22
Thomas Freeman's work, 21
Thompson, Francis, 70
thou fliest, 70
thou hadst, 48
Thou hast, 142
threat, 31, 81, 165, 173
  age-long, 95
  first full-blown, 74
  first grave, 74
  throngs, 92, 115
  untold, 142
Thy, 9
Thy will be done, 112
tidal flow, 122
Timaeus, 49, 53–54
time Anglican parish priests, 39
time church, 147
time God, 11

time idolatry, 93
time immemorial, 118
time Jesus, 111
time Julian, 172
time Mark, 130
time merchants, 177
time Paul, 115
time religion, 164
Tintern Abbey, 18
titles, 10, 27, 104–5, 115, 169
Titus, 139, 142
token mark, 136
Tollinton, 149
tone, 108, 119
tongue cleave, 92
tooth, 106
Torah, 92, 110
tower, 47, 69–70
towering peak, 44
towering peaks, great, 124
town, 175
  sizeable pagan, 22
track, 98
trade, 21, 92, 164
  lucrative, 96
  old established, 165
traders, 134, 156
tradition, 86–87, 115, 131, 133, 157–59, 166
  ancient Greek, 106
  best, 138
  early church, 159
  established, 169
  good, 110
  long, 110
  long academic, 165
  long Judaic, 123
  old pagan, 175
  oral, 131
  rabbinic, 64

rabbinical, 64
strong, 60
tribal, 106
unique, 87
valid, 111
tragic act, 82
tragic events, 91
trail, 10–11, 18
transcendence, 20, 41, 82–83, 98, 100, 146
transcendence of God, 64, 66
transcendent, 18, 20, 41, 60, 83, 101, 117, 146, 160
Transfiguration experience, 125
transformation, gradual, 95
transgressions, 69, 100, 121
transition, 176
  settled, 169
transitory, 9, 132, 150
translation, 115
  famous, 141
trauma, real, 100
treatises, early, 154
tree, 47, 57–58
  olive, 175
trek, 10
  long historical, 91
treks, long, 33, 164
trepidation, 162, 164
tribal mores, violated, 106
tribes, 93, 95
  hostile Anglo-Saxon, 137
  northern, 94
tribulation, 87
tributaries, 144
trinitarian dogma, 172
trinity, 113, 148–49
trio, 118, 154
triumphant spectrum, 68

triumphs, 27, 90
trust, 136
  persistent, 10
truth, 26, 29, 34, 42, 45, 51, 64, 66, 71, 74, 77, 129, 133, 150, 152
  ethical, 94
  great, 70
  theological, 79
truth God, 83
Tubingen School of theology in Germany, 166
tumultuous years, 105
tunnels, long, 91
turnaround, 68, 71
  complete, 168
  great, 90, 127
Tuscaloosa, 28
Tuscaloosa County, 28
twentieth century, 23, 25, 29, 36, 39, 59, 80–81, 96–97, 115, 136, 147, 149, 166, 168
  early, 20
twentieth century theology, 120
twenty-first century exploration, 51
twilight, 139, 142
Tyre, 115

U
ultimate, 16–17, 41, 55, 182
ultimate destiny, 178
ultimate fulfillment, 90, 122
ultimate goal, 160
ultimate promise, 12
uncompromising, 156
unconscious assimilation, 111
undated past, long, 63
understanding, 26, 31–32, 34, 39, 45, 48, 60–61, 75, 82, 94, 102, 111, 145, 147, 149
  best, 75
  complete, 149
  human, 64
  limited, 64
  philosophical, 21
unfavorable winds, 11
unification, 172
  gradual, 182
unified national state, 137
uniqueness, 116–17
United States, 2, 23–24, 32, 71, 81, 108, 132, 136
  eastern, 182
United States Supreme Court, 70
unity, 83, 149, 172
  coming world, 178
  developing, 173
  forging, 137
  national, 93
universality, 168
universe, 13–21, 26–27, 29, 31–34, 36, 38–41, 47, 51–52, 54–55, 61–62, 64, 74–77, 83, 147–48, 158
  eternal, 52
universe function, 75
universe stemming, 40
universities, 22
University, 28–29, 93
unnumbered assemblage, 142
unpretentious circumstances, 106
unravel, 65, 147
unremitting, 81
unremitting encouragement, 108

unremitting flow, 67
unrighteous, 117
unspeakable complexity, 41
unstoppable progress, 132
untold number, 105, 145
unworthy petitions, 100
Upanishads, 69
upheaval, 90, 139, 142
upper-class support, 108
Uppermost, 123
ups, experienced, 9
Ur, 85, 152
Ussher, 23, 39
Ussher's calculation, 24
Ussher's estimate, 24

V
vacuum, 17, 88
vain, 42, 153, 172
vain effort, 172
Vandals, 170
vanished coin, 139
vantage point, 63
variance, 14, 76
variant stages, 33
variations, 35, 59, 149
varied first century Church, 113
vehemence, growing, 102
vehicle, 52, 66
veneration, 115, 182
   highest, 113
ventures, new, 134
venturesome, 175
Venus, 155
verge, 90–91, 154
verse, 119, 142, 153, 158, 178
   sublime opening, 13
very good, 31, 60–61, 74, 78
Very useful in serving me, 137

veterinarian, 102
vicissitudes, 11
Victorian Age, 37, 71, 132
Victorian England, 31
Victorianism, 32
Victorian peace, 169
village, 35, 59
   large, 22
   neighboring, 35, 59
village chief, 35
village folk, 35
vindication, 91
violence, 64, 114
violent, 104, 120
violent death, 102
violent fate, 121
violent persecutions, 123
violent ways, 21
vision, 20, 42, 84, 120, 168
   far-reaching grandiose, 178
   new, 171
voices, 69, 84–85, 168
   blended, 84
   great historical, 84
   human, 69
   ringing, 62
voices of God, 84–85

W
walls, 109
   mud, 35
war, 21, 24–25, 90–91, 101, 105, 125, 136, 160
   provoked, 103
   tumultuous, 108
War II, waning following World, 171
Washington DC, 99
water, living, 172
water brooks, 34

waterbrooks, 68
waters gathered together, 36
watersheds, great, 148
wave, new, 156
waver, 19, 64
ways God, 84, 146
  variant, 99
weakening tribalism, 137
wealth, 70, 77, 129, 141–42
  prized, 143
wealthy caste, 103
wealthy Englishmen, 25
we always knew there was a god, 46
Webster, Daniel, 113, 139
weight, 116, 126, 174
  unique, 126
Weightier, 167
weightiness, 138
weighty, 38, 53, 149
Weiss, Bernard, 145
Weiss, Johannes, 145
welcomed Jacob, 43
well-earned renown, 134
well-educated Christian, early, 177
Wellington, 98
well-intentioned people, 135
the West, 182
West Africa, 2, 5, 10–11, 20, 22–23, 34, 46, 57–59, 69, 102, 104, 119, 156, 159, 165
West Africa alienation, 58
West African, 21, 119
West African people, 21
West African Pioneer, 22
West African reason, 59
West African tradition, 166
West Church, 162
West Coast, 21

Westcott, 145, 178
Western Christendom, 173
Western Church, 39, 162
Western churches, 162
Western Civilization, 32, 38, 52, 60, 63, 74, 79, 88, 94, 117, 158, 169–70
Western civilization in Europe, 163
Western Coast, 164
Western Europe, 23, 66, 119, 127
Western European Christianity, 182
Western Hemisphere, 106
Western historiography, 89
Western history, 164, 169
Western life, 79
Western mind, 23
Western Philosophy, 14
western pope, 162
Western Roman, 73
western society, 34, 133, 180
Western theology, 80
western thought, 89
Western world, 78
we will never get home again, 99
wheat, 81, 180
Wheeler Robinson, 42
in which sin reigned, 17
wholeness, 63, 83
  unalloyed, 80
Whyte, 124
  Alexander, 124
wilderness, 109, 118, 121
wilderness temptations, 90, 102
William, 14–15
William Allen Poe, 2

William Edward Hartpole Lecky, 32
William Jewell College, 10
William Mitchell Ramsay, 157
wind, 81
winter, 133
  famous, 51
wisdom, 13, 24, 27, 47, 120
withdrawal, 64, 124
without delay, 140
witness, 21, 35, 59, 139, 141, 147, 164, 170, 182
  incidental, 140
witnessed absentee priests, 180
witnessed Rome, 172
woman, 63, 67, 72, 80, 114, 129
  old Yoruba, 82
  wealthy, 77
women, 11, 67, 89, 142
Wonderful Counselor, 95
wood choppers, 57
wooded area, 99
the Word, 16
word chronology, 101
word economy, 18
word logos, 73
Word Pictures, 154
words, 13, 16, 24, 26, 28, 77, 79, 92–93, 98, 109–13, 135, 140, 145, 152, 154
  best-remembered, 37
  inspired, 37
  interpreting, 107
  longest, 165
  much-loved, 72
  stately, 165
words about, 176
Wordsworth, 84
William, 18, 40, 88
work, 10–11, 20, 22, 24, 30–31, 38–39, 57, 59, 61, 65, 67, 82–83, 89–90, 154–57, 179–80
  attentive, 86
  commenced, 96
  completed, 61
  daily, 78
  earthly, 73
  finished, 60, 74
  great, 170
  literary, 51
  magnificent, 165
  new, 156
  respected, 25
  solid, 24
workers, 57, 180
work undoing, 91
work vocabulary, 151
world, earlier, 14, 27
world culture, 181
world empire, 95
world history, 67
world knowledge, 50
world religions, 143, 182
  great historical, 89
  modern, 163
world rulers, 82
world's past, 177
world system, 29
worldview, 30
  standard, 28
World War I, 32, 90
  following, 177
World War II, 23, 28, 66, 71, 81, 90, 101, 179
World Wars, 10, 116
World War writings, 108
worldwide edifice, 178

worship, 92, 115, 155, 158, 180
wrangling, academic, 49
writer, 51, 63, 65–66, 75, 80, 102, 106, 109, 137, 145–46, 149–50, 154, 156–57, 165, 169
writer's favorite definition, 62
www.parsonsporchbooks.com, 2

Y
Yahweh, 16, 42–43, 61, 78, 87, 89–90, 94, 103
   he whose salvation is, 115
   sacred name of, 87–88
Yahwehism, 87–88
   succeeded, 87
Yahweh's purpose in history, 88
Yahweh's regality, 39
Yahweh's religion, 93
Yahweh's Servant, 90
Yale, 25–26
Yale College, 25
Yale University, 13, 25
yearns, 19, 143
years, silent, 110–11
Years War, 51
Yoruba lady, 125
young Africans, 10
young Baptist missionaries, 134
young Christian faith, 95
young Clement, 148
young confederates, 137
young days, 161
younger, 99, 136
younger Americans, 51
younger brother, 99
younger members, 110
younger years, 132
young Indians, 144
a young man, 140
young mission fields, 154
youth, 102, 140, 142
   early, 99
   single, 140
youth's conviction, 119

Z
Zealots, 103, 124

[Created with TExtract / www.Texyz.com]

www.ingramcontent.com/pod-product-compliance
Lightning Source LLC
Chambersburg PA
CBHW071312110526
44591CB00010B/862